D1713399

Jurists: Profiles in Legal Theory

General Editor:
William Twining

John Austin

W.L. Morison

STANFORD UNIVERSITY PRESS

Stanford, California   1982

Stanford University Press
Stanford, California
© William Morison 1982
Originating publisher: Edward Arnold (Publishers) Ltd, London, 1982
Stanford edition printed in the U.S.A.
ISBN 0-8047-1141-0
LC 82-80924

Contents

To John Anderson and Mary Morison
whose Specific Resemblance in John Austin's sense is referred to the reader's literary experience.

Preface

There has never been a comprehensive full-length study of Austin in the English language. More than a century after his death, the opportunity usefully to present a systematic analytical account of what Austin said about law generally and particular topics within it has passed. So much of what he says has been effectively superseded.

Yet a great deal continues to be written about Austin, most often because his errors are regarded as instructive. He was always ready to take the chance of going wrong clearly, lacking the guile to compromise his theorizing with qualifications to serve as protective devices. A typical form of argument in which Austin figures runs: There is a long-standing problem of legal theory, 'X'. To this problem Austin gave the answer 'A'. Another thinker gave the answer 'B' and yet another the answer 'C'. All these answers turn out on examination to contain the hidden factor 'Y' common to 'A', 'B' and 'C'. The beginning of an attempt to find the true answer to the problem is to eliminate 'Y' from the answer.

I hold it truth with those who sing that legal scholarship may rise on stepping-stones of Austin's dead self to higher things. But the divers tones of the singers are attuned to no one clear harp. All the following are disputed questions: What were the problems which Austin saw? Were they real problems or did he misconceive them? What were the answers which he attempted to give? Wherein do the errors in his answers lie? Who, after Austin, has correctly analysed his problems and his errors and thereby moved legal scholarship to higher things? Who has gone wrong about these matters and thereby substituted an impression of progress in legal scholarship for true progress in areas of special Austinian interest?

In the introduction to this book I have given an outline of my own answers to these questions in the area which I see as of fundamental Austinian interest. But, when all is disputed, the presentation of the evidence is what is important, and most especially that the evidence should be presented in its own proper context.

It is this last consideration which largely determines the form of the present book. The contributions of the thinkers influencing Austin to his thinking are presented as far as possible in the manner in which they presented them, with the relevance for Austin indicated by running commentary. Austin's own jurisprudence is presented as far as possible in the manner in which he presented it, with the most central difficulties which later thinkers have seen, as well as what I see as Austin's strengths, indicated by running commentary. I have presented later thinkers who traversed Austinian problems, again, by seeking to give a general impression of their views, with relationships to Austinian thinking emphasized and assessed by running commentary. From the evidence presented in this way, I believe that the conclusions expressed in the introduction fairly emerge.

I am greatly indebted to the General Editor for help and encouragement with the writing of the work and to the editorial staff of the publishers. I am also indebted to Miss Marie de M. Youngman, Secretary to *The Sydney Law Review*, for production of the manuscript, to Miss Joanne Morris, Lecturer in Law in the University of Sydney, for reading the manuscript, and to Dr G.L. Certoma, Senior Lecturer in Law in the University of Sydney, for assisting me with the understanding of Professor Arduino Agnelli's *John Austin*. I had the advantage of general assistance from Mr Peter Norman and Miss Narelle Kitzelmann, Research Assistants in the Department of Law in the University of Sydney. Unfortunately, considerations of space exclude consideration of European Continental reactions to Austin's work. Unavailability in Sydney in time prevented reference in the body of the work to Wilfrid E. Rumble, 'The legal positivism of John Austin and the realist movement in American jurisprudence' (1981) 66 *Cornell Law Review*, 986.

W.L. MORISON

University of Sydney, November, 1981.

Introduction: The argument of this book

John Austin believed that the first 'moral' (now it would be called social) science to be established was political economy, as expounded particularly by David Ricardo and epitomized by James Mill. It was Austin's own ambition to establish a second such science, jurisprudence, exhibiting the scientific features which he admired in political economy. These features were, firstly, its presentation of its subject matter as patterns of observed mental and physical events. It was an empirical science. Secondly, it presented its patterns of events by reference to the universal features which all events have: their logical features as these are discerned by the traditional logic associated with Aristotle. It was a logically systematic science.

James Mill transmitted his fascination with logic to his son John Stuart Mill. Austin made it plain to his students that in logic he considered himself the student of the young man who was his own student of longest standing in law. The most prominent in Austin's lectures of the logical notions which Mill canvassed in his published work are the five predicables of Aristotelian logic: firstly, the real kinds, as Mill called them, to which a thing belongs – its genus and its species; secondly, the differentia which must be added to the connotation of the genus to arrive at the definition of the species; thirdly, the propria which things necessarily have in addition to the definitional features when they belong to a given species; lastly, the accidentia, meaning the features of some or all things in a species which lack the necessary connection associated with propria. Austin sought primarily in his work in jurisprudence to define the species law by its genus and its differentia, and to investigate what propria were exhibited by all systems of the legal species: what features necessarily accompanied their being of the species law.

In this sound enterprise Austin was hampered by his adoption, and often by his mishandling, of notions of Jeremy Bentham, whose disciple Austin was at the beginning of his career. In one matter of logic Mill and Austin did not follow Bentham, namely, in hypothesizing a logic of the will for some aspects of social science which would substitute in those areas for the logic of the understanding, as Bentham called Aristotelian logic. But Bentham's more general attack on syllogistic reasoning as employed in Aristotelian logic had an undesirable impact, as we see it, on both Mill and Austin, causing Austin in particular a tentativeness about some logical matters, over which he puzzled when he might have been developing his legal theory.

1

Much more damaging to Austin's project of a scientific jurisprudence was the influence of the distinction which Bentham drew between a universal expository jurisprudence (as distinct from a particular expository jurisprudence dealing only with the legal system of one country) on the one hand, and a censorial jurisprudence on the other. The latter dealt with questions of the goodness or badness of laws, and Bentham stressed the importance of avoiding confusion between this kind of question with other questions one could ask about laws. The priority which Austin habitually gave to considerations of precision and clarity in thinking produced a drastic but characteristic response to these considerations. He excluded censorial jurisprudence altogether from his field of inquiry and called it the science of legislation. There was no warrant for this either in the practice of Bentham or of the political economists, who habitually included a treatment of the desirability or undesirability of economic measures in their work. Austin himself was unable to adhere consistently to his policy of not discussing these matters.

Austin's performance was further adversely affected by overtones in the word 'expository', which suggested, in the context in which Bentham spoke of 'universal expository jurisprudence', that its subject matter was aspects of legal *provisions*. This is an absurdly narrow focus for a scientific approach to the way legal phenomena behave. Bentham appreciated this, saying that it could scarcely deal with much more than necessary legal vocabulary.

Further damage to Austin's work was done directly by the suggestion that universal expository jurisprudence would largely deal with universally applicable legal terms. John Stuart Mill divided the ways in which the propria of a species are connected with its definitional characteristics by distinguishing propria arising by demonstration and those arising by causation. The former are properties without which the species itself would be inconceivable. The elaboration of terms to describe properties necessarily accompanying law in this way is a dominating area of Austin's concentration.

Here was a sharp contrast between Austin's performance in jurisprudence and his political economy model. The political economists, while not neglecting Austin's main type of inquiry, concentrated upon principles of cause and effect which were to be observed operating in all economies: much the most instructive kind of 'laws of nature'. Austin did not exclude this kind of inquiry by definition, but he thought that the common principles in legal systems attributable to universally operating causes were few.

The definition of law which Austin adopted largely from Bentham was both good and bad, though Austin's adaptation of it was largely bad, consisting as it did in restricting its scope in various ways in the interests, as always, of clarity and precision. The definition of law as mandates of a sovereign habitually obeyed by his subjects was good because it kept the aspiration to represent law empirically, as something we can readily understand in terms of observable occurrences, before both Austin and his students. It was bad because it did not in fact portray empirically observable occurrences as it purported to do, for two major reasons.

In the first place, the Benthamite definition was developed from a notion which some legal practitioners tend to assume and some legal theorists hypothesize. This is that there is a source of authority of certain laws in society against which the authority of no prescription from any other source is to prevail. What the Benthamite definition did was to represent this source as a top person or body of persons in society, recognizable without reference to the kinds of lawyers' thinking to which we have just referred. This enterprise was an abject failure. Austin was unable to identify his sovereign, if indeed he could identify him at all, without recurrent surreptitious reference to legal rules for that purpose. So his definition became circular.

In the second place, the Benthamite theory represented the hypothesized source of authority of overriding legal rules as the fount of all legal authority. This is how what otherwise might have been a definition applicable only to laws promulgated by the sovereign came to be a definition of all laws. The generalization was achieved by a transparent fiction to the effect that whatever mandates the sovereign allows to take effect and does not countermand, he adopts as his own mandate. No significant subsequent jurist has ever been able to swallow this proposition.

Because of the ways in which both his self-imposed restrictions of scope and his fundamental errors about law affected his labours, Austin's achievements in furthering the enterprise of developing the science of jurisprudence, on the model of the political economy, tend to be interstitial to his main exposition, or to occur when he deliberately went outside the confines of his own brief to himself. In his earlier lectures, his notions about areas which he distinguished from law in locating it for himself are often instructive; for example, his account of positive morality, and his distinction between what is positively regarded as moral and what is truly moral by application of the test of its utility for the general happiness. His account of utility is instructive because it presents a model of what is involved in seeking to give an empirical account of ethics, even though his particular picture must ultimately be seen to be false. His attacks on approaches to ethics which are not empirical are likewise instructive.

In his later lectures published through the labours of his widow, Austin's treatment of some of the notions implicated with that of law − its propria by demonstration in John Stuart Mill's sense − are also instructive as exercises in Austin's empirical manner of proceeding. Thus, his treatment of what we call legal positions in this book − rights, duties, and the like − can be seen as attempts to present these complex examples of legal relations in the manner in which John Stuart Mill saw relations generally, adopting his father's notion, and saw legal relations in particular. Austin, however, took an insufficiently comprehensive view of legal positions and his empirical account of their character is affected by his erroneous view of law. His treatment of 'injury', which means for Austin disobedience to sovereign commands, is also instructive. In this context, Austin expounds the psychology which he adopts from James Mill and then applies it to the mental and physical events involved in what may amount to an injury.

Austin's treatment of sources of law in the later lectures is sadly affected by the deficiencies in his definition of law, but instructive about the difficulties of determining what is authoritative in a precedent. Austin appears to reach his solution to this problem only by making a logical mistake to the effect that there is an *infima species*, or narrowest category, to which a set of facts belongs. Austin's map of the legal system, comprising the final incomplete portion of his published lectures, is equally instructive in its efforts to give empirical accounts of classifications within a legal system. But even here Austin's view of law adversely affects his performance especially through the implication he drew that the supreme source of authority in a legal system can have no legal position under it.

When we proceed from the character of Austin's work to its reception, we find that it was placed under prejudice by the extent to which Austin's views on particular political and economic matters were influenced by conclusions suggested by what have since turned out to be errors in his political economy model. Austin's adherence to what would now be considered reactionary middle-class values is demonstrated by an examination of his political pamphlets, though their existence is also made clear by his lectures on jurisprudence. Nevertheless it does not seem to be demonstrated either that Austin's motives fell short of proper standards of academic integrity, or that his influence on the development of the law was reactionary by the standards of the period in which it exerted its greatest effect. Bentham's and Austin's influence on colonial constitution-making was highly constructive, as it was in codification of areas of colonial law, which proceeded more along the limited lines suggested by Austin's work than according to the grand designs of Bentham. The same was true of codification in England itself. Constructive influence of Austinian thought on textbooks and decisions in common law areas is also discernible. Admittedly, in all areas of legal development the useful Austinian influence may now be regarded as all but spent because of its limitations.

On the other hand, Austin's particular brand of empiricism applied to law is of continuing potential productiveness, not only because of its soundness in operation, but because no other significant English jurist has ever taken a view quite like it. This applies even to Bentham, for Austin's approach has distinguishing features owing much to the Mills.

Putting Austin's empiricism in its strongest form – and in putting Austin's notions into what we think their strongest form we are following H.L.A. Hart's precedent – the vital characteristics of Austin's theory are as follow. Everything we say is true, false, or senseless. When it is senseless, this does not mean that the making of the statement does not perform other functions for the speaker than making sense. The implication is only that it does not convey meaning. Significant true statements are accurate pictures of an observable reality, once we have adapted our linguistic expression to put what we really mean. This involves representing the facts we observe in the forms which they always actually possess – the forms of propositions of traditional logic. The distinctive character of the philosophy which Austin sought to apply to law is its combination of empiricism – the view that reality consists of observed occurrences – and formalism – the view that our language represents patterns of occurrences in their true logical forms.

Taking an Austinian approach, in the light of its general features, involves rejecting special imperative or 'ought' propositions which do not figure in traditional logic. One is also involved in rejecting approaches to law based on suppositions that scientific statements depend on a conceptual building out or 'interpretation' by the scientist of what is experienced, yielding scientific propositions which are valid in the light of criteria adopted for the purposes of the science in question. It further involves rejecting the notion that the truth of propositions depends on criteria determined by usefulness for some purposes (pragmatic criteria).

Those who interested themselves after his death in the questions about law which Austin had raised were generally legal scholars with little interest in the philosophical springs of Austin's thinking. Even Mill's account of Austin's work after his death was calculated to cause confusion and only Sir J.F. Stephen commented at that time on the publications brought to light by his widow in such a way as to give a clear understanding of what Austin was about. Sir T.E. Holland described jurisprudence as a formal science without appreciating whence Austin's interest in matters of form derived. Sir John Salmond defined law as the rules acted on by the courts, but he conceived the courts by reference to their end, supposedly justice, as he did the State, of which the courts were conceived to be organs. Justice itself was defined by reference only to homely phrases like common sense and Salmond did not make it clear whether he considered that courts always aimed at justice or whether he thought that was what they ought to do. After him, Sir C.K. Allen took what was to become the standard view that the sanctioning power which Austin presented as the sovereign was the creation of law rather than vice versa, as Austin's theory supposed. But Allen presented law in vague fashion as a kind of hardening of the arteries of society.

The development in America among those who concerned themselves with the questions Austin raised about law is similar, except that the disregard of Austin's empiricism was more explicit. J.C. Gray confronted Austin's view that law could be understood in terms of happenings by insisting that legal phenomena were ideal creations of the courts, though involving a degree of relationship with facts. Gray leaves the reader fuddled about where facts end and where fiction and ideal creation take over. Wesley Hohfeld resembles Gray in this despite his acutely perceptive account of legal positions, which at least can be reinterpreted in empirical fashion even though Hohfeld himself insisted it was not to be so understood. Albert

Kocourek completed the task of wrenching Austin away from his philosophical roots by saying that Austin's notions were all fundamentally sound if they were reinterpreted as ideal conceptions. That Austin did not see them that way was all that was wrong with Austin.

By the middle of the twentieth century the torturing of Austin's notions had given rise to a tissue of misunderstandings about the kinds of things a theorist of his type – usually called positivist – stood for, especially on more fundamental matters. Insofar as the cause of producing an empirical theory of law like Austin's was advancing, it was through theories in which the connection with Bentham's theorizing was indirect, and which owed little or nothing to reflections about Austinian thinking.

Perhaps the theory of Lasswell and McDougal of Yale comes closest to indicating how Austin's philosophy can be applied to law, even though it cannot be regarded as directly aligned with it. Their focus for their legal studies, corresponding in function to Austin's definition of law, is in terms of things that happen – certain community decisions. Lasswell's and McDougal's legal studies themselves can be seen as raising kinds of questions to which the answers must be simply true or false, even though they cover a wide range of inquiries which Austin inhibited himself from undertaking.

In England itself the philosophical notions invoked by Austin's work and their application to law were squarely faced in the second half of this century in the work of H.L.A. Hart. Yet now Austin's philosophy was not adopted, but instead a different kind of philosophy was applied to law. It confronted what we see as the desirable direction of Austin's philosophy on its most fundamental points. In the closing pages of this book we seek to defend the features of the Austinian approach in which we follow him, and to show how the phenomena by reference to which Hart's legal philosophy is developed can be better understood on an Austinian basis.

1

Personal and social influences on Austin and his work

The dynasty at Norwich

There is a view that economics is not a department of human activity but a pervasive aspect of it. It consists in the allocation of scarce means to whatever ends are to be pursued. There is in any case a habit of mind which reflects this approach and it was the habit of mind Susannah Taylor displayed in her written advice to her daughter Sarah, who was to become Mrs John Austin and to accept the major responsibility for ensuring that her husband did not live and die in obscurity. Mrs Taylor moves easily through care of the personal appearance, domestic economy, the acquisition of social goodwill, and the cultivation of the mind, subjecting each to a single method of calculation. Personal vanity is the antidote to slovenliness; but if it leads only to a love of decoration without inducing a habit of attention to the good order and neatness of one's garments, it does not answer its genuine purpose. In social life, one does not indulge oneself by endeavouring to make others feel one's consequence, but rather takes an interest in others' interests. By many little innocent and even laudable methods one may gain goodwill without ruining oneself by expensive entertainment, or giving up too much valuable time. The useful evergreen, goodwill, is not to be sacrificed to the gaudy flower, admiration. In regard to the mind, the feeling of vanity, contemptible in itself, can be made to serve the noblest ends. For, at the same time, the accomplishments which are a passport to superior company will lay up a store of gratification for the time when the pleasures of society diminish and one's resources for happiness depend chiefly upon oneself.[1]

The mother wrote with some claim to filial attention. For whether or not we join with later economists in objection to her measurement of success by reference to stores of happiness or gratification, she had achieved success in terms of her own listing of objectives to be sought. We are told that she was known as the Madame Roland of Norwich and, while this is supposed to have been due in part to facial resemblance to the famous Frenchwoman, it was also attributed to her conduct of a political *salon*.[2] This was undoubtedly modest by comparison with that of her namesake by her friends' adoption, but she compensated by retaining her store of gratification until she died a peaceful death in 1823. At one stage a source of the gratification had been the revolution which disposed suddenly of the original Madame Roland.

Four years before Sarah's birth, the family had gathered to celebrate the fall of the Bastille.[3]

The incident lends colour to the suggestion that Sarah Austin was of radical origin.[4] But the label is misleading. The formidable Taylor – Martineau group were certainly dissenters in religion. The patriarch was John (or William) Taylor, a Unitarian divine who died at the Warrington Academy in 1761.[5] But this kind of orientation marched well with the development of the family as the centre of a cultural circle of the kind which Leslie Stephen sees as typical of those formed by middle-class interests in increasingly important manufacturing towns of the period.[6] Cultural improvement was an asset for material and social improvement, as Susannah Taylor makes it clear she understood.

John Austin himself was the son of a miller in Suffolk, Jonathan Austin, who improved his own material fortunes by contracts during the Napoleonic wars. John Stuart Mill ventures the opinion that the father must have been a man of remarkable qualities because all his sons were of more than common ability and all eminently gentlemen.[7] John Austin, born on 3 March 1790, entered the army as an officer at the age of 16 and served for five years, first as an ensign and then a lieutenant, some of it in Malta and Sicily under Lord William Bentinck. His sale of his commission in 1812 is attributed to family pressure following the death of his younger brother Joseph in service as a naval officer. But in any case his journal in his last active three months in the army indicates a restless dissatisfaction turned in part upon himself. He complains of his own indolence but goes on to record his reading in weighty matters of general philosophy. In a letter to his father he had already expressed his regret at ever entering the army.[8]

Upon his return to civilian life he began to read for the bar in the chambers of equity draftsmen, his father having assured him that his circumstances were sufficiently easy for John to make any choice of employment which he could reasonably desire. He evidently was introduced to the Taylor – Martineau family very early in this period. He became engaged to Sarah Taylor late in 1814.

His letter of 'merely conditional proposals' of 12 November 1814 posed their problem as whether their well-being would be promoted by yielding to mutual inclinations, assuming always that they existed in her case. He proceeded by elaborating the faults with which she would take him, under Latin ordinal numbers. He added by way of prediction rather than undertaking that, assuming that she could answer in the affirmative the interrogatories which he required her to administer to herself before accepting, and which he elaborated at length, he would not forget that he was her hope and stay – even though his maintaining her at some remote future period was only a 'contingentability' – and that he might be urged on to heroic industry by 'the full and exclusive and proud possession of a thinking, feeling, high-minded woman'. He requested finally: 'When you have subjected to this ordeal of self-examination make me acquainted with the issue of your scrutiny', which turned out to be favourable.

Austin justified the 'plainness of this language' by his misgivings concerning whether he should believe that she was 'in truth that volatile, vain and flirting thing, hackneyed in the ways of coquetry, and submitting its light and worthless affections to the tampering of every specious cox-comb'.[9] This was evidently a school of thought to which W.J. Fox, a colourful Unitarian divine and intellectual of the period, and a friend of the Taylors, had belonged. He expressed astonishment at the transformation when Sarah put Austin's injunctions for her amendment into practice, and wondered whether they could be permanent.[10] But her own testimony indicates that she was attracted not only by Austin's serious-mindedness and talents but by the mixture of imperiousness and gloomy uncertainty about his future which had made their appearance even this early. On re-reading after his death what she described as letters full of love and reason, she picked out as particularly moving a passage in which, after exhorting her to read Adam Smith, Matthews, Bacon and Locke, he concluded by pressing on her the study of Latin and the reading of Tacitus 'for I shall desire to talk with you on all subjects which engage my attention'. But she records with equal affection his forecasts of adversity and his need for her as a prop and comforter.[11]

In these circumstances, Sarah's records of her reading in the years following her engagement are some indication of what was then engaging John Austin's attention. During 1815 and 1816 Tacitus was prominent, but in the latter year the first entry is 'Bentham, "Traité de Législation" '* and a later one 'Blackstone, "Comment" '. And in 1817, while 'Lord Bacon's works entire' have been caught up from her husband's original injunction, the entries also include 'Bentham, "Des Peines" &c' and 'Bentham on "Parliamentary Reform" '. In 1818, the entries include 'Bentham, "Defence of Usury" ', also his 'Church of Englandism'. In 1819, the year of her marriage, she read 'Bentham on "Judicial Establishments" ' and 'Bentham's "Letters to Lord Pelham" '. The change of environment after her marriage is reflected in the facts that in 1820, as well as reading Bentham's *Fragment on Government*, she began to read James Mill's *History of British India* and finished his pamphlet on Parliamentary Reform in the following year.[12]

Austin was called by the Inner Temple to the bar in 1818, after which he set out to make a living as an equity draftsman from 2 Old Square, Lincoln's Inn.[13] But his efforts did not begin under favourable auspices. Describing his reading in Chambers as early as 1816, he had complained of his inability

* In his notes to Exhibit 6, University College London, Faculty of Law, *Laws at the University College London 1827–1838. Annotated Catalogue of Exhibits* (London, 1977) A.D.E. Lewis suggests that Austin himself was reading Bentham's own version of the *Principles of Morals and Legislation*, rather than the Dumont version which Sarah refers to here, at this time. Lewis's suggestion is based on internal evidence of Austin's annotations to his copy, which survived the destruction of nearly all Austin's library (till then preserved in the Inner Temple) during the 1939–45 war.

to turn from one subject to another, and in the following year of the effect of equity draftsmanship in cramping his writing style.[14] In a letter to Jeremy Bentham in 1819, he spoke of his preoccupation with the *Grimgribber* – technical legal jargon – of practice as a reason for his inability to be active in the propagation of Benthamism.[15] We have again, in all these things, the mixture of contempt for the activities of many of those with whom he found himself in contact, coupled with uncertainty about his own capacity to cope with the tasks involved. In fact his practice at the bar, which may not have extended beyond equity drafting, was to be unsuccessful and his efforts to last only about seven years.

Austin had been introduced to Bentham just before his marriage to Sarah Taylor in 1819. There is some speculation that he met Bentham through his wife, but her manner of describing the introduction does not suggest this. She further writes that Austin idolized Bentham at the time[16] and this no doubt explains the fact that after the marriage the newlyweds took up residence in Queen Square, Westminster, with a view of Bentham's garden.[17]

The neighbours at Queen Square

At this time, Bentham was just over 70 years old and had finally settled to uninterrupted residence in Queen Square where he was to spend the last 14 years of his life. He had acquired the house on the death of his father, Jeremiah Bentham, in 1792.[18] But he had had other residences as well in the intervening period where he had spent substantial parts of his time. In 1807 he had taken a house at Barrow Green, in Surrey, but in 1814 he had rented a statelier house, Ford Abbey, near Chard in Somersetshire.[19] His ability to sustain the outgoings associated with the possession of a very large country house has been attributed to a government payment of £23,000 in the preceding year by way of compensation for its failure to proceed with his Panopticon scheme and a successful investment in the socialist Robert Owen's venture at New Lanark. But less successful investment followed and he had relinquished Ford Abbey in 1818.[20]

The other neighbours of significance were James Mill and his family, described as living 'almost next door' to the Austins.[21] James Mill had become associated with Jeremy Bentham about 1808 when Mill had assisted Bentham in getting his materials on judicial reform in Scotland into print. In the summer of 1810 Bentham had moved the Mill family into an old stone house in his garden once occupied by John Milton. But the damp soon drove them away and they were unable to return until 1814 when Bentham's new-found affluence enabled him to assist for the time being with the rent of the house the Mills occupied at the time the Austins arrived. James Mill and his eldest son, John Stuart Mill, had also spent much time with Bentham at his country residences as well as foregathering with Bentham and his visitors in Queen Square.[22]

The admiration of Austin for Bentham, coupled with his legal training, achieved immediate intimacy between the Austins and their neighbours, and this was reinforced by his wife's intellectual and social accomplishments and physical attractions, particularly having regard to the matrimonial situations of the different neighbours. Bentham had remained a bachelor. The objects of both his and James Mill's more refined passions were aristocratic. Bentham's were centred around those he met during his first month long visit in 1781 to Bowood, the country seat of the future Lord Lansdowne, who had befriended him because of his reactions to Bentham's *Fragment on Government*. Stephen tells us that the ladies 'petted' him and Bentham was particularly attracted to Lady Lansdowne's niece, though she was then only 13 or 14. After waiting a decent interval, he proposed to her in 1805, when she refused him with expressions of regret at the pain her refusal would inflict. Perhaps she remembered something of Bentham's hedonism from his readings to the ladies, which Stephen claims were received with 'feminine docility'. After waiting a further interval, Bentham proposed again in 1827, but was once more rejected.[23]

James Mill, for his part, conceived a strong affection for the daughter of Sir John Stuart, for whom Mill's eldest son was named, who sponsored Mill in his studies at Edinburgh and who transported him to London in 1802 to make a career there. James describes the daughter as a beautiful woman, in point of intellect and disposition one of the most perfect human beings he had ever known, and the best friend he had ever had, while he was also hers and she spoke of him with almost her last breath.[24] But she had married the banker Sir John Forbes and James married Harriet Burrow in 1805, as soon as he had established himself in London as a journalist and editor. She was the daughter of a woman who successfully conducted an establishment for the care of lunatics. She was unwilling or unable to participate in her husband's literary and political activities, becoming a drudge while she bore a long succession of children with names which Charles Dickens was to satirize in *Hard Times*.[25] Her difficulties were increased in the early years of the marriage by the fact that the family stock of financial capital reduced as its members inflated. James Mill had abandoned his editorships after his marriage in order to work on his *History of British India*, which took some 12 years to write.[26] The book itself was, however, a success and led to a comfortable post in the London operations of the East India Company. But, though restored in fortune, it is claimed that he continued to be unkind to his wife. John Stuart Mill ignores her existence in his autobiography and on this absence of information a psychological theory of the springs of his actions has been erected.[27]

By contrast, Sarah Austin's graces rapidly established her in the good opinions of Bentham and James Mill, as did the qualities and knowledge of her husband. Their house − or rather part of a house − became a centre for the Benthamite circle. Part of this arose from the attentions of both of them to the young John Stuart Mill's education. The young Mill had been born on 20 May 1806 and had been subjected to an intensive private education by James Mill himself, both at Queen Square and at times in one or other of Bentham's country houses. He worked at Ford Abbey in the same large room as his father and Bentham, who took a very active interest in the educational proceedings. The severity of the young Mill's régime was increased by his being required to accept responsibility for the education of his younger sisters, and Sarah Austin's first acknowledged assistance to him was in her assumption of these responsibilities while he extended his visit to the family of Sir Samuel Bentham, brother of Jeremy, in France during the period from May 1820 to July 1821. In January of the latter year he wrote to Sarah Austin to express his gratitude.[28] Sarah was by then pregnant with her only child, Lucie, who was born on 24 June 1821, and the young Mill came to make appropriate response by playing with Lucie. The facts that she called him 'Bun Don', that she retained the title of 'Toody' into adult life, and that she continued then to call the austere John Austin 'da' are perhaps not especially significant for the purposes of the present narrative.[29]

Soon after John Mill's return from France, John Austin took a hand in his education. It had been determined that John Mill should follow in the footsteps of both Jeremy Bentham and John Austin by reading for the bar and he read largely Roman law and some English law with Austin in the winter of 1821 to 1822. Mill explains that his father, notwithstanding his abhorrence of the chaos of barbarism called English law, had turned his thoughts to the bar as on the whole less ineligible for John than any other profession. He adds that Austin had made Bentham's best ideas his own and added much to them from other sources and from his own mind. In Mill's view, the readings were not only a valuable introduction to legal studies, but an important portion of general education. The readings included Heineccius on the Institutes of Justinian, as well as the same author's *Roman Antiquities* and part of his exposition of the Pandects; to which was added a considerable portion of Blackstone.[30]

The sympathy between Mill and Austin deepened towards the end of the Austins' period in Queen Square, most particularly after Austin had left the bar, had been appointed to the first Chair of Jurisprudence upon the formation of the University of London, and had returned after the period he had spent at Bonn studying and preparing his first course of lectures. At this time, as the twenties of the century ended and the thirties began, Mill says that among the persons of intellect he had known of old, Austin was the one with whom he had the most points of agreement. He attributed this partly to old ideals which they continued to share, partly to changes in himself, and partly to changes in Austin. The major ideal which they continued to share was the fundamental Benthamite objective – the achievement of the greatest happiness of the greatest number. Mill says that, like Mill himself, Austin never ceased to be a utilitarian, and this was to be said again by Sarah Austin after Austin's death.[31] On the other hand, Mill points out that Austin had always been opposed to the Benthamite 'sectarianism', by which Mill appears to mean the belief that no human activity was worthwhile except the furtherance of the object of general community happiness.[32] Mill himself became dejected about the rewards for him of a life dominated by this objective during his famous mental crisis which began about 1826.[33]

Mill did not consult Austin during the period of dejection, when he did not consult anyone, or in his period of reorientation when Austin was either not available or going through crises of his own, or both. Mill found Austin when they did talk much softened by his German experiences. He attached much less importance than formerly to outward changes, unless accompanied by a better cultivation of the inward nature. He had a strong distaste for the general meanness of English life and held even the kind of public interests which the English cared for in very little esteem. He thought there was more care particularly for education and mental improvement under the Prussian monarchy than under the English monarchy and saw the real security for good government as *'un peuple éclairé'*, which was not always the fruit of popular institutions. If it could be had without them, that would be preferable. Austin predicted that the Reform Bill would not produce the great immediate results which were expected from it, because the men who could achieve the great improvements did not exist in England. Austin was at this time, Mill says, cultivating a German religion of poetry and feeling with little of positive dogma. Mill most differed from Austin, in spite of their degree of sympathy on this last kind of matter, because of Austin's indifference, bordering on contempt, for the progress of popular institutions.[34]

The circle around the Square

Politicians active in the furtherance of the electoral Reform Bill of 1832, two years after Austin left Queen Square, were one of the groups of visitors to the Square with whom he came into social and intellectual contact during the years of the family residence there. Bentham's own view of the need for democratic reform was stimulated at this period by his experiences in attempting to persuade the authorities to adopt his 'Panopticon' scheme for the disposal of convicts following the pressures created by the loss of the American colonies, and Bentham's disapproval of the conditions in the new site for transportation provided by New South Wales. Under the Panopticon scheme, the convicts would support themselves in England by labours subjected to the close supervision made possible by the design of the prison. Bentham had had assistance from the engineering skills of his brother, but had laboured over years on the project himself only to have it come to nothing with its final rejection a few years before the Austins' arrival. The kind of government which would do this was not in Bentham's view conducive to the furtherance of the objects of Utilitarianism.[35]

Bentham's connections with practical politicians prior to his involvement in the Panopticon scheme were few, the most conspicuous exception being

Lord Shelburne, later Lord Lansdowne, who, at a time when he was in opposition, had been impressed by Bentham's attacks on the legal system, as represented by Blackstone's *Commentaries*, in Bentham's *Fragment on Government*. He therefore sought Bentham out in his chambers in 1781 and invited him to Bowood in the same year. But Bentham made a largely unfavourable impression on the politicians who passed in and out during his extended visit, though he impressed Samuel Romilly whom he met at Lord Lansdowne's table in 1788, and Romilly became thereafter an expounder of his theories in Parliament.[36]

Thereafter Bentham's political radicalism began* to develop as he ran into continuous trouble with his attempts to get his Panopticon scheme accepted and English opposition developed to the French revolutionary activity, which Bentham saw as creating a vacuum offering opportunities for the application of his art of legislation. As early as 1792 he had attacked Mr Justice Ashurst for comparing the English legal position favourably with the position in France as demonstrated by the massacres, and he offered gratuitous advice to the French from time to time. His political reputation was enhanced by the publication of Dumont's account of his views in 1802. This included material from Bentham's *Introduction to the Principles of Morals and Legislation*, not a success when Bentham himself published it in 1789, as well as from later manuscript. Thereafter Bentham's house in Queen Square became the centre not only for casual visitors of the politically interested, prominent or distinguished, but a centre for frequent resort of those with radical political views, especially after the advent of James Mill, whose twin planks for achievement of the objects of utilitarianism were the democratization of government and the enlightenment of the people.

In these activities the Austins became involved. Speaking of the Austins' residence at Queen Square and afterwards, John Stuart Mill says that Sarah Austin, who began to be known by her translations, took the principal conduct of the active and practical part of their life. For, although Mill explains that Austin always felt like a gentleman and judged like a man of the world, in the good sense of both those terms, Mill adds that he retired as far as he could from all business or contact with worldly affairs. She, on the other hand, laid herself out for drawing round her as many persons of consideration or promise of consideration as she could get, and succeeded in getting many foreigners and some literary men. Many who came for her remained for him.[37] Mill's reference to foreigners is perhaps in some degree, though not necessarily exclusively, a reference to Sarah's activities in the early part of the Austins' residence in befriending dignitaries displaced by political troubles in Savoy.[38]

Among the political members of the Benthamite group, the Austins formed the longest standing friendship with the George Grotes. Born in

---

* See William Thomas, *The Philosophic Radicals* (Oxford, 1979) for a general account of his associates.

1794, George Grote, from a family of bankers, had been introduced to the group by the economist Ricardo, and by 1821 was defending James Mill's theory of government and in 1822 publishing the *Analysis of Revealed Religion*, based upon Bentham's manuscript. He was to become a Member of Parliament after the passage of the Reform Bill of 1832 and to resign upon the collapse of the Benthamite-inspired Philosophic Radical Party at the close of that decade. His matrimonial situation, as represented by Packe, has parallels with that of the Austins as represented by Mill, Mrs Grote is said to have been a high-powered woman, forcible, ambitious and loquacious. She pushed or inspired Grote into the life-long task of writing a *History of Greece*, into which he ultimately retired after his resignation from Parliament. For her part, she launched a political drawing-room. In the late 1820s, their residence in Threadneedle Street was the headquarters of discussions among John Stuart Mill and some of his political friends who had disturbed the equanimity of the Mill household by arguments with James.[39]

Charles Buller, born in 1806, also belonged to the group of those who became members of the reformed Parliament after 1832, and he and his wife were also intimates of the Austins in the latter part of their residence at Queen Square and afterwards. It has been said that while most of the entertaining for John Stuart Mill's immediate coterie was done by Sarah Austin and Mrs Grote, a little later on the more glittering chandeliers of Mrs Charles Buller, whose household joined the circle in Queen Square after the Mills had left it in 1831, revealed to him the world of wit and quality.[40] But the following comments of Waterfield indicate that the drawing room of Sarah Austin was colourful enough:

> To her house came Sir Francis Burdett, who had been sentenced to three months' imprisonment and a fine of £2,000 for his attacks on the authorities at 'Peterloo'; courteous Lord Lansdowne, who had been a member of the All Talents Administration on the death of Pitt; Daniel O'Connell, and the younger Radicals, like Macaulay, Molesworth, Roebuck, Charles Buller, John Stuart Mill, Charles Austin and John Sterling. 'It was', said *The Times*, 'as remarkable an assemblage of persons as ever met in a London drawing-room.'[41]

It will be seen that the Austins' assemblage included literary figures as well as Parliamentarians and Thomas Carlyle, the poetic historian, was included among these in the last part of the Austins' first period in England, following in this respect in the footsteps of fellow historian Thomas Babington Macaulay.[42] Carlyle's introduction was evidently effected by Buller, though with trepidation, and took place in September 1831. Buller wrote to Carlyle on 12 September of that year that he was happy to hear from Mrs Austin that Carlyle had called, though he was half-afraid to effect the introduction. While, he said, she being a Benthamite had taken on herself human form and nature, and was a most delightful specimen of the union of Benthamite opinions and human feelings, the more regular Radicals rendered the approach to her house dangerous. But Buller was pleased that the important purpose of the meeting was to meet John Stuart Mill.[43] Nevertheless, Carlyle took occasion in passing to describe John Austin to his wife. He pictured Austin as a lean grey-headed painful-looking man, with large earnest timid eyes and a clanging metallic voice, that at great length set forth Utilitarianism *steeped* in German metaphysics, not dissolved therein; a very worthy sort of limited man and professor of law.[44]

It appears from Mill's account of Austin that he was not easily drawn into Sarah's social, intellectual, and political gatherings, though in Mill's view he was highly effective in discussion at least on informal occasions.[45] He was also capable at this period of being drawn into writing for the political periodicals in which Mill at different times had an active interest, despite Mill's reservation about Austin that he tended to expend himself on oral discussion and would make himself ill when he came to write because of his dissatisfaction with what he produced. It was the 19-year-old Mill who performed the editorial tasks on Bentham's *Rationale of Judicial Evidence* about 1825, though perhaps because Austin was not interested rather than that he was thought unsuitable, and perhaps because the project was thought important to Mill's education.

Austin did, however, contribute along with other members of the circle to the *Westminster Review* in 1824, the year of its foundation, which journal was launched with the aid of funds provided by Bentham himself. It was the venture of the Utilitarians as a distinct body into political journalism. Austin's contribution was an attack on primogeniture in the interests of equality, replying to an article then lately published in the *Edinburgh Review* by McCulloch. John Stuart Mill described it as of great merit.[46] The editorship of the journal fell largely into the hands of Bowring, Bentham's latest protégé, in whose lap he was to die eight years later. The immediate result of Bentham's attitude to Bowring was friction with Bentham's older friends and the review was relatively unsuccessful after its initial impact, passing out of the ownership of the Benthamites after the first few years, at least for the time being. It does not seem that the Austins were deeply involved in the friction, and by the time Bentham dramatically took back his library from James Mill in 1827,[47] the Austins were temporarily leaving or gone from the scene. Bentham presented Sarah with a ring at the end of his life.[48] However, Sarah Austin, much later, wrote that her husband's relations with Bentham cooled during the later period of their stay at Queen Square, and for generally similar reasons to those which affected Bentham's other long-standing associates. She points out that in the early period of their residence his associates were men of eminence such as Romilly, Dumont, Brougham, and Bickersteth (later Lord Langdale). But in the later period, she says, Bentham became impatient of contradiction and surrounded himself with sycophants, a part which John Austin was ill-qualified to play, and which led to Austin seeing less and less of Bentham.[49] Bowring himself seems to have been a charlatan, and his literary executorship of Bentham is accounted a disaster by later writers. Much corrective and additional work has had to be done on Bentham's manuscripts in our own day. The other publishing venture of the circle during this period was the *Parliamentary History and Review*, an annual review of parliamentary proceedings, which again was short-lived. James Mill and John Stuart Mill contributed articles, and Austin another on the subject of joint-stock companies.[50] The editorship was in part the responsibility of Charles Austin, John Austin's younger brother, who achieved all the success at the bar which the elder brother could have hoped for himself, and yet retained his intellectual interests. Launched in 1825, it lasted only three years, but John Stuart Mill considered that the best strength of the Philosophic Radicals was put forth in it, and its execution did them much more credit than the *Westminster Review* had ever done.[51] At the time of the launching, John Stuart Mill's relations with both the Austins obviously remained cordial. He had read law with John and now Sarah was teaching him German, after which he sometimes wrote to her as '*Mütterlein*' for many years up to 1848.

Austin at Bonn

During the years 1827 and 1828 the Austins' residence in Queen Square was interrupted through events associated with his appointment to the foundation Chair of Jurisprudence in the University of London, established in 1826, which was to become University College. The proposed initial subjects of study set out by the Education Committee of the Council as early as February 1826 included Jurisprudence, English Law and Roman Law. The inclusion of the first subject was dramatically innovative and solid testimony of the Benthamite influence in the councils of the institution. It was only in 1758 that Oxford had recognized that even English Law itself was a proper subject of academic instruction by the creation of the Vinerian Chair, and Cambridge did not follow suit until 42 years later. Meanwhile Jeremy Bentham's initial fame, such as it was, arose from his attacks on Blackstone's lectures, among other things, for their lack of pursuit of scientific principles. The guess has been hazarded, based on cryptic references in Bentham's diary, that he may have personally interested himself in Austin's appointment to the Chair of Jurisprudence which was formally made on 27 July 1827 at the same time as the appointment of Andrew Amos to the Chair of English Law. Possibly of more importance was that Brougham, a somewhat patchy supporter of Austin in later years but a friend of the family at this time, took a leading part in the agitation for the establishment of the new institution. James Mill was also active, and the Council included the Austins' particular friend George Grote. Among the Utilitarians, Austin and McCulloch both obtained chairs.[52] It would have been a walkover for Austin even if there had been serious competition, which apparently there was not.[53]

At some time after the foundation stone of the University was laid in April 1827 Austin determined to go to Prussia in preparation for his first course of lectures, anticipated to begin in Michaelmas Term, 1828. Austin's reasons for deciding to go to Germany are obscure, though there has been speculation. It has been pointed out that since the end of the eighteenth century some English literary and learned circles had begun to show an interest in new currents of German intellectual life. Kant and post-Kantian philosophers, above all Hegel, gradually became better known in England. Niebuhr's *Roman History*, which revolutionized Roman historical studies, made a great impression in England, and at the foundation of the University of London the impressions made by German life and institutions, and Bonn in particular, had a suggestive influence.[54]

Austin was only interested in University institutions for the purpose of conducting his lectures. He held determinedly aloof from academic struggles during his tenure of his chair[55] and he must have been preoccupied with the enormous problems of producing satisfactory subject matter for his course. On a very mundane level, it seems that Austin may have desired to get away to escape the activity in his drawing-room. At an earlier period one solution for him appears to have been to get away to talk with Bentham, and an idyllic picture has been painted of them strolling around Bentham's garden deep in discussion while John Stuart Mill played happily with Lucie in the model Panopticon along the lines of which the garden had been re-designed.[56] But by now, according to Sarah's later account already noticed, Bentham had turned largely to other confidants.[57] Austin's stratagem, if such it was, succeeded in a measure. Bonn, where he settled in October 1827, after a brief period in Heidelberg, is described as a quiet little university town charmingly situated on the sunny bank of the mighty river Rhine, opposite the lovely hills of the Siebengebirge. It was the seat of the youngest Prussian university, founded barely 10 years before but including on its staff Niebuhr, already mentioned, and August Wilhelm von Schlegel, the translator and philologist.[58] In this environment Austin did in fact settle down to work and Sarah was bored to tears. In January 1828 she was appealing to Mrs Grote, in God's name, both to write herself and rustle up any other people she could to do so out of Christian charity.[59]

Apart from Bonn's virtues as a quiet and removed spot, and the fact that its selection would have won the approval of the university authorities in London when it had been held up to them as a model,[60] Austin no doubt saw it as suitable in ways directly related to the subject of his work. Bentham had received a great deal of stimulation from the study of Blackstone, not because Blackstone appealed to him, but because he found Blackstone's errors stimulated him to develop his own views in opposition, to lend them excitement, and to make them seem important. Austin had long been thoroughly familiar with his way of proceeding from his earliest studies of Bentham's works even before he met him. He could well expect similar stimulation from pitting himself against German metaphysicians, whose notions were equally unsatisfactory to Benthamites. But Austin's gladiatorial efforts in controversy were hampered at the outset by language difficulties. Speaking apparently in the context of political issues, Sarah says that her 'glorious man' laid into the Germans with all the force he could muster in a strange tongue, but the Hercules was in chains and felt it and grew very angry sometimes. From his wife's account, it seems further that Austin was inclined to withdraw into the contempt which we have noticed earlier he tended to develop for those with whom he was concerned in difficult situations. She complains of the labour and research which the German press is always putting forth without regard to the *end*, the typical Benthamite complaint of failure to approach any activity from the standpoint of its utility. She points out, no doubt reflecting the views of her husband, that jurisprudence is a subject which seems difficult to treat without regard to the end, and adds Austin's comment that this difficulty the German jurists labour, with no trifling success, to overcome. Thus many of their books appeared to belong more to the department of bibliography – histories of Editions, Codes etc.[61] The statement of Austin's about the German labours is plainly not a compliment but a sneer – that they find means of going on writing about jurisprudence which enable them to evade the matters to which they should be properly directing themselves. In the main intellectual controversies which did go on at the University of Bonn, between Niebuhr, the ancient historian, and Schlegel, the linguist, Sarah says the Austins held aloof and does not trouble to explain what they were.[62]

Nevertheless, Sarah Austin expresses her husband's satisfaction with his progress in the preparation of his lectures and he expresses his own satisfaction with this in a letter to George Grote in December 1827. After describing his exacting daily régime of work, he says that he took the Institutes of Gaius, *not* as his guide to the *rationale* of jurisprudence, but for the purpose of helping his memory to the subjects with which it dealt.[63] Austin was well advised to say to a fellow Benthamite like Grote that he was not looking to the Institutes of Gaius to provide him in itself with an appropriate classificatory system for his jurisprudence. Bentham had severely criticized Heineccius for following the classification of the Institutes of Justinian when he wrote in 1727 more than a thousand years after they were written.[64] It is inconceivable that Bentham would have thought any better of anyone following the classifications of the Institute of Gaius dating from the same era as those of Justinian.

On the other hand, Austin makes one unguarded statement in his letter to Grote which indicates that his distaste for classifications not worked out under the auspices of utility was evaporating, which surely would have angered Bentham as well as being in conflict with Austin's own Benthamite stance up to that time. After describing to Grote the four hours a week he was spending reading with a young *privatim docens*, he concluded that 'though the Philosophy of Law is in a backward state among the Germans, such of their expository books (particularly on the Roman Law) as I have run through appear to me to be *models of arrangement* (italics supplied), and to abound with learning.'[65] Here he speaks as if there need be no relation between the classifications one regards as satisfactory for the purpose of presenting particular legal systems and those needed for the purposes of legal philosophy, such as working out an ideal system.

The *privatim docens*, not referred to by name but only by label in both Austin's letter and Sarah's biographical sketch of Austin, was described as a friend of Niebuhr and as having studied at Göttingen under Hugo and at Berlin under von Savigny. It has been guessed that he was Ludwig Arndts, later Ritter von Arnesberg, who had been lecturing in Bonn and who later produced a widely used text on Pandect law.[66] Gustav Hugo is accounted the forerunner of the historical school which developed in opposition to the older natural law notions, rejecting the view that law could be presented as the product of philosophical speculation and insisting that it must be the product of historical development. Von Savigny, however, while an expositor in the first instance of Hugo, came to be reputed the founder of the historical school.[67] Austin thus found himself with an instructor brought up on an approach which had points in common with the Benthamites in its attack on natural law notions, but sharp points of difference in the insistence on law being a product of history, which precluded codification, a subject on which von Savigny was in hot dispute with Thibaut of Heidelberg whence Austin came to Bonn. The Utilitarians were being attacked about this time for the Benthamites' lack of any sense of history,[68] and the young Mill had been shaken as much by what he regarded as his father's insensate opposition to all the criticisms Macaulay made as by the force of some of the criticisms themselves.[69] It was the beginning of a transformation in Mill's thought concerning the importance to be attached to historical factors and perhaps Austin was sufficiently influenced for this to be one of the bases of the younger Mill's continuing sympathy with Austin after Austin's return from Bonn to which we have referred. The historical school did not, however, influence Austin to the extent of inducing him to abandon his Benthamite passion for codification as the practical object of the art of legislation. He was later to condemn von Savigny in round terms in his work.

It has been said that the historical school, for all its emphasis on developmental influences, never ceased to construct dogmatic systems of current law.[70] Even Hugo and von Savigny were authors of such dogmatic systems, despite their objections to attempts to freeze the law for the future by legislative codification. It is in such systems that Austin appears to have been particularly interested. After this, a continuing theme of Austin's was to be the extent to which English law could be clarified by seeking to understand it in terms of Romanist models.

The University of London

Austin returned from Germany in the spring of 1828, according to his wife's biographical sketch.[71] But it appears that she drew a veil in that sketch and perhaps in other places over precisely what happened next, though the

...and social, and was sure she would not disappoint him in the w...
...en bitterly disappointed herself. But these statements to the p...
...robably much less than the 'merely conditional proposals' that Au...
...t to her in 1814. She mourned, but appeared to accept, that 'one ...
...love you so much should be for ever parted from you'. When ...
...s finally determined to go abroad and the prince invited them to go ...
...tle, the Austins went instead to Boulogne and the correspondence fel...
...Sarah's main expressed concern being that the prince should not...
...e what had passed. She warned him away from a projected visit. After
...ere was only an occasional epistolary relapse into longing for the one
...leased her 'spiritually and sensually'. They are said to have met on
...ne occasion years afterwards out of a curiosity confined to each other's
...ance.[87]

...e context of this correspondence, Waterfield recalls Austin's state-
...n his letter of proposal to Sarah that no hypocrisy could conceal the
...f mental purity from the earnest gaze of a lover. Waterfield concludes
...ustin's gaze no longer answered this description, but alternative
...ilities are that this Austinian theory is false or that Austin was aware at
...f some estrangement and could have been distracted. His wife was,
...ver, expanding her drawing-room activities at the time he was teach-
...nly in some degree on behalf of his students, and this may have
...ed further distractions. He may have been led away into making the
...f informal perorations on social occasions which in any case he seems
...e much preferred to preparing and delivering lectures to a timetable.
...lt that he was too prone to expend himself in this way.[88]

...ast years in London

...ne period during his lectureship Austin removed his establishment
...Queen Square to Park Road, Bayswater, separated at that time from
...t's Park only by a hedge. The move was attributed to financial
...ms and Packe[89] and Waterfield[90] fix the year as 1832. But this appears
...post-dating the move by two years. The financial stringency had
...ped because of the visit − or visits − to Germany and no doubt also
...e of the postponement for a year of the beginning of Austin's lectures
...vember 1829. By 30 April 1830 Sarah was writing that the Austin
...es were recovering after two cruel years which had put them sadly
...n everything. But the economy move had obviously already been
...for the letter explaining this is addressed from Park Road, and Jeremy
...am's letter to her asking her to visit him three months later assumes
...ust come from a distance.[91] The fixing of the location is unlikely to
...aused friction to develop between John Stuart Mill and Sarah Austin,
...rek infers it did through Sarah's gossip about their neighbour, for the
...gement came very suddenly 18 years later. It is true that the Austins
...erhaps not by coincidence, found themselves living with their garden

sketch may have been intended to convey the impression that he then began
to lecture while avoiding any explicit statement to that effect.[72] If so, her
granddaughter and perhaps others were misled. Janet Ross states that in
1828 the Austins returned to London *and* Mr Austin's lectures opened with
a class which exceeded his expectations.[73]

However, letters exhibited by the Faculty of Laws of University College,
London, in 1977 and utilized by A.D.E. Lewis in later writing,[74] establish
the incorrectness of all the above. In a letter to the Warden of the College
Austin mentions the ill-health which, together with the difficulty of the
subject matter of the course, compelled him to postpone his lectures. A letter
to the clerk who dealt with correspondence in the Warden's absence indicates the intention of beginning the lectures on 16 November 1829, when
the first session continued into July 1830.[75] Bellot also relies on a newspaper
report for the statement that this was the first series. It is apparent, from
quoted excerpts of a letter from Sarah Austin, written at some unspecified
date in 1829, that Austin had been subject to recurrent illnesses prior to the
time when he eventually began to lecture, and that Mrs Austin did not
consider that they were entirely of physical origin. She spoke of him having,
at the time of the letter, passed two months without having an attack, which
she called a pittance of time for a man engaged in the most extensive and difficult of all studies, to rearrange all his dissipated ideas and to collect the long
and nearly perfected chains of thought and arrangement. Although at the
time of the letter Austin was described as 'going on with spirit', his wife adds
that he had many times entirely despaired of being able to commence his
public career and she had accustomed herself to look steadily at the abandon-
ment of all their prospects in London forever as a result of any decision
which her husband might take. She proceeded that the contemplation of 'the
terrible consequences to a hypochondriacal man of living without a fixed
employment' had embittered her otherwise very pleasurable gardening.[76]

It appears from the above description of Austin's activities that this letter
antedates the actual beginning of the lectures, and by the time the first series
of lectures was well advanced into April 1830 Sarah wrote more cheerfully.
Her husband had held aloof from the struggles of the professorial body with
the Council and from the struggles within the Council itself, confining his
attentions to his class. With them, Sarah recorded, he was on the most
delightful terms and he had received notice that his guarantee would be continued for a further year, extending the Austins' financial security till
towards the end of 1831. Moreover, there were indications of students wishing to enrol for classes in the following year.[77]

The first class was unfortunately to turn out untypical, including as it did
distinguished representatives and associates of the Benthamite circle, whose
reactions to what Austin said, at least on the broader subjects included, were
bound to be approving. In addition to John Stuart Mill and Charles Buller of
whom we have said something, Lewis lists Edwin Chadwick, Edward Strutt
(later MP and thereafter Lord Belper and President of the Council of

University College 1871–79), John Romilly (later MP and MR, the last Master of the Rolls to sit in the Commons), the future Lord Clarendon (Lord-Lieutenant of Ireland 1847–52, Foreign Secretary 1853–58, 1868–70), his brother Charles Villiers (later MP and vigorous opponent of the Corn Laws, a member of Palmerston's Cabinet 1859–66) and George Cornewall Lewis (Chancellor of the Exchequer 1855–58).

But the assurances which Sarah says Mill and Romilly had given her of others wishing to attend Austin's classes in the following year were not borne out.* Sarah wrote in April of 1831 that he actually had no class at the November starting date and the classes were therefore deferred till January. The University College exhibition referred to above contains his letter of 12 November, confirming Sarah's statement that on the starting date he had no class, and when this only rose to three in the following week he postponed his lectures to January, when matters were not much better. According to Sarah, Austin made up his mind at that time to resign at the end of the current course of lectures, which would have meant towards the end of 1831. Sarah attributed Austin's difficulties at that time to the fact that nothing else could be expected in England, where all was treated, not merely as a science, but only as a craft. Austin's inclination was to retire to Paris to construct such a complete *Corpus Juris* as 'might live for ever and be a text-book for all future codifiers'.[78]

Austin did not resign at the end of the second session, though he now entered upon the projected literary activity by preparing the earlier part of his lectures for publication. *The Province of Jurisprudence Determined* was in print by mid-year 1832. There is no suggestion from any source that there was any improvement in student attendance during the third session,** and doubt has been expressed whether any lectures were given at all.[79] Sarah claims that Austin's last lecture was at the end of this session – in June, 1832,[80] – but other authorities indicate that he persisted with a fourth session until June, 1833.[81]

It is claimed that Austin's fourth and final series of lectures apparently gave him no difficulty after he had begun in December, 1832.[82] But he did not in any case succeed in correcting the fundamental fault in his lectures

* In response to a request from Sarah for a written assessment at the end of the first session, Mill had warned her that the second session would be badly attended because of deficiencies in the lectures. Those delivered needed to be much abridged and repetition excluded. But the major defect was failure to cover anything like the programme which Austin himself had projected. The initial impact of the course was unfortunate because the introductory material contained no substantive matter. The endeavour to rely on oral exposition rather than written preparation was a failure (Mill, *Collected Works* XII, 51–3). It appears also that the number of lectures delivered in any form was curtailed (Lewis, 'Austin', 21).
** Waterfield, *op. cit.* 42–3. A rather pathetic prospectus for the third session ((1832) 8 *Law Magazine*, 534–5) complained about continuing lack of support for the classes while at the same time proclaiming Austin's willingness to expand his activity to cover the Law of Nations. Mill was at this time trying to allay Sarah's fears about Austin's future (Mill, *Collected Works* XII, 71–2).

adjoining that of John Taylor and Harriet Taylor,[92] who was to become John Stuart Mill's wife many years later and with whom Mill was to become on increasingly affectionate, though not adulterous, terms as the 1830s progressed. There are at least three theories of the connection between Mill's relations with Harriet Taylor and his relations with Sarah Austin. One, which its author himself describes as outrageous, is that Sarah had conceived a passion for Mill and he at first for her because she reminded him of his father, and she resented his subsequent deep affection for Harriet.[93] The second theory is that Mill became angry with Sarah because of her gossip about his relations with Harriet. Hayek attaches importance to the fact that Sarah was in a strategic position to observe after the Taylors moved to Park Road and was regarded by Mill as chiefly responsible for the talk.[94] Still a third theory is that the Austins and their particular friends conspired jointly to ostracize Harriet.[95] But none of these theories will explain the time and suddenness of the estrangement.*

The public activities of John Austin during the period after he ceased to lecture at London consisted in a series of appointments brought to premature terminations without satisfying fulfilment. In August 1833 he was appointed to the Criminal Law Commission at the satisfying salary of £500 per annum.[96] But the powers of the Commission were limited and Austin was frustrated by his inability to work upon the largest possible canvas and to set about codifying the criminal law of England. He retired after his health was affected by the shackles in which he had to work.[97] In 1834, he was engaged to deliver a course of lectures in Jurisprudence at the Inner Temple, but did not find the audience rewarding – in fact it shrank to only five[98] and the frustrations of teaching in this environment also reflected themselves in feverish attacks which led to repeated cancellations of lectures.[99] He gave up within a short time and withdrew to Boulogne in the interests of tranquillity and inexpensiveness of living. Sarah estimates the period spent there as about a year and a half, extending into 1836, and the tranquillity appears to have been broken by little else than Sarah Austin's exploit in helping rescue castaway women convicts bound for New South Wales from the wreck of the 'Amphitrite'.[100]

In 1836 the Austins returned briefly to London to prepare for their period in Malta. Austin and his former student G.C. Cornewall Lewis were

---

* Carlyle refers with disapproval to Sarah's gossip about Harriet Taylor in 1834 (Packe, *Mill*, 120 – 4, 178 – 9) but there was affectionate correspondence between Mill and Sarah about the *London and Westminster Review* shortly after this (Packe, *Mill*, 196 – 7, 209) in 1837, about James Mill's death (Mill, *Collected Works* XII, 306, 321 – 2), on Mill's side at least about a contribution of Carlyle's to the *Review* in the same year, and about the prospect of Austin being interested in a chair in Glasgow (*ibid.* 333 – 5). As late as the mid-1840s Mill was in friendly correspondence with Sarah about the affairs of Auguste Comte and the Austins' own personal affairs, and as late as February, 1848 was sending changed pages in the second edition of his *System of Logic* to Austin, following on Austin's warm reception of the first edition (Mill, *Collected Works* XIII, 506 – 7, 521, 527 – 9, 541 – 3, 571 – 3, 579, 622, 653–4, 711 – 15, 730 – 1).

appointed by the Colonial Office under Lord Glenelg to inquire into conditions in the island in the light of local discontent with the British administration, the offer being transmitted by the Austins' friend in office, Sir James Stephen. They arrived in Malta in October of that year. While Lewis and Austin devoted themselves to formulating recommendations about political and economic conditions, Sarah utilized her knowledge of Italian to establish relations with the local aristocracy and to institute cultural and educational projects at the expense of her more general continuing literary activities. In 1837 their movements were restricted by a serious outbreak of cholera. At that time the Commissioners came under attack in the *London Times*. In mid-1838 the Commission was abruptly terminated by a changed Colonial Office.[101]

Austin's reaction to this further reverse was predictable. His health broke down seriously. During the winter of 1838 to 1839 he is described as very ill, and similarly during the following winter. When his daughter Lucie married Sir Alexander Duff Gordon in the spring of 1840, the anxiety was not about whether the bride would be left at the altar by the groom, but whether the bride's father could be got to the altar to give her away. To the 'inexpressible joy' of his family he was got there, though whether or not on time is not disclosed.[102]

Austin's pain of mind and body is attributable in part to the consequences of what the Commissioners did do in Malta and in part to the effect on him of what he did not get to do there. The Commissioners faced the difficulties of dealing on the one hand with the governmental authorities, under a virtually absolute system of personal rule by the governor, and on the other with a population swollen to over a hundred thousand much disturbed by the absence of their ancient popular council and fallen into serious poverty. The people had great expectations of the Commissioners which were immediately damped by the Commissioners' view of the necessity for extensive inquiry into political, economic and legal matters. The length of the inquiry also angered the British because of the interference with the ordinary functions of government caused by the authority given to the Commissioners. So complaints were made to the effect that it would have been more satisfactory to pursue grievances through the Colonial Office and the Commissioners were recalled after about 18 months with their recommendations far from complete and what recommendations they had formulated still to be fought over in England to the anxiety of the Austins when they returned. The Commissioners apparently made some effort to continue with their work after they returned. As late as 28 May 1840 an anxious Maltese inquirer was informed by Sarah that Austin had not lost sight of the matter of the *Consiglio Popolare* but was constantly meditating on it and improving his recommendations.[103] By that time he was on the verge of departure for Germany for the sake of his health.

The chief controversy in England over what the Commissioners did put forward was provoked by the discussions over the Ordinance in Council of

14 March 1839 which established freedom of the press. Lord Brougham attacked the consequential proposal for a rigid code of libel, and what he said was found very hurtful by the Austins, coming from a friend.[104] Brougham also attacked aspects of the opening up of offices in government administration to Maltese, though he spoke kindly of the Commissioners' efforts in retrospect.[105] These included provision for changes in various import duties. The Commissioners also succeeded in remodelling the police force, effecting changes in the education system and in Malta Government charities and in the administration of courts of justice.[106] But while they had suspended recently promulgated codes of law during their inquiries, these were in the end put back again, and the Commissioners appear ultimately to have made no progress towards the democratization of the governmental system.[107]

Of more immediate practical hurt to the Austins was the delay and uncertainty about payment of the Commissioners. Apparently none of the remuneration, as distinct from expenses falling on the Maltese, was paid until May 1839, when it was fixed at £3,000 total for the two years. Some of this the Austins earmarked for the Duff Gordons, whom they expected to have to assist, for Sir Alexander was titled but impecunious.[108] Moreover Lucie herself was delicate. She was to spend long periods abroad for her health apart from her husband, at first in Capetown and then in Egypt. Her recipe for ameliorating her condition, smoking cigars, though quoted by a family biographer as among the things placing her in the twentieth century, was unhappily as ineffective for this particular purpose as a twentieth-century medical practitioner might have expected. She survived her father, for all his chronic illnesses, by only 10 years, and her mother by only two.[109]

In addition to all this, Austin was subject to the usual frustration that circumstances prevented him from proceeding to the grand design of codifying any major branch of the law of Malta.[110] Whether the fact that Austin was unable to proceed to codification was a disaster for him or a protection to him, in the light of what happened when he was left to execute grand designs, posterity can only be left to wonder. In any case, this was the end of his prospects of executing a substantial exercise in the kind of project in practical codification which was so dear to the heart of Jeremy Bentham and in which proclivity Austin followed him.

The later years in Germany and France

At the time of their daughter's marriage the Austins had already determined to go to Carlsbad and their departure was imminent.[111] Its mineral waters had been commended by medical friends to Austin as a recipe for the improvement of his health. From mid-1840 to some time in 1844, the Austins' pattern of life was to spend much of the pleasanter parts of the year in Carlsbad, with other times in Dresden and Berlin, varied by an occasional visit to London. The result was soon shown in an improvement in Austin's health, but at this period his wife had given up hope that he would in the future be well enough for a regular employment. She felt bitterly what a great teacher was 'lost to the world', when she witnessed Austin expounding to a young judge. But Austin's audience, she added, was now largely feminine and his discussion was of matters of broad philosophy.[112] His health remained delicate, preventing a presentation at the Court in Saxony, but did not prevent him from beginning work late in 1841 on a highly critical review of Friedrich List's *Über die Nationale Oekonomie*, which was published in the *Edinburgh Review* in 1842. List was a pioneer of the idea of the *Zollverein*, the economic association of German states, a notion antithetical to Benthamite economic doctrines of free trade, and he called particularly for the protection of urban industries. Meanwhile Sarah pressed on both with her more serious and lighter German translations as well as articles and letters.[113] In 1842 Austin was feeling well enough to make the offer to review Mill's *System of Logic* for the *Edinburgh Review*,[114] but this does not appear to have come to anything.

The Austins removed to Paris in early 1844 and in the same year Austin was elected as a corresponding member in the Moral and Political Class of the *Institut de France*.[115] It is obvious from the date that the election was not due to any extended activity of Austin himself at the time. It may not unfairly be attributed in part to his wife's influence. By this time her friendship with the French philosopher and politician Victor Cousin, whom she had met by accident in Germany on Austin's earlier visit, was of 16 years' standing and lasted till his death shortly before her own, with only one contretemps on a visit to her at Weybridge much later. It seems that when a French correspondent concluded a letter formally with an assurance of exclusive devotion Sarah liked to think it was true, only to be disillusioned during that visit by Cousin's lack of attention to her and to her programme for him.[116] She was also by 1844 already friendly with the leading conservative politician and academic historian of the Louis Philippe era, François Guizot, who headed the government at the time of the 1848 revolution. At some stage she also formed a continuing friendship with Cousin's friend B. St Hilaire, who, in a lesser capacity, had the same kinds of interests as Guizot. Sarah rapidly developed a political-academic salon during the stay in Paris and the Austins both came to have associations and sympathies with academics and others connected with the Louis Philippe régime.

As for jurisprudence, the gap between Austin's project and performance was as complete as it had been ever since he had left the University. Austin had written to Sir William Erle in 1844 saying that he would now set to work in good earnest and, if his unlucky stars would allow him a little peace, he hoped he would turn out something of considerable utility. Austin's specifications for what he proposed were on the grandest scale according to Benthamite notions, and perhaps more. He intended to show the relations of positive morality and law, and of both to their common standard or test; to show that there are principles and distinctions common to all systems of law (or that law is the subject of an abstract science); to show the possibility and conditions of codification; to exhibit a short body of law arranged in a natural order; and to show that the English Law, in spite of its great peculiarities, might be made to conform to that order much more closely than is imagined. Austin was prepared to concede that the questions involved in this scheme were so numerous and difficult, that what he would produce would be very imperfect. He thought, however, that the subject was one which would necessarily attract attention before many years were over, and that his suggestions would be of considerable use to those who would pursue the inquiry under happier conditions.[117] But there is no evidence that Austin took any action on this project at this time except to formulate a prospectus.[118] The next year Mill was raising with Sarah the question whether there was any chance of a reprint of the *Province of Jurisprudence Determined*, with the second volume, representing his later lectures, which Austin had projected.[119] Austin had been subjected to pressure for a reprint from others, but was not prepared to reprint the *Province of Jurisprudence Determined* except as part of a larger whole and with corrections. This effectively stopped even the smaller enterprise. Austin might continue to indulge romantic notions of solving all the jurisprudential problems he saw at a blow, but Sarah was to say later that any fresh requests for a reprint or his second volume made him react as if someone had hit him. The published part of his lectures thus remained out of print for many years before his death.[120]

The only minor piece which Austin wrote during this period was his article 'Centralization' in the January 1847 number of the *Edinburgh Review*.[121] Mill warmly praised it as a thorough discussion, eminently calculated to give clear ideas and correct vague feelings and confused notions, and to educate the minds of those who wished to study such subjects.[122] But he gently chided Austin himself for setting about a work which compromised between diffusion of knowledge among the uninitiated, and Austin's own particular forte in Mill's view, the analysis of a subject down to its ultimate scientific elements. Mill urged Austin that every thinker should make a point of either publishing in his life if possible, or at any rate leaving behind him the most complete expression he could produce of his best thoughts, those which he had no chance of getting into any review. Mill continued that there were two books of which he had heard Austin speak as projects: a continuation of the *Province of Jurisprudence Determined* that was in fact a publication and completion of Austin's lectures; this would be the easier to Austin as much of it was already done: the other which would be more important was a systematic treatise on morals. We may comment that if Austin did not proceed with the major tasks he claimed to have set himself it was not for any want of badgering from those who thought most of him.[123]

Revolution broke out in France on 23 February 1848. Louis Philippe abdicated on the following day and Lamartine on behalf of the provisional government proclaimed a republic. Mill warmly applauded the actions of the provisional government in taking its stand on electoral reform and allaying fears at the acts of violence which had occurred. Mill felt inspired.[124] Mill had, however, been made aware of the Austins' alarm that they were in danger and that they were concerned about the initial suspension of passports. In his letter to Sarah Austin he showed a new note of testiness with her about this, and went on to complain of a letter in *The Times* which bore the signature 'John Austin', in which Mill said there were several things Austin should not be supposed to have written. Mill had been led to believe by what he called a 'disavowal' in *The Times* that it was not Austin's letter.[125] But Sarah proceeded to send the letter to him and Mill returned it, shocked. He conceded that there might be some unfavourable consequences arising from the revolution in France, but to suppose that they preponderated was to him as much a 'dream' as the contrary expectation appeared to Sarah. Mill never thought, he said, that he should differ from Austin in feeling on any public event as he did on this.[126] Nevertheless, Mill did not lose his respect for Austin over the matter. It is plain he did lose what respect he had for Sarah, who had the misfortune to conduct the acrimonious correspondence while Austin stayed in the background. Subsequently Mill would have nothing to do with her.*

Closing scenes at Weybridge

The Austins' reaction to the revolution of 1848 in France was the opposite of that of Sarah's family to the revolution of 1789, and they returned to England early in March 1848. They took up residence first at 8 Queen Square, where Lucie had established a drawing-room in the tradition of her mother and grandmother, the frequent visitors including Dickens, Thackeray and Tennyson.[127] Sarah at this time was developing a correspondence with Whewell, a leading disputant with Mill on matters of logic. She confided in reply to Whewell's letter congratulating them on their safe arrival, that her husband could not think with patience of any Englishman exulting in the awful ruin in France, which displayed gross insensibility to the sufferings of others.[128] At that time Sarah was busy trying to get the fallen Guizot housed on his flight from France as well as looking for a more permanent abode for herself and her husband, finally settling at Weybridge.

In her biographical sketch of Austin, Sarah represented his nine years at Weybridge as a period of tranquillity, saying that the battle of life was now not only over, but had hardly left a scar. But the suggestion she goes on to

---

* Harriet by this time had developed a poor opinion of the Austins as typical of those who were successful in England (Packe, *Mill*, 338). There appears to be a suggestion that Sarah criticized Harriet in the context of her reaction to receiving a copy of Mill's *Political Economy* dedicated to Harriet at a time when Sarah was affronted by Mill's encouragement of revolutionaries (See Mill, *Collected Works* XIV, 4–5). In the early draft of his autobiography Mill disparaged Sarah for her sharp tongue and lack of worthwhile opinions, in a passage deleted in the final product (Mill, *Early Draft*, 147).

make that at this stage Austin was content to pour his knowledge into his wife's receptive ear is not true, and the fact that, in Sarah's words, 'he showed no inclination to devote these years of improved health and tranquil leisure to the work he had so long ago projected' did not always preserve the atmosphere of what she calls 'the calm evening that followed on so cloudy and stormy a day'.[129] Austin was at first apparently making efforts. Sarah wrote in January 1850 that Austin got books and exhausted their whole contents, turning every part of his subject over a thousand times in his mind. But though the head worked, the hand was absolutely inert. He would take refuge in a kind of *découragement* – as if there were nothing to be done for mankind. Sarah added that he was greatly disquieted about France, things appearing blacker and more threatening to him than when there was fighting in the streets.[130] Things did not appear to have altered in the slightest when Sarah again reported his state of mind to Guizot in November. She said only: 'My husband is tolerably well – as well as a body subjected to the attrition of such a mind, revolving on itself, can be.'[131] Nor was Austin's mind any easier about events in France. In December 1851 George Grote was sympathizing with Sarah about Austin being 'struck down' by the brutality of Napoleon III's *coup d'état*.[132] The bitterness on which Mill comments in his autobiography was increasing. Sarah says to Guizot: 'My poor husband grows misanthropic. He cannot say with your indulgent smile, *"Ah, chère amie, les hommes sont si faibles!"* He execrates them: *Il y a de quoi.*'[133]

In 1857, Sarah was reduced to final despair about Austin's writing prospects, but certainly not to resignation. Guizot had inquired after Austin's *Province of Jurisprudence Determined* and Sarah was unsure where he might get a surviving copy. She writes that 'as he had bound himself to this notion of a revised and altered edition *and* a second volume, the result is that he has never touched it, and *never will*.' 'What reason can he give to me or to himself?' she asks, 'Health? But, to *me*, he can hardly urge *that*.' She adds that he had made the causes which conspired to disgust him with men and their affairs an excuse to himself for obeying his own reluctance to set about work. She summed up Austin as 'an immense, powerful, and beautiful machine, without the balance wheel, which should keep it going constantly, evenly, and justly'.[134]

Guizot dutifully responded to Sarah's distress, as others had done before him, by putting his shoulder to where the balance wheel should have been, and Sarah was duly grateful. But Guizot's mixture of flattery and cajolement of Austin, made on behalf of all that Austin owed to 'mankind, to his country, to himself, and to God', set the machine working in what Mill had earlier impressed on Austin was the wrong direction.[135] He wrote an article, the 'Plea for the Constitution', opposing any extension of democratic reform. Mill felt called upon to write a courteous answering article in *Fraser's Magazine*[136] and Sarah herself displayed nervousness about its effect on her French correspondents. She wrote to St Hilaire: 'I do not know whether it will interest you, my dear friend, for it is very anti-democratic, and only treats of England.' But she added that in England it had made a considerable effect, and she hoped that her husband would be encouraged by its success.[137]

Unfortunately, Austin himself was no longer in a position to be encouraged for there was little time left to him. He wrote the article in the latter part of 1858, and he died in December, 1859, after a seven-week illness which set in at the beginning of November. Among the condolences Sarah received, Mill's was conspicuous by its absence. He wrote to her granddaughter Janet and did not mention Sarah in the letter, which Janet notes greatly distressed Sarah.[138]

Sarah now herself began work on the project of producing a new edition of the lectures which had been published and producing the second volume which Austin had envisaged covering the later lectures. Despite a severe illness in June 1860, during which she at times was not expected to recover, she was able to report that the first volume would be printed immediately, and she was working ahead with the second volume despite increasing difficulties as she proceeded.[139] She had written to Mill about a month after Austin's death and asked for his advice and assistance and his copy of the tables of the lectures. Mill wrote a few terse lines in reply saying that she could not have better advisers than Sir John Romilly and Sir George Cornewall Lewis – who had also attended the lectures – and that he had lost his copy of the tables.[140] However, three years later he compromised by assisting in the project while continuing to avoid Sarah. He wrote to Henry Reeve, her nephew, saying that he had in his possession notes of lecture 40 – which was missing from the materials Sarah had – and offering to put this at Sarah's disposal as well as any others of his notes, including those which represented Austin's extemporaneous exposition. The result was that this lecture was able to be published in the edition of the work in 1869, revised and edited by Robert Campbell, and Campbell made acknowledgment for this and for parts of lecture 39 on Codification, to Mill.[141] In addition to this assistance, Mill wrote a warm review of Austin's work in the form in which Sarah had now completed the publication of it, in October 1863 in the *Edinburgh Review*.[142]

Sarah's policy in preparing the 1861 edition of the *Province* was to alter nothing of what had appeared in 1832, except the position of the outline, and to add some scattered memoranda. These appear appended to the text with labels such as 'Ms fragment' as well as an occasional comment by Sarah herself. At the time of the production of the new edition of the *Province*. Sarah declared her intention to produce the remaining lectures as they stood, but to attempt to collate Austin's notes of his Inner Temple lectures, which constituted a much shorter group, with the longer collection of University of London lectures. On closer examination, she found that the author had himself marked the parts of the Inner Temple lectures which were to be added to, or substituted for, the earlier lectures. Thus the lectures printed in 1863 were the two sets of lectures consolidated by Austin himself.[143] Sarah Austin had intended herself to prepare a further edition of the whole of the work with the assistance of the notes by Mill which had reached her in the indirect manner we have described, but she did not live to complete the task,[144] though she did live to see her edition immediately welcomed at Oxford and prescribed for the new Honours school of jurisprudence.[145] In 1865 she was discussing a new edition with legal friends but by the end of the following year she was confessing to her declining energies and her powerlessness to complete the second edition.[146] On 8 August 1867 she died, and the work with Mill's notes was completed by Robert Campbell, who had both a Scottish advocate's and an English barrister's qualifications, in the next two years.

2

Literary influences on Austin and his work

Early literary influences

John Austin, we are led to believe, was always a reserved, 'bookish' person. It is said he inherited a gentle, nervous disposition from his delicate mother. As a boy, he used to spend many hours reading the bible to her and he was nearly always to be seen with a book in his hand. This is not to say that he always enjoyed it. His first recorded words are to the effect that he was making himself do it as a matter of duty and this was at least one battle with himself which he frequently won. He said on the last day of December 1811, when he was framing his New Year resolutions, that 'the expectations of my father, which I am bound in honour and gratitude to fulfil, command me to arouse myself from this lethargy of the faculties: and I am, too, convinced that my happiness is commensurate with and inseparable from the progress I make in the acquisition of knowledge.' He goes on later to record his success in reading Dugald Stewart's *Essay on the Beautiful*, commenting especially on the author's defence of metaphysics, Locke's *Human Understanding*, Mitford's *Greece*, Enfield's *History of Philosophy* and Drummond's *Academical Questions*.

His object in all this was to master the world around him and thus make a name for himself. A staccato entry in his diary reads: 'Reading. Fears of never emerging from obscurity. Height 5 ft $9\frac{1}{2}$ in. in boots.'[1] It is perhaps not remarkable that he should have sought to emerge from obscurity through reading. Education was a path to rising in the social scale for one in his social position, as the history of his later associates shows as well as his own, though he never attained the degree of wealth and position in his lifetime which Jeremy Bentham, James Mill, John Stuart Mill and others did. What is a little more remarkable is his choice of reading in that he began at the very base, systematically working through books which dealt with the conditions of human knowledge or the historic cradle of our Western ways of looking at the world around us. But perhaps this is intelligible, too. One type of person to whom the idea of a systematically ordered world which can be mastered by an understanding of the principles of its order – the *Weltanschauung* of German philosophy with which Austin came to be familiar – is said to appeal, is the intelligent, insecure person, and Austin was obviously both of these things in a very high degree.

The picture of Austin thus presented may be thought to be disturbed by the fact that he entered the army. But we are led to believe that he was caught up in the spirit of the days following Trafalgar, and it is probably an understatement to say that not everybody who enters the army knows what it will be like. There is little evidence that Austin was at this time a man of action. One biographer does indeed say that when he entered France in his later years he must have reflected on the fact that he first entered the country over the Pyrenees under very different conditions.[2] But if Austin had been caught up in the forefront of the peninsular war, surely someone else would have noticed it – even the professor himself. In the days which his diary covers, Austin was reproving himself for the times when he allowed himself to become involved in the contentions of his fellow officers and was unsuccessfully trying to escape the strictures of the colonel. He uses the word 'row' with the distaste with which he subsequently came to react to the word 'revolution'.[3] Books, Austin's preferred field of activity, are unlikely to react with hostility to being read.

The simple picture of Austin we have given may also be thought to be disturbed by the fact that the theory of law for which Austin became famous is a theory which looks upon law as imperatives and, moreover, selects among the kind of imperatives which are characteristic of law the kind which are issued in what H.L.A. Hart has described as the case of the gunman who says to the bank clerk, 'Hand over the money or I will shoot'.[4] Hart points out that, though Austin used the military term 'command' to describe this situation, this is not really appropriate, because the word 'command' is ordinarily used to describe orders given with authority, even if also backed by coercive sanctions, whereas Austin's theory of law concentrates exclusively on the coercive aspects. But Hart does not suggest that any military frame of mind in Austin himself contributed to the fact that this kind of theory appealed to him. Nor does Hart suggest that he misunderstood it because of any military frame of mind. There is in fact no contradiction in persons with a horror of violence adopting this kind of theory. In fact this is one kind of person to whom such a theory is particularly attractive.

For the central strategy of law on such a theory, to whatever ends it is ultimately directed, is to seek to monopolize and control force and by this means to pacify society. The stimulus to the production of this kind of theory may well be the observation of chaotic conditions associated with the use of force, to which is attributed the adoption of this approach by Austin's famous predecessor Thomas Hobbes, reacting to the violence between the Puritans and the royalists in the seventeenth century. The approach is less likely to appeal to those who have a taste for violence than those who seek an escape through law from the uncontrolled manifestations of it which they see. Austin was observing such manifestations all the time from his period in the army onwards, through successive continental revolutions and wars associated with the emergence of national states. At all this, we are told, he desponded.

Further, though Austin was predisposed towards pessimistic attitudes, this type of attitude should not necessarily be associated with undue pessimism. There is some justification for those espousing this approach when they call it realism. It stands in opposition to the kind of historical approach which supposes that law is only in its primitive stages preoccupied with the control of force and moves afterwards progressively to higher levels – the sort of view which Mill tells us became attractive to him after his mental crisis. But the Austinian may rightly claim that to suppose that law must move in this way is to suppose that there are factors controlling the development which are fundamental in the sense that they are not themselves subject to control – that this kind of historical theory is metaphysical. In practice, there is no doubt that, whatever may be said about its lack of comprehensiveness, or of the psychological springs in those who espouse it, a theory of the Austinian type points to functions of law of continuing pressing importance.

After John Austin severed himself by degrees from the army, the acquaintance he made in the first instance with the Taylors and Martineaus of Norwich may have been purely adventitious from the direction of our interest in literary influences. Sally Taylor, as the future Sarah Austin was then known to her intimates, identified her fiancé to a friend, at the time of her engagement, by saying that he was the elder brother of her dear friend Miss Austin, whom the correspondent had heard Sally mention. The two families are said to have known one another.[5] But the literary background and interest of the family no doubt contributed to the common cause Austin was able to make with them and especially with the youngest of the seven offspring.

We have noticed that the patriarch of the Taylors and Martineaus was John Taylor, an eminent Unitarian divine who died at the Warrington Academy in 1761. The Warrington Academy was a famous dissenting seminary, first located in Liverpool and later in Manchester. In the year in which John Taylor died there, its most famous luminary, Joseph Priestley, was appointed as tutor. J. A. Passmore has pointed out that Joseph Priestley is often described as the founder of modern perfectibilism – the doctrine of the perfectibility of man.[6] The *Weltanschauung* of Priestley was not confined to establishing an understanding of how the world works, though it certainly included this, or the means of making it better, though it included this too. His inspiration was millenarian and a particular object of his interest and inspiration his studies of the book of Daniel. 'Whatever was the beginning of this world', he said, 'the end will be glorious and paradisaical, beyond what our imaginations can now conceive.'[7]

When it came to the questions of the means of perfecting mankind, Priestley, in the first place, accepted the associationist theory of psychology put forward by David Hartley. Hartley rejected the view that men are ineducable because they have innate passions which irresistibly incline them to particular courses of action. Self-love, resentment of injuries, the passion between the sexes, and the pursuit of happiness all derive from the working of associative mechanisms upon our original experiences of pleasure and pain. The burnt child comes to fear the fire by associating touching the fire with pain and avoids doing so.[8] Apart from his psychology, Priestley saw in the history of science an exemplification of the road to progress and improvement, and in the French and American revolutions, grounds for confidence that governments could be liberalized.[9]

Leaving aside the religious inspiration of Priestley's supreme optimism, there is much in common between the manner in which Priestley saw aims and objects, and the means to ends, through a survey of human knowledge and its various branches, and the broad and systematic approach of Austin's future close associates, the Benthamites. This is no accident. Bentham discovered the principle of utility which is associated with his name with all the sense of drama with which Archimedes discovered the principle which goes by his. But Bentham did not discover his in the bath as Archimedes is supposed to have found his, unless indeed he read Priestley in the bath. Bentham says that he discovered the principle in 1768 in Priestley's *Essay on Government*.[10] There it appears in the form that 'the good and happiness of the members, that is of the majority of members, of any state is the great standard by which everything relating to that state must be finally determined.'[11]

Joseph Priestley died in 1804. He does not figure in the accounts which are given of the Taylor ménage during Austin's association with it at the time of his courtship and engagement and the early years of his marriage. But Priestley's ideas breathe through the letters of Susannah Taylor to her daughter which we mentioned at the outset of this book, as we did the connections of the Taylors with the most famous Unitarian intellectual minister at the time of Austin's association with them, W.J. Fox. What may have been the detailed contacts of Austin with Priestley's work one does not know. It is not included in the list of works in Austin's library, unfortunately destroyed in the war of 1939 to 1945, which appears in Campbell's *Austin*.[12] The influence may have been indirect.

There is, however, one suggestive incident pointing to its actuality, through whatever channels it operated. When John Stuart Mill was going through his mental crisis and valued Austin's sympathy and understanding, he talked with Austin about the perfectibility of man. He records Austin as professing great disrespect for what Austin called 'the universal principles of human nature of the political economists', and insisting on the evidence which history and daily experience afford of the 'extraordinary pliability of human nature'. Mill goes on to say that this is a phrase he has somewhere borrowed from Austin. Austin, Mill adds, did not think it possible to set any bounds to the moral capabilities which might unfold themselves in mankind, under an enlightened direction of social and educational influences.

All this is pure Priestley, even though Mill speaks of it in the context of saying that Austin had cultivated at this stage a kind of German religion of poetry and feeling with little in it of positive dogma.[13]

Mill himself had never had any religion, though he occasionally speaks of, for example, philosophy, as if it were a kind of religion-substitute after the style of Aldous Huxley's pregnancy-substitute. It is a little puzzling, however, that Mill attributes importance to Austin's influence over him on the matter of the importance of the pliability of human nature for the perfectibility of man, for Austin's views do not seem, as far as Mill retails them, to be distinctly different from his own father's views as Mill had earlier recounted them. The discussion perhaps went further than Mill suggests into Unitarian views of the kind which came from Priestley.

The Austins themselves appear to have been Unitarians throughout their adult lives, taking a restricted part in parish affairs at Weybridge on this account, though they became friendly with the Anglican Archbishop Whewell in their later years and their daughter Lucie turned to Anglicanism in her youth. Unitarianism was associated with Benthamite utilitarianism to the point where Unitarians were described as utilitarians in their Sunday best.[14] We shall see that Austin himself treated utility as the index to the laws of God in those many instances where these laws were not the subject of revelation, following in this respect the general Benthamite approach.

Jeremy Bentham

At the time Austin went to live at Queen Square, obviously because Bentham was there, he was described as a disciple of Jeremy Bentham, and we have already referred to evidence of his avid reading of Bentham's works before that time. In his own writings, however, he was anxious from time to time to make the point that he did not continue an uncritical disciple. In some part, this may have been due to an effort by Austin to maintain his own self-esteem as an independent thinker. But some differences are attributable to Austin's attempt to escape criticisms of Bentham which he encountered in public and professional attitudes of the period, while others of greater intellectual importance are attributable to the influence of his other neighbours at Queen Square.

For all the access which Austin had personally to Bentham in the early part of his residence, his most intimate association over the whole period of importance for Austin's writing was with the young John Stuart Mill. This persisted through the period in which Mill was reading law with Austin, the period following Mill's intellectual crisis when the two engaged in intimate discussions, and the period when Mill attended Austin's lectures and was himself giving advice about Austin's problems. Because of his intensive education by his father at the time when he came to Austin, one function the young Mill performed was to act as a conduit pipe impressing James Mill's notions upon Austin, as Austin's own work shows. Because of the young

Mill's subjection particularly to Bentham's work at the same period, and particularly to the *Rationale of Judicial Evidence*,[15] the young Mill came to have problems with questions of logic in which he was at that time particularly interested. Austin's work reflects these, too. An important theme in reviewing Bentham's work for our present purposes is, therefore, how that work came to raise these issues.

It is our good fortune currently to have access to the two most general works of Bentham relating to law, *An Introduction to the Principles of Morals and Legislation*[16] (let us call it the *Principles*) and *Of Laws in General*[17] (let us call it the *Laws*), in fine editions, the first by J.H. Burns and H.L.A. Hart, and the second by Hart alone. The first of these works was available to Austin at the times of importance for our purposes, having been first published by Bentham in 1789 and an account of much of it having been published in French by Étienne Dumont in 1802. The second was not published in any edition until 1945,[18] when the manner of publication still called for improvement until 1970. Nevertheless Austin was able to pick up its more general threads from other works of Bentham available to him* and from his oral discussions with Bentham himself.

The project which became the manuscripts of the *Principles* and the *Laws* was designed by Bentham as an introduction to a plan of an ideal penal code, though even this was only a part of a grander design which Bentham had conceived. When the further splitting which separated the *Principles* and the *Laws* took place, the *Principles* came to be devoted largely to an explanation of the desirable objectives of laws, and factors in, particularly, the human situation with which legislators and judges were faced, affecting the implementation of those objectives. The *Laws* came to be devoted to definitions and classifications going to the character and structure of a legal system.**

Accordingly, the *Principles*, firstly, expounds the principle of utility. That principle, Bentham explains, approves any action according to its tendency to promote happiness − its utility − which means, as applied to the proper

* The works of Jeremy Betham surviving in Austin's library as presented by Sarah Austin to the library of the Inner Temple as listed in the Campbell *Austin*, ix – xii were: the *Principles* (1789), the Dumont version of it (Traités de Législation civile et pénale (1802)), the *Constitutional Code for the Use of All Nations and All Governments Professing Liberal Opinions* (1830), the *Fragment on Government* (1776), and *Draught of a New Plan for the Organisation of the Judicial Establishment in France*. But this list would not have been exhaustive of what in fact Austin read of Bentham.

** The history of the development of Bentham's grand design is traced by Burns and Hart in their introduction to the *Principles* and by Hart in his introduction to the *Laws*. An important published work issuing from the scheme in addition to those already mentioned was the *Theory of Punishment*, in Dumont's 1811 version, which Sarah Austin read on Austin's bidding. Of the interruptions which Bentham indulged to the development of his systematic writing the *Fragment on Government* (1776) was available to Austin, but the *Comment on the Commentaries* was not published until 1928 by C.W. Everett. Both are now available in Jeremy Bentham, *A Comment on the Commentaries and a Fragment on Government* edited by J.H. Burns and H.L.A. Hart (London, 1977).

objective of governmental measures, the happiness of the community.[19] Bentham called sources of pleasure or pain, when considered as giving binding force to laws or rules of conduct, sanctions. These might be physical, political, moral or religious, the first arising in the ordinary course of nature, the second through the judge giving effect to the will of the sovereign, the third through reactions of a man's associates, and the fourth through divine will.[20] In working with punishments, the legislator had to understand the force of the pleasures and pains which were his instruments, making detailed calculations of the effects of his actions by way of pleasure and pain on the various individuals in the community and summing up the values of pleasures and pains on both sides.[21]

The calculations which Bentham envisaged in all this would strike any reader as massive and we shall see that Austin was led, either because of his own misgivings or because of criticisms of their impracticality, to suggest ways in which they might be minimized. Thus he became in some degree a heretic in this area of Benthamite theory.

Austin did not, in his major work in jurisprudence, adopt Bentham's system of classification of pleasures and pains, to which Bentham next proceeded in the *Principles*, nor did Austin substitute anything for it, so that this is a gap in Austin's work. Bentham said that pleasures and pains may be simple or complex. Simple pleasures he identified as those of sense, wealth, skill, amity, good name, power, piety, benevolence, malevolence, memory, imagination, expectation, those dependent on association, and relief. Pains were classified according to a largely corresponding scheme. Bentham thought that virtually all these pleasures and pains must come under the consideration of the legislator in making a law: in determining what is mischievous and should be an offence, what is the temptation to commit it, and what should be the means of punishment.[22] Bentham also considered systematically the causes of pleasures and pains and how their operation varied with various aspects of the individual affected. Some of the effects of pleasures and pains he thought were of sufficiently general character to be taken account of by the legislator, others could be more easily taken account of by the judge dealing directly with individuals.[23]

Austin took more interest in Bentham's analysis of the ways pains and pleasures, and the prospects of pains and pleasures, affect acts of individuals in differing circumstances. Pleasures and pains had to operate on individuals through their understanding and their wills, particularly in regard to the formation of intentions and the part played by motives.[24] Bentham also considered the way in which an act was related to its consequences, and was especially concerned with these consequences where they were mischievous. Where the consequences were mischievous the acts, in Bentham's view, should often be made offences by the legislator, but not always. One of Bentham's most influential points was that punishment was an evil because it inflicted pain, and could only be justified where it avoided a greater evil. Even then it must be appropriately variable and equable, be commensurate with other punishments, have easily understandable characteristics, operate with exemplarity and frugality, serve to reform, disable from future offending, compensate, gain popular acceptance, and have means of remissibility.[25]

While Bentham's primary interest in the analysis outlined in the preceding paragraph was the reformative one of constructing an ideal code, Austin's interest was more in the opportunities for systematic treatment of whatever laws one might encounter at any place or at any time, desirable or not, which such an analysis provided. His analysis in any case varied from Bentham's. The same is true of Austin's approach to classification of offences, the matter to which Bentham proceeded in the *Principles*, and true for the same reasons. Austin and Bentham agreed on the need for a logical division of the subject matter of law. But their immediate objects in making the analysis were different, even though Austin had no wish to minimize the importance of what Bentham was doing.

On the logical aspect, Bentham said that to understand a thing, one has to understand the points on which a thing agrees with other things (its genus) and the points on which it disagrees (its difference). A perfect knowledge of objects constituting a logical whole is to be obtained by repeated bipartition of them.[26] Bentham thus quickly reaches four major classes of offences – private offences (primarily against assignable individuals), semi-public offences (primarily against a whole class narrower than the entire community), self-regarding offences (primarily against the offender himself) and public offences (against the whole community). To these he adds a fifth class of multiform offences, and then proceeds to divide each class and again subdivide, though with various difficulties, until he leaves further subdivision to the major body of the work to which the *Principles* was intended to be introductory.[27]

Thus far – and this means as far as the beginning of the final chapter of the *Principles* – Bentham's exposition was in general orderly. He had expounded the proper general objective of law, the means which the legislator, particularly, had at his disposal for implementing that objective, and the considerations of which he had to take account in framing offences and punishments, which had by this time emerged as the primary task in framing laws in the light of the considerations earlier expounded. Bentham had intended in his final chapter to deal with the relation of the penal branch to other branches of law, but by now the question was very sharply raised concerning what functions other branches of law had to perform at all in a proper legal system. It was easy enough to say that the complicated relationships between penal and other branches of law in existing systems were the outcome of legislative incompetence, and Bentham did say this, but what would be the division of penal and other branches in a sensibly constructed system was a matter which he found it necessary to leave tentative when external pressures forced publication in 1789 of the *Principles* in what was substantially its 1780 form.

Bentham explains in his preface to the *Principles* in 1789, as well as in the final chapter of the *Principles* as published, that the answer to the above question depends on the answer to the question 'What is an identifiable and complete law?' which means for him an expression of the will of the legislator sufficient for submission by subjects and implementation by officials. This could not be discovered by examining existing systems because no system consisted of a body of laws complete in this sense. It had to be constructed and one had to begin with the character of laws in general to find what was required.[28]

That was where the *Laws* began. That, too, was where Austin began his whole theory of jurisprudence, and he was to develop it in a way which was, deservedly or undeservedly, to obtain for him a reputation as a retrograde or backsliding Benthamite. The function of the definition of a law in Bentham was to advance the task of constructing an ideal code by attending to the proper manner of its exposition; for Austin the definition was the basis of the general jurisprudence upon which he concentrated his attention. Bentham, in the final chapter of the *Principles*, divided jurisprudence into expository, concerning what the law is, and censorial, concerning what the law ought to be. Bentham said that expository jurisprudence might be local or universal, and because of the differences of law from place to place in substance, universal expository jurisprudence would be virtually confined to the terminological, dealing with the meanings of words like law, power, right, obligation, liberty and others.[29] These were matters of central concern to Austin.

Austin follows Bentham very closely in the definition of law at the beginning of the *Laws*. Bentham's definition is

> an assemblage of signs, declaratory of a volition conceived or adopted by the sovereign in a state, concerning the conduct to be observed in a certain case by a certain person or class of persons, who in the case in question are or are supposed to be subject to his power; such volition trusting for its accomplishment to the expectation of certain events which it is intended such declaration should upon occasion be a means of bringing to pass, and the prospect of which it is intended should act as a motive upon those whose conduct is in question.[30]

Bentham points out what is significant for the understanding of Austin, that this definition is broader than might be suggested by what is commonly understood by a law, for it comprehends much that would be denied that title on the insufficient ground that the sovereign is not the immediate source, though he is the ultimate source.[31]

For Bentham, as for Austin, the ultimate source of a mandate of the kind in question is the will of the sovereign in a state − a person or assemblage of persons to whose will a whole political community is (no matter on what account) supposed to be in a disposition to pay obedience (not necessarily in all cases) in preference to the will of any other. A given mandate may be so by conception or adoption of the sovereign, the first where he issued it as it stands, the second where it issues from some other person but the sovereign's will is known to be that that other person's will should be looked upon as his own. The adoption may be by susception (tacit acceptance) of mandates already issued, otherwise by pre-adoption. Susception applies to the mandates of former sovereigns and subordinate power-holders, pre-adoption cannot apply to the acts of future sovereigns because an attempt at this by the present sovereign would be nugatory.

Pre-adoption by the sovereign of the mandates of subordinate power-holders applies to all the mandates of persons to whom the law gives powers of ordering and countermanding orders, whether beneficial or fiduciary, and whether for the benefit of particular individuals or the public at large, so that in the latter case they are seen as constitutional powers. Conveyances and covenants have all the connection they have with the legal system because, tacitly adopted by the sovereign, they are converted into mandates. Legal mandates generally are domestic or public, the latter being sovereign or subordinate. Subordinate legal mandates are judicial if issued on the occasion of a suit, otherwise they are subordinate laws or by-laws if capable of perpetuity, if not, executive orders.[32] Although Austin did not always pursue the above notions to their full length, and there are differences in terminology, these notions of Bentham are at the root of Austin's treatment of sources of law.

Equally fundamental to Austin's theory are Bentham's notions that where the sovereign directs a law to himself it can only be a royal covenant, where directed to future sovereigns only a recommendatory mandate. He can employ no sanction against the future sovereign, and those sanctions affecting covenants of his own cannot be physical or political, only religious or moral.[33]

As the *Laws* progresses, however, Bentham covers ground over which Austin does not follow him. Austin was content to confine his definition of laws to general laws, whereas Bentham stresses that powers of issuing general mandates require complementary powers which may diminish or destroy their force. Powers to bring particular objects within a class laid down by a general law, or exclude them from it, are necessarily part of the total exercise of power in a community. Even a despot cannot bring all individuals under his notice so as to legislate for everyone *de singulis*.[34] Bentham makes the further point when dealing with laws commanding officials to apply sanctions (subsidiary laws which are 'adjective' rather than 'substantive') that circumstances may arise in the course of administration which have the effect of enabling the punishment to be escaped or imposed by manipulation of the adjective laws.[35] Problems in the application of laws certainly did not escape Austin's attention, but his definition of law did not bring them within the field of his study in such a way as to provide for systematic treatment of them.

Bentham proceeds towards the performance of his task of describing a complete law by discussing the ways in which various laws may apply to other laws.[36] The principal concern of Austin with this sort of matter was with the question whether a declaratory or a repealing law would fit the general definition of law which Austin largely adopted from Bentham – a different concern from Bentham's own at this point. Then Bentham tells us that directive laws need to be reinforced by subsidiary laws such as punitory and remedial laws, the last seeking to obviate a mischief by making compensation for what is past, by curing what is present, or by guarding against what is to come. Thus there may be as much as a threefold satisfactive clause annexed to a directive law, with the help of trains of remoter subsidiary laws.[37]

Austin did not get in his main lectures to these matters at all, though there are brief references to some of Bentham's distinctions here in his outline of his projected course for students. The problems of classification here did not have the same bearing for him as they did for Bentham, for Austin began his map of the legal system with the substantive civil law, not with a cataloguing of criminal offences. Bentham, naturally in the light of what we have seen to be the direction of his interest in its functions, does not systematically consider the civil law until after he has explained what is involved in a complete law. This, at the point in his exposition we have reached, he is now ready to do.

In point of degrees of fullness, Bentham says, a law may be merely directive, or it may be this and incitative, the incitement being comminatory (threatening with punishment) or, rarely, invitative (rewarding).[38] Austin excluded the latter type from his account of law by definition, possibly just for the sake of tidiness. Bentham continues that the law may be tempered by specifications of circumstances extenuative or aggravative, and further have satisfactive clauses attached (remedial appendages). A law may fail in the matter of completeness in expression, the connection of its parts, or its design (relation to the will of the legislator). If liberal interpretation seeks to arrive at a will of the legislator which in fact was lacking because of failure of the legislator's understanding, interpretation becomes a euphemism for alteration.[39] Austin shared Bentham's concern about judicial legislation of this sort, even though he explicitly distinguished his position from Bentham's by favouring judicial legislation more generally.

Austin does not, however, share Bentham's concern at all with arriving at a notion of a single complete law adequately expressive of the legislative will. Austin founded his map of a legal system largely on classifications of rights, following in this respect more conventional notions than Bentham's. Even on that basis later commentators had to notice that Austin would talk rather undiscriminatingly of a right in the singular or rights in the plural, using the term in the singular sometimes for what, on the basis of what he said elsewhere, would have to be regarded as a collection of rights. For Bentham a single law creates a single offence, delineated by reference to its being the narrowest species of that kind of offence of which the law will take account without recognizing differences in circumstances affecting the responsibility – the *infima species*. The relevant differences, however, may not appear exclusively in the actual expression of the directive which sets it up, which has to be as broad as the imperfect precision of the language used will require. Bentham calls the narrowest classes provided with names *genera infima*.[40]

The problem of specifying the further differences, necessary beyond what language conveniently permits, in order to arrive at a single offence – the *monad*, which is the smallest element in a legal system – may be solved in Bentham's view by attaching narrative or expository matter to the mandate laying down the offence. For example in an offence against property the offence will not be committed by the owner or those to whom he grants permission, and the multitudes of exceptions here involved can be reduced to an almost infinite degree of compression by presenting them in narrative form.[41] It is through this expedient that the fundamental division of penal and civil laws emerges. In any law there must be a penal and civil part. But if the expository matter is attached separately to each offence, there will be enormous duplication in the setting out of legislation. The description of the act itself or the punishment would occupy small space, but the quantity of circumstantive matter is voluminous and will be the same – repetitive – over classes of offences. A quantity of circumstantive matter applying alike to various classes of offences is therefore placed contiguous to none and constitutes the civil code.[42]

Bentham proceeds to find the major difference in civil and criminal *procedure* in the circumstance that, as he sees it, the offence in the former case is ordinarily created by the judge in his order at the end of the case, while in the latter it exists beforehand.[43]

Whatever Austin may have thought of all this, it cannot easily be rendered consistent with his mode of presenting his map of the legal system. He began with what was for Bentham expository matter, and which for Bentham could be rendered intelligible only in relation to a catalogue of offences which Austin did not reach in detail at all.

Bentham concluded the *Laws* by saying that it supplied the plan of a complete body of statute law for every purpose, and, together with the *Principles*, a complete and pretty detailed plan of a complete body of laws. The *Principles* gave an idea of the substance, the *Laws* the proper form in which it should be cast to disclose the true nature and mutual connections of the laws, enabling the customary law to be digested without a single loss of an ancient and respected institution.[44] While Austin profoundly agreed with this last point and stressed it himself, Bentham's plan for a code which would enable it to be done was not Austin's plan of presenting his own map of a legal system. Nor was Austin's notion of a scientific exposition generally that with which Bentham concluded by describing as his own: the fruits of a method planned under the auspices of utility, in which laws are ranged according to the ends they have in view.[45]

Austin might have displayed more interest in Bentham's inquiry into what was required for a complete expression of the will of the legislator in a single law if Bentham had not attempted to give it a special kind of scientific foundation, both in the preface to the *Principles*[46] and the concluding chapter of it,[47] as an exercise in working out what was involved in the logic of the will, as opposed to the Aristotelian logic of the understanding. Neither the word 'logic' nor the word 'will' could have been less happily chosen in the light of the powerful influence of the Mills, especially James Mill reflected in his son, upon Austin. James Mill, in his *Analysis of the Phenomena of the Human Mind*,[48] drawing upon late eighteenth-century philosophy, demolished the will, leaving it in much the same state as the Benthamites generally left the moral sense. It was a spurious mental phenomenon constructed by mistakes of thought out of very ordinary mental happenings. There is something anticipatory here of the idea that constructions of some ideas of mental events by scholars amount to construction of 'ghosts in the machine', which was to appear in Gilbert Ryle's *Concept of Mind*[49] over a century later. The internal evidence of Austin's work is that he accepted Mill's conclusions in this respect enthusiastically, as we shall see.

The natural outcome of the rejection of the will was the rejection of any special logic associated with it, and the insistence instead on the analysis of human behaviour proceeding largely according to the logic of sciences generally. John Stuart Mill was to say in his *System of Logic*[50] that his book, concluding that work, on the Logic of the Social Sciences could only be a supplement to his general work since he must already have described the methods of investigation of the social sciences if he had succeeded in describing those of the sciences generally. It was only a matter of which methods were more specially suited to the various branches of moral inquiry.[51]

Bentham's manner of speaking of the logic of the will, in contrast to the logic of understanding which he saw traditional logic as an attempt to grasp, has been seen as having relations with modern deontic logic, especially having regard to Bentham's emphasis on the importance of imperative propositions in law as expounded in Chapter X of the *Laws*.[52] Bentham himself used deontology as a synonym for ethics, but he obviously considered in speaking of a logic of the will that the imperative, as opposed to narrative, propositions there involved were not confined to ethics. John Stuart Mill considered the imperative mood as characteristic of art, as opposed to science. For him, whatever speaks in rules or precepts, rather than assertions of fact, is an art.[53] But Mill did not consider that any special logic was required in reasoning about the application of precepts to facts. This was one case where the traditional Aristotelian syllogistic logic was adequate, since it was merely a matter of working out what was involved in a formula.[54] Further, Mill considered that the reasons used to arrive at a precept in the light of an already established objective, were ordinary scientific factual propositions.[55] A special kind of reasoning was required only for validating the first principles of an art − justifying their desirability − for example, justifying utility as the end of law or other arts. Mill called this teleology.[56] But this area of special logic, as understood by Mill, does not appear to be involved in understanding the structure of positive law, in which area Bentham thought a special imperative logic of paramount importance. It must be stressed here, as elsewhere, that Mill's *System of Logic* was not available to Austin at the times important to us, though he applauded it when it appeared. What is clear is that Austin wished himself to construct a science of law rather than involve himself in Bentham's art of legislation, and to do it on the model of James Mill's science of political economy, which was a behavioural science elaborated in laws of nature, not teleology.

To a thinker of the school of the Mills and Austin, Bentham left the relation between the science of law and the art of legislation in some confusion. He considered that the science of law was the most important part of the logic of the will, insofar as the form of the science was concerned. It was to the art of legislation what anatomy was to medicine.[57] But then later, he divided jurisprudence into expository, concerning what the law is, and censorial, concerning what the law ought to be, the latter of which he *identified* with the art of legislation.[58]

On this latter basis, Austin's work has to be classed as universal expository jurisprudence, which, as we have seen, Bentham thought had a very narrow field because so little coincided from nation to nation. But where does this leave the science of law which is to the art of legislation what anatomy is to medicine? It is not an exposition of legal provisions, it is, from the Mill point of view, an account of laws of nature determining things about legal provisions wherever they appear, in any code actually appearing at any given time, or which might ideally appear. That is what Austin sought to write about. To say disparagingly of such a person that he is only concerned with the 'is' and not the 'ought', as Bentham's contrast between the expository and censorial might suggest, is unfair. The 'is' propositions employed are statements to the effect that if one encounters a given phenomenon – or equally if one produces that phenomenon in pursuit of a given objective – then one will encounter another, too. These laws are as important to the art in a field as to other kinds of investigation in it. There are a number of reasons for regarding Austin as a conservative. But to regard him as conservative because he espoused an 'expository' science in this sense is not a cogent reason.

Although the present writer would take his stand with Bentham's younger associates concerning the very general matters last discussed, it is not intended to suggest that by taking that stand one disposes of the question whether Austin should have devoted attention to the question of what is involved in a single complete law. All that can be said is that, for one who takes the Mills' point of view, it is unfortunate that Bentham surrounded his special points in this respect with philosophical panoply. James Mill, while he disposed of the will, did not pretend to dispose of volitions and Austin, as we shall see, accepts Mill's account of the latter. What Austin may have been distracted by the unacceptable philosophy from doing was to give sufficient attention to the complexities of legal volitional mandates with which Bentham was concerned.

James Mill

Since the influence of James Mill's *Analysis of the Phenomena of the Human Mind* is acknowledged explicitly in a special context in Austin's own work we defer consideration of it until it arises there. But James Mill's economic writing has a much more generalized influence. Two of Austin's minor works at least, his earliest article about primogeniture in 1824 and his review of List's work in 1842, have as their major object the support of James Mill's economic views. But, most importantly, Austin considered that James Mill's account of economics was the very model of what an account of any social field should be like, and this applied to jurisprudence as much as anything else. Some writers suggest that Austin's model was mathematics, but we believe this gives rise to a fundamentally false interpretation of Austin's whole objectives. Mathematics was not his model. It was what was then known as political economy, for the scientific achievements of which Austin had an unbounded admiration, which he somehow reconciled with his strictures on the narrow assumptions the science made about the springs of human action. And what is fundamental about political economy as presented by Mill is its character as a logical pattern of laws of nature exhibiting necessary connections between things.

At the time when John Austin arrived at Queen Square, James Mill was working on his *Elements of Political Economy*. John Stuart Mill was then 13 years old, and the elder Mill's notes of his lectures to his son became the outline of the book, of which the first edition was published late in 1821.[59] By this time the younger Mill's immediate further education had been turned over to John Austin, his father's gift to his son on the handing over being a copy of Dumont's exposition of Bentham's *Principles*[60] and other Benthamite matter.

The *Elements* was Mill's attempt to do for David Ricardo what he had sought to do for Bentham in the field of law and government. Mill and Ricardo had been close friends for 10 or 11 years at the time of the publication of the *Elements*, during which time Mill was giving advice and assistance with Ricardo's economic theorizing and publication, especially in the light of his experience as a journalist. He pushed and encouraged Ricardo with the writing of his *Principles of Political Economy*, and accepted the results wholeheartedly. By the time this work was published in 1817, Mill was already pushing Ricardo to become the parliamentary spokesman for correct economic principles and good government and Ricardo obtained his seat in 1819, Mill continuing to educate him for this purpose in Benthamism until Ricardo's sudden death in 1823.[61]

In 1810, at the beginnings of his Benthamite close associations, Ricardo was already 38 years old and had 13 years to live. He had been developing his thoughts on economic theory for 10 years and specially interested Mill in him through his first publication at the time. Ricardo's original inspiration was Adam Smith and he thus represents a force independent of Bentham himself operating upon the thinking of Bentham's associates, whatever the points of contact might be, and later upon the thinking of men who were to be far more radical than the Benthamites, including Karl Marx. The implications of Ricardo's views for matters not confined to the economic field, especially as filtering through the elder Mill, were problems for the younger Mill and Austin to discuss together.

The *Elements* deals first with production, designating labour the primary instrument of production and calling attention to the fact that its productive powers can be augmented chiefly by limiting the number of each man's productive operations – division of labour. Capital, the secondary instrument of production, owes its existence to labour of which the first capital is the result, though subsequently capital is the result of capital and labour combined. For the purposes of proceeding next to distribution, Mill classifies what is produced into the rent of land, the wages of labour, and the profits of stock. Rent arises from the fact that earth does not continue to yield produce in equal abundance to successive portions of capital, rent being the excess of what is yielded to the more productive portions above what is equal to the produce of the least productive portions. The genuine effect of labour and capital in cooperation after rent is taken out of account, is left to be divided between the labourer, as the wages of labour, and the capitalist, as the profits of stock. In respect of the proportions going to each, as the share of one is increased, so the share of the other one falls. In this sense wages and profits depend upon one another, but in respect of the absolute quantities of produce which those shares may contain, the productive power of the instruments of production is the determining cause.[62]

Proceeding to interchange of commodities, Mill identifies demand and supply as what determines in the first instance how much of one commodity exchanges for how much of another. But what ultimately determines the matter is cost of production. In this capital and labour are commonly combined, but since the value of all capital is determined by labour, the exchange value of commodities is determined by labour. Capital is only hoarded labour. But, although exchangeable value is proportioned to quantity of labour expended in production, labour cannot be used as the measure of value. The degree in which produce is shared between the two kinds of labour varies, there is no practicable means of ascertaining in advance the exact quantity of hoarded labour which goes to production, and labour is not constant in its productive powers. Nor can an accurate measure of value be found in anything other than labour, but gold is less imperfect than almost any other, because it is produced under conditions close to the medium of the variable factors above mentioned.[63]

Exchange takes place between different countries when one of the countries alone can produce one of the commodities or one has a greater relative facility in producing one of the commodities than the other, unless this difference be insufficient to cover something more than the expense of carriage. The benefit is in what is imported, not in what is exported.[64]

Wants may be best supplied if there is a medium of exchange, a commodity which, in order to effect an exchange between two other commodities, is first received in exchange for one and then given in exchange for the other. Certain metals are found to be suitable for this purpose because of their divisibility, portability, indestructibility and steadiness of value. Governments can exclusively undertake their stamping for quality and quantity, and put them into convenient shape, whereupon they become money.[65]

The value of money — what exchanges for a portion of commodities — is determined by the quantity of money in a country. Whenever coining is left free, the value of money is determined by the value of the metal, which in turn is determined by its cost of production. A government can only raise or lower the quantity in relation to its natural level to an inconsiderable extent. Sometimes two metals may be used, but this causes great inconveniences because they may fluctuate in relative value, unless one is only legal tender to a small amount. Substitutes for money may be attempted, of which paper money is a type of written obligation to pay money. Bills of exchange save the transport of gold and are useful not only between country and country but may perform the functions of paper money within a country, as may promissory notes, especially of banks. Paper money is highly advantageous to a country because it saves what of national production would otherwise go to provide the medium of exchange, and paper is more convenient. One inconvenience is the failure of the parties to fulfil obligations but to this there are spontaneous corrective forces under free competition and the evil of forgery is minimized under the same conditions. Another inconvenience is change of the value of the currency, which is highly injurious, but follows only from an act of government and the security against it is dependence of government upon the people.[66]

Because when gold is cheap, other commodities are dear, an increase in the quantity of gold, which cheapens it, will destroy the power of a country to export other commodities, and a fall in the quantity of gold in the country will encourage export of them — assuming freedom from government interference. The quantity of things for which gold will exchange — its value — is not the same even in all parts of the same country and for the same reason as it is not the same in different countries. The cost of living may be higher in one country — the value of the precious metal is lower — by the amount only of the cost of carriage of commodities from one country to the other. Gold distributes itself from where it is produced throughout the globe because of the effect of the mutual relations of gold and other commodities' prices on the importing and exporting of both — producing a balance.[67]

The business of money transactions between nations is carried on much more by the medium of bills of exchange than by transporting gold. If the amount of bills wanted and offering between two countries is the same there will be neither premium nor discount in the sales and purchases – the exchange will be at par. But if the amounts are unequal, there may be variations limited by the cost of transporting gold, or metallic money to the same real content of gold.[68]

There may be bounties or prohibitions aimed at making more or less production or exchange flow in the profitable channels than otherwise would. The effect is then to induce the industry of a country to employ itself less advantageously. No commodity which can be made at home will ever be imported from a foreign country unless it can be obtained by importation with a smaller quantity of labour, that is, cost, than it could be produced at home. The merchants will always buy in the cheapest market and sell in the dearest. The case of the landlord is peculiar. A high price of corn is profitable to him because the higher the price, the smaller the portion of the produce which will suffice to replace with its profits the capital of the farmer, and all the rest belongs to the landlord. To the farmer and to the rest of the community it is an evil tending to diminishing profits and enhancing the charge to consumers. Colonization may take forms restricting desirable free trade, the mother-country gaining advantages in cheapness of goods from the colony. But this must be at the expense of the colony and under free trade both parties gain. There is no advantage even to the mother-country from a captive market in the colony.[69]

Production, Distribution and Exchange are means of which the end is Consumption. Firstly, consumption may be for the sake of production – the necessaries of the labourer, machinery, and materials. From this productive consumption, unproductive consumption is distinguished – the end which is not a means, satisfaction being what is derived through the loss of property to the individual and the community. What the productive powers produce in a year is the gross annual produce, and after replacement of capital productively consumed, the net annual produce. A year means in political economy a period including a revolving circle of production and consumption such that what is produced in one year is consumed in the next. An individual only produces to the extent he wishes to consume and likewise the demand and supply of all individuals in the nation, taken aggregately, must be equal. So the amount of the annual produce is limited to annual demand. But there may be a lack of adaptation of parts of demand and supply, with gluts and deficiencies of particular commodities, having effects on their prices, so that production is drawn into the correct channels and balance restored.[70]

Consumption is by individuals or by the government. Government consumption is unproductive and must, on any permanent basis, be derived from rent, profits of stock, or wages of labour. It cannot be derived on a long-term basis from capital without desolating the country. For the government to take a share of the rent of land does not affect the industry of the country for the capitalist is indifferent whether he pays the surplus after profits of stock to the landlord or the government. But where land has been converted into private property rent could not be taken exclusively to supply wants of governments without injustice to adjusted expectations. However, only the present rent is entitled to protection from tax on these grounds; increases effected through government action would be an appropriate source for defraying government expenses, and the fact that this cannot occur at a stroke but through a gradual process does not affect this. Taxes on profits, if on a basis of equality, do not affect most factors in the economy, providing no incentive to switch production, and not affecting the aggregate of demand and supply or the value of money. A tax upon wages cannot be made to fall on the labourer if wages are only sufficient to sustain the supply of labourers, for in such a case the tax must cause a rise in wages. But if they are not at this lowest rate, the tax can be made to fall on the labourer.[71]

Where direct taxes are imposed which are made to fall equally upon all three sources of income above, Mill says that insofar as they are paid by the landlord or the profit-maker, they fall on that person. Where a tax is paid by the wage earner, it falls on the profit-maker through a rise in wages if wages were formerly only sufficient to sustain the labourer, otherwise on the labourer himself. In both cases, adjustments will occur which prevent an effect on the total level of prices. But the question in what proportions taxes ought to fall is a question which must take account of the real value of incomes to individuals with all their feelings including those for their children, which depends on the security and permanency of the incomes as well as their amount. A tax ought to leave the relative condition of the different classes of contributors the same after tax as before it. An item of income worth only half the number of years' purchase of another should attract only half as much tax to preserve the natural equilibrium.[72]

Mill turns to the effect of taxes on commodities. The effect of a tax on one single commodity is to raise its price and it falls on the consumers of it. By various adjustments, if a tax is imposed equally on all commodities it falls upon all consumers. Taxes upon the produce of land, such as corn, fall on the consumer as in the case of any commodity, not on the farmer or the landlord. Taxes on the instruments of agricultural production fall also on the consumer, in the same way as taxes on the profits of the farmer, partly for the benefit of the government and partly for the benefit of the landlord. Tithes imposed generally upon the produce of land operate within the above principles and fall on the consumer. Poor rates as levied operate in a mixture of the ways already covered: where a tax is imposed proportionally on rent it falls on the landlord, where on land proportioned to the produce it falls on the consumer, and where on land proportioned to the farmer's profits it falls on the consumer and incidentally benefits the landlord. Where a tax is laid on land at so much per acre, it does not affect the cost of production and hence the price if there is no discrimination between cultivated and uncultivated land. But where the tax is levied only on cultivated land the tax must be included in the price. The landlord benefits, the consumer loses for the landlord's benefit and that of the government and there is a retardation of descent of capital to inferior species of land.[73]

Mill deals next with some special cases at the edge of taxes on commodities, first, taxes on transfer of property, which he finds will fall according to the type on transferor or transferee, and taxes on law suits which are both a tax on suitors and the demand for justice. Taxes on coinage, on the other hand, through requiring payment of more for the coins than the bullion of which they are composed, raise the currency in value so that the tax falls on nobody and this tax ought to be carried as far as the incentive which it creates to illicit coining will permit. But if paper currency is issued without restriction, the quantity of currency may rise so high that paper-holders have an incentive to demand coins for melting and cause adverse effects in sudden contraction of the paper currency by banks. But if an obligation is imposed on the bank to pay the paper-holder bullion or coins at his option, the check on the issue of paper is made to operate earlier. Taxes on precious metals when produced or imported, as distinct from coinage, would fall on the consumer so far as used for ornament rather than coinage, but rather more slowly than on many commodities because of the high ratio of quantity in use to annual supply, as applies to some other commodities like houses.[74]

In concluding at once his discourse and his account of taxation, Mill asserts that capital is most advantageously employed when no inducement whatsoever is employed to turn it from the direction which the interest of the owners would give it into another. If, for example, a tax is imposed upon English broadcloth which is exchanged for German linen, the people of England will suffer through the adjustments set in train both by paying tax on the broadcloth and being obliged to pay more for their linen. This does not mean that a highly taxed country cannot export to as great an extent as if she had not been taxed at all, but if care has not been taken to compensate for established duties by countervailing duties and drawbacks, it does not export with the same advantage. If drawbacks of duty and countervailing duties are appropriately applied, the prices of commodities in one country may be raised to any extent above their prices in the surrounding countries.[75]

We have said that the above picture of the workings of the political economy was Austin's model of what a social science should be like, including jurisprudence. His admiration for it will become clear as we trace the course of his lectures in the next chapter. Some features of it need to be stressed for the interpretation of Austin.

Mill's account of the economy is presented primarily as a science, not as an art. The logic employed is the logic of the understanding, even though Mill is presenting what was then known as a 'moral', in the sense of social science. Mill prided himself especially on his logical method, and saw it reflected in the tight arguments by which he displayed the operations of causes and effects in the economic field. This was one source for him of the mental pleasure deriving from the study of political economy.[76] Austin obviously derived such pleasure from imitating this in jurisprudence, insofar as he was capable of deriving pleasure at all in his circumstances, most especially because he saw universal logical propositions as expressing real necessary connections between things as Mill did in his political economy.

Certainly, Mill also claimed to derive pleasure from what he conceived to be the utility of what he was doing,[77] as Austin did in his own work. Mill's science of political economy had, for Mill, lessons for the art of government in dealing with the economy, by wise practice of which a government could contribute to the wealth of the whole community, extending to the world community. Mill introduces these questions of the art of government, however, incidentally to his account of the science, and often, though not always, the art of government is seen to be the adoption of a 'hands off' policy, permitting market forces to operate unchecked to the supposed advantage of all. This could be connected, and was importantly connected in Benthamite theory and practice, with Bentham's point in the *Principles* that legislation was *prima facie* an evil because it operated ordinarily through the production of pains (the sanctions). So legislation should be repealed where it damaged the economy, by interfering with beneficial market forces, and this was the source of the Benthamite campaign for the repeal of the corn laws.

Austin accepted all this enthusiastically, and carried the lessons to the point where he could be accused not only of conservatism, but inhumanity. We shall see that he thought industrial problems should be solved, not through amelioration of the workers' condition through positive legislation, but through achievement of industrial peace through education of the workers in Ricardo's and Mill's principles, this education carrying with it recognition on the workers' part that the institution of property was beneficient and that what remedies there were for their ills lay in their own hands through limitation of their own number by birth control.

In Charles Dickens's caricature of James Mill's approach in *Hard Times*, emphasizing the inhumane aspects of it, Mill's approach is presented as if the selfish interest which Mill presented as operating to maximize the wealth of all in the workings of the economy were, on Mill's approach, appropriate to all departments of human activity and were calculated to maximize happiness in all respects. But how far this charge can be validly brought against any Benthamite is questionable. We shall see that Austin believed, as Bentham did, in the reality of and value of human benevolence, while at the same time, on what basis is not clear, accepting the dependence of economic laws on the inevitability of motives of self-interest operating in that sphere. It is not clear, either, how the assumptions of self-interest manifested in economic laws were reconciled by Austin with the view he expressed to Mill of the infinite pliability of human nature in the hands of the legislator. There is difficulty in reconciling an approach to social areas like Bentham's in which prominence is given at the outset, and throughout, to the notion that they are areas for human will, effectively designed and expressed, playing on features of human nature as an instrument, with an approach like Austin's treating social areas as ones in which laws of nature operate and an art like legislation has to face at least some important ones which are intractable.

We have said we do not blame Austin for treating social areas initially as sciences, but perhaps he is more vulnerable to the criticism that he did not show more concern for the problems his approach raised for the art of legislation and how they might be tackled. The younger Mill was certainly concerned with these things, but the aspects of his work in which his problems were Austin's problems related rather to general logic and the logic of the social sciences and the science of law in particular. Mill's approach to these matters, insofar as they were of special importance to Austin, we now discuss.

John Stuart Mill

In the younger Mill's literary education, the political economy strain in the general picture of Benthamite thinking was forced upon his notice before he read work of Bentham himself. First James Mill lectured John on the *Elements* in the course of writing it, John prepared the marginal notes on his return from France in 1821, and it was only immediately following this that John was called upon to read Dumont's work including an account of Bentham's *Principles* as an introduction to his reading law with Austin. Mill says that the *Principles* struck him with the force of a revelation, strengthened his passion for principles of classification, and offered him a vista of improvement for mankind. He went on to read Bentham's other works as private reading while his father was pressing John's formal studies into psychology. It was in 1823 that John entered the service of the East India Company, and in 1824 that he undertook the editing of Bentham's *Rationale of Judicial Evidence*, published in 1827.[78]

Mill thought the five volumes of this work among the richest in matter of all that Bentham produced. It continues Bentham's theme of the mystifications in English law in the hands of the judiciary, and rejects the practice of having rules of evidence altogether, as a hindrance to the fundamental objective in this area of arriving at the truth. In the early stages of his first volume, Bentham discusses the relations between evidence of facts, probative force, degrees of persuasion and, most importantly, causes of belief in testimony – not as an exercise in law only, but as a general inquiry. Bentham stresses here that the source of belief in testimony is experience – because of the conformity of experience with the truth of things. Because Aristotelian logic is not founded on experience, which would produce physics instead, such logic produces in Bentham's view, only propositions each of which is nothing more than an *ipse dixit*. Bentham therefore calls Aristotelian logic 'nonsense physics', just as he calls ethics which is not tested by utility, but instead relies on mere assertions by way of *ipse dixit*, nonsense ethics. Bentham says nothing in this context about the logic of the will as opposed to the logic of the understanding. He is concerned to launch a fundamental attack on Aristotelian logic going beyond the charge that it is too restricted to be capable of dealing with the social sciences. His distinction between the understanding and volitions appears instead in the *Rationale* when he is classifying the causes of incorrectness in testimony into intellectual and moral causes.[79]

His involvement in the *Rationale of Judicial Evidence* was to influence Mill in more than one way when he came to write his own *System of Logic*. In some matters he adopted Bentham, as in his treatment of logic as a matter of what truths are evidence of what other truths. In others Bentham set him the problems, though Mill did not adopt Bentham's solutions. And this applied particularly to the place of the Aristotelian syllogistic reasoning in logic. The problem for Mill was whether he was to reject this reasoning as useless as Bentham had done, or adopt it as the basis of his logic, or find a compromise or compromises. In the end, he adopted compromises.[80]

But at the time Austin had Mill in his lecture class, was raising logical questions with the class, and promising the class that Mill's researches were about to clear up outstanding problems, in fact it would be 12 years before Austin was to see the complete manuscript. The evidence provided by what appears in Mill's *Logic* of Austin's views is therefore indirect. But at least Austin acclaimed it when he saw it, and spoke of reviewing it so as to forestall critics of what he saw as views of his own as well as Mill's. He would scarcely have done this if it presented a view of the logical character of propositions of social science which was markedly different from what he understood to be the character of his own propositions of jurisprudence. Moreover, in important respects for the assessment of Austin's activity, Mill adopted statements from his father's *Analysis of the Phenomena of the Human Mind*, which was familiar to Austin.

From the internal evidence of his lecture materials, it emerges that what was most bothering Austin, at the time when Mill was in his class, was what one would expect, from what we have already said, to be bothering Mill at the same time. Did the syllogism have a useful place in logic? Austin was hesitating over the question whether a syllogism really took us from the truths stated in the premises to a fresh truth in the conclusion, or whether it only repeated something of what was in the premises. Austin's tentative conclusion was that the syllogism did not give us any new truth and therefore it was the most futile part of logic.[81] The important point, however, is that this question did bother Austin. It has come to be thought by many that Austin imagined his own fundamental activity was analytical in the sense, or some sense like it, in which Austin was inclined to think the syllogism was analytical. But Austin's own conclusion was that this kind of activity was futile, and he could scarcely have meant this adjective to apply to himself.

Austin said in the same context that, apart from other than syllogistic kinds of reasoning like induction, the methods of which Mill was to make the central part of his own work on logic, the important things in logic were terms, propositions, definitions, and divisions (abstracted from all particular matter). These were the major subjects of Austin's central activity in jurisprudence and the account which Mill gives of them has a clear message which is wholly consistent with Austin's approach generally: in treatment of them the main burden of what is required is investigation of the facts. The verbal arbitrariness which is involved is minor.

While Mill classes a definition as a merely verbal proposition, he says also that the arrival at a definition is not a merely verbal operation. Although definitions are strictly of names of things, and not of things themselves, how to define a name may involve considerations going deep into the nature of the things which are denoted by the name. The definer is confronted at the outset with a language which has not been made but has grown. It may have passed by successive links of resemblance from one object to another until it denotes a confused huddle of objects. Thus, if we ask 'What is justice?', the first question must be: What is the attribute which men mean to predicate when they call an action just? To which the first answer is, that having come to no agreement on the point, they do not mean to predicate distinctly any attribute at all. Nevertheless, they believe there is such a common attribute. So the second question is: 'Is there a common attribute?' And the third question is: 'What is it?' Only the first of these inquiries is into convention or usage, the others are into matters of fact. If, further, the answer to the second question is 'no', then an inquiry must be made through what portion of them such a general resemblance can be traced, and what common attributes give that resemblance. When these are ascertained, the name when applied to them becomes susceptible of definition. It should then be defined by reference to the most important scientifically of those attributes. Since, upon the result of this inquiry respecting the causes of the properties of a class of things, there incidentally depends the question what shall be the meaning of a word, some of the most profound and most valuable investigations which philosophy presents to us have been introduced by, and have offered themselves under the guise of, inquiries into the definition of a name.[82]

It is probable that this is one of the parts of the *System of Logic* which most pleased Austin, for he would surely have recognized in the approach Mill described his own approach to the definition of law. It is even possible that he thought that he had provided Mill with an exercise in definition which helped Mill to develop his views about what was involved in definition. He had a right to think that. Mill makes it clear that, in the type of situation which he last describes, there is no single 'proper' definition which can be identified, but the definitional lines should be drawn upon considerations of helpfulness towards the scientific objectives involved – what will lead in the most illuminating directions for subsequent scientific investigation. On this point the present writer would support Mill, but while Austin appears to take this view at times, at others there may be some suspicion, as we shall see, that he thought that things have an 'essence' which can be identified rather than selected. For Mill himself one selects rather than identifies the essence through the definitional exercise itself. Neither Mill nor Austin accepts that it is impossible to define at all in some areas, including some areas of law, by the ordinary method of genus and difference, though this is suggested by Bentham and is associated with modern linguistic philosophy by Hart. In this last matter, the present writer has to confess that he aligns himself with Mill.

Mill thought that the most important function of classification, like that of definition, was as a logical process subservient to the investigation of truth.[83] But classification is implied in the use of general names functioning as the predicates of propositions at all. Therefore we have to look at the five kinds of predicables posited by Aristotle: a *genus* of a thing, its *species*, its *differentia*, a *poprium* of it, and an *accidens* of it. These are all terms which have to be understood relatively to the subject of the proposition. Distinctions which are drawn by allocating things to a genus or a species are differences in kind, or natural divisions. The predicate constituting the class name implies (connotes) attributes which are thought of as the essence of the class. This is because these features, denoting the objects belonging to the class, carry with them multitudes of other properties which also belong to objects within the class, and not just a few determinate ones. Every real Kind (genus or species) admitting of distinction into real Kinds, is a genus to all Kinds below it, a species to all Kinds in which it is itself included. The most specific Kind to which an individual belongs is its *infima species*.

Mill sees the *differentia* as a word which signifies the attribute distinguishing a given species from other species of the same genus – what must be added to the connotation of the genus to complete the connotation of the species. A *proprium* of a species is any attribute which, though not connoted by the name of the species, follows from an attribute which the name connotes. The *proprium* may follow by way of demonstration (because its absence would be inconsistent with some law of our thinking faculty or the constitution of the universe) or causation. In either case we say it follows necessarily. Under the remaining predicable, *accidens*, are included all attributes of a thing which are neither involved in the signification of the name nor have any necessary connection with the attributes which are so involved. If they are in fact universal to the species, we call them inseparable accidents, otherwise separable.[84]

Mill was later to go on to deal with demonstration and necessary truths, and there to argue against Whewell that even the hypotheses of geometry are either real facts with some of the necessary qualifications omitted, or just experimental truths. The theorems of geometry are only necessary truths in the sense and to the extent that they follow from those hypotheses.[85] The dominant message in this general treatment of classification and the associated matter about necessary truths is the same as it is with Mill's treatment of definition – the large extent to which the operations of classification are bound up with what we find in experience – the dominant extent to which what we observe empirically enters into the process. The various notions which Mill puts forward here were discussed by Austin in his lecture materials, and once again there is no reason to suppose that he took a fundamentally different view of what was involved from Mill's. This is especially important because of the theories of Austin's work, which reach the conclusion that it was somehow divorced from empirical investigation, because he referred in places to necessary notions in law. The later misinterpretations in this respect are a major part of an historical process which MacCormick[86] rightly sees as having cut Austin from his philosophical roots, and as having contributed to the whole tradition going stale.

Unfortunately, Mill himself may have given some initial stimulus to this process. Paradoxically, Mill gave some currency to the idea that Austin's approach was conceptual and not empirical by developing a theory of conceptions, even though all the time stressing that the principal requisites of clear conceptions are habits of attentive observation, and extensive experience, a memory which retains an exact image of what is observed, the use of names with a clear connotation, and consequently the perception of those agreements between things on which important consequences depend.[87] However, Mill did not explain this when he used the word 'conception' in his article about Austin's work after Austin's death.[88] Some of what Mill says there is reflected in condensed form at the beginning of Holland's *Jurisprudence*, with empirical implications largely excluded.

Of especial importance, in the search for light from Mill about Austin, is Mill's treatment of relations. From any point of view, law has especially to do with relations. However, only some of the more complex of them are likely to be given the title 'legal relations' or 'jural relations'. These particular ones of them are given names like 'rights' or 'privileges' or 'powers' or 'immunities'. These are the relations we call later in this book 'legal positions', to distinguish them from others, having regard to the fact that when a lawyer advises his client of his legal position, he is likely to be talking at least about the aggregate of these involved in the client's concrete situation. But we look at Mill's approach to relations generally as well as his legal example.

Mill claims that the 'simple and clear' explanation of relations which he gives was first given by James Mill in the *Analysis of the Phenomena of the Human Mind*, which, as we have mentioned, was known to Austin and from which Austin adopted other material in his own lectures.[89] This explanation is that, when we predicate of A that he is the father of B, and of B that he is the son of A, we assert one and the same fact in different words. That fact, when analysed, consists of a series of physical events or phenomena, in which both A and B are parties concerned, and from which they both derive names. What those names really connote is this series of events. A name is relative when, over and above the object which it denotes, it implies in its signification the existence of another object.

The facts which are involved in a legal relation are, for Mill, states of consciousness, but this must be understood in relation to his view, stated by way of introduction to what now follows, that all we know of *any* fact is the sensation it excites in our consciousness. The foundation of the relationship of debtor and creditor is, on this basis, the thoughts, feelings, and volitions (actual or contingent), either of the persons themselves or of other persons concerned in the same series of transactions; as for instance the intentions which would be formed by a judge, in case a complaint were made to his tribunal of the infringement of any of the legal obligations imposed by the relation; and the acts which the judge would perform in consequence; acts being (as Mill has already said) another word for intentions followed by an effect, and that effect being, no doubt, but another word for sensations, or some other feelings, occasioned either to the agent himself or to somebody else. There is no part of what the names expressive of the relation imply, that is not resolvable into states of consciousness; outward objects being, no doubt, supposed throughout as the causes by which some of those states of consciousness are excited, and minds as the subjects by which all of them are experienced.[90]

It is perhaps a little unfortunate that Mill chose to be so careful to insist here on the tenets of his general philosophy that all we can know of objects is the sensations excited by them. Most of the time he is ready enough to talk for convenience about the objects which he says we suppose excite the sensations. But, allowing for this, his approach is wholly consistent with Austin's, even if not complete, and may be used to explain Austin's approach.

Mill's account, of course, is not complete and does not pretend to be, nor are we for our part approving it as accurate. What is important is the kind of account it is – of relations as being involved in a pattern of experienced happenings. What is also important to notice is that Mill's view is that when we talk of a thing having a relation, we are talking of one kind, though a special kind, of attribute that it has. It is implied that we can classify things by their relations as well as by other kinds of attributes, and even discover a genus and a difference. Austin acts on this view in his lecture materials. Bentham's suggestion that we cannot classify a right in this way, which later has been regarded as very important, is inconsistent with the way in which Mill and Austin act. Austin does indeed say that some legal terms will not admit of definition in the formal or regular manner in his introductory remarks in *Uses of the Study of Jurisprudence*, probably just retailing recollected Bentham. But then he proceeds to his work on the opposite basis.

The influence of German writings

The influence of the Romanist German literary influence on Austin is scarcely separable from other Romanist influences which had their origins further back in his career than his period in Germany. He was reading Latin histories at the beginning of his preparation for the bar and no doubt earlier and it was Roman Law which John Stuart Mill read with him, though not exclusively, during Austin's period at the bar. He was thus familiar with the Latin language and with major works on Roman Law before he went to Bonn and built on this while there through now having access to the Institutes of Gaius. On the other hand, during his brief period at Bonn, he was troubled at least at first, by unfamiliarity with the German language, by the fact that apart from his studies he was expected to familiarize himself with the workings of the institution as a respected model for the University of London, and by the fact that the most considerable intellectual contacts he had there were, as we have seen, in different degrees outside the legal field. We have, however, also seen that the distaste he at first showed on Benthamite grounds to the German material appears to have evaporated and that he gained some familiarity with German legal literature while reading with the *privatim docens*. No doubt under the tutor's guidance, Austin brought a great deal of German legal literature back with him for use in the writing up of his lectures in the next few years. This ultimately found its way to the Inner Temple, and Campbell's editions of Austin preserve a list of it, though we have noted that the library itself was ultimately destroyed. In the list of works in Austin's library German works are predominant; close to 100 of the 136 volumes. They are mostly works on law published before the time he wrote his lectures. It is noted in Campbell's list that the book full of analytical notes by Austin is the Commentary on the Institutes of Gaius.[91]

Professor Andreas Schwarz had access to this library before it was destroyed. He wrote that the books showed clearly enough by their wealth of marginal notes and underlinings as well as by the volumes and passages obviously unread (to which von Savigny's *History of Roman Law in the Middle Ages* and the volumes of the *Zeitschrift für geschichtliche Rechtswissenschaft*, the leading organ of the historical school, belong) where the owner's interests lay. His first and main studies were some German textbooks of Institutes and Pandects, current at this period of transition from natural law and dogmatic exposition in the direction of historical studies. These were the Institutes of Haubold and Mackeldey, the Pandects of Thibaut and in a still higher degree the *Doctrina Pandectarum* of Mühlenbruch, written in Latin, and the original and short dogmatical and historical outlines of Hugo. Schwarz claims that he obtained from them not only his main knowledge of Roman law, but also a great part of his juristic training. Other materials showing evidence of careful reading were articles of Thibaut especially on the interpretation of real and personal rights, von Savigny's early work on Possession combining research into texts with natural law speculation, systematic text-books on criminal law by Anselm von Feuerbach and C.F. Rosshirt, and encyclopaedias of legal science of Hugo and especially Falck.[92]

While there is some evidence of examination of Kant, Schwarz does not consider that Austin penetrated into the depths of contemporary German philosophy. Indeed, Schwarz finds in what Austin said when he asked to postpone his first year of lectures – that the lectures delivered by the German professors as introductions to positive law are written in a manner which Englishmen would not relish – an inadequate appreciation of the extent to which the Germans had arrived at general statements of legal science which could offer him a model for his purpose. The major efforts of eighteenth-century German literature to establish general principles of law and jurisprudence, Schwarz finds, were 'apparently not immediately known to Austin'. He could, however, gain a suggestive survey from Falck's *Encyclopaedia*, the earlier parts of which Schwarz finds he thoroughly studied and rather overrated, though emerging with notions which were in any case different from Falck's. Further, Austin borrowed a name 'Philosophy of Positive Law' as an alternative title to Jurisprudence from one of the small books of Hugo, but Schwarz adds that, apart from this expression, Austin's work had not much in common with the substance of Hugo's book.[93] The expert assessment by Schwarz of the extent of the impact on Austin of general German intellectual ideas and general German ideas about law is thus much more deprecatory of the influence than the much less instructed ones of Mill and Carlyle, which as we have already noticed, were formed after Austin's return from Germany.

Of particular areas of Austin's work, Professor Schwarz considers that in the most mature part of Austin's work, published as *The Province of Jurisprudence Determined*, German influence is scarcely noticeable. Where it contains ideas which are to be found in German writers, they are equally to be found in English writers with whom Austin was more familiar. On the other hand, in the later parts of Austin's work the characteristic German training in Roman and pandect law can be clearly recognized, affecting Austin's treatment both of concepts and sources. The Austinian attempt to clarify legal concepts coincided with a movement to the same end in Germany and Austin utilized the German work on particular concepts. Most important among these were the notions of '*jura in rem*' and '*jura in personam*' rooted in Roman Law but modernized by Thibaut particularly in an article which Austin carefully studied. Austin refers again and again to the distinction between these notions. Further, although a legal division of persons is to be found in Blackstone's commentaries, Austin's exposition of legal personality is clearly influenced by German books to be found in his library. Again, Austin's work on the theory of tort and crime evidences German influence both through what his work contains and the extent of the marginal annotations on the German works on these subjects to be found in his library.[94]

We have called attention earlier to the indications in Austin's prospectuses for continuance and expansion of his work, both in the dying days of his lectures in London and even much later, that it was these parts of his work which Austin particularly hoped to develop. He believed that English law could be treated in terms of the Romanist German model to a much larger extent than Englishmen recognized, and that such a treatment would be of considerable utility in establishing it on a systematic basis suitable for codification. In this respect his aspirations were something of a reversion to pre-Benthamite activity, for those giving systematic accounts of English law on a broad basis for hundreds of years had been suspected of distorting it by forcing it in varying degrees into Romanist models. But in any case the project remained an aspiration, and despite Sarah's great efforts on the manuscript, the expert assessment was that Austin had not reached a degree of expertise in the Romanist models sufficient to make this part of Austin's writing significant work of scholarship.

3

Austin's jurisprudence

The province of jurisprudence determined: jurisprudence and moral sciences

The *Province* is the only part of Austin's lectures for which he was prepared to take responsibility to the extent of proceeding to publication.[1] But it will be recalled that he had second thoughts about the satisfactoriness of even this portion and resisted re-publication for as long as he lived in the hope of making revisions.

He begins by saying that the matter of jurisprudence is positive law: law set by political superiors to political inferiors. Positive laws are a species of what are laws in the sense of rules laid down for the guidance of an intelligent being by an intelligent being having power over him, which embrace laws set by God to men (the Divine law) and laws set by men to men. Within the latter class are those set by political superiors in independent political societies. The term law as used simply and strictly, applies exclusively to these and these are the appropriate matter of jurisprudence. Austin restricts the term positive law to these, even though there are other laws in the proper signification of the term which are also established by position (exercise of power). Thus Austin excludes from positive law even laws set by men to men where the former are not political superiors – which are properly though not strictly termed law – and those objects improperly termed laws which are rules set by mere opinion rather than by defined persons, within which Austin mentions International Law along with laws of fashion and honour. The objects which Austin specifies here as being excluded, whether properly or improperly termed law, he designates in the aggregate 'positive morality'. Laws governing the conduct of lower animals and inanimate objects are only metaphorically termed law and are excluded from positive law as well. So we finish with divine laws (which are one class of what is properly called law), positive laws in Austin's sense (alone strictly law), positive morality (straddling what is properly and improperly called law) and finally the laws so called merely by a metaphor which induces muddy speculation.

Laws or rules properly so called are, then, a species of command, and the understanding of what is a command is the key to the sciences of jurisprudence and morals. A command is a signification of desire with a power and purpose in the party commanding to inflict an evil in case the desire be disregarded. The liability to evil of the party commanded means that he is bound or obliged by the command: that he is under a duty to obey it. Command and duty are correlative terms, such that whenever a command is signified a duty is imposed and *vice versa*. The chance of the evil in case the duty be broken is frequently called a sanction, punishments being a class of sanctions. The magnitude of the sanction and of the chance of its being incurred are not relevant to the definitional exercise. To include rewards within the term sanctions strains the signification of the term command and can only generate confusion. Logically, each of the three terms command, duty or obligation, and sanction signify the same notion, but each denotes a different part of that notion and connotes the residue.

Commands are either laws (or rules) obliging generally to acts or forbearances specified as a class, or occasional or particular commands directed to an act or acts specified by their individual natures, for example a legislative order stopping the exportation of corn shipped or in port at a particular time, or enjoining a punishment in a specific case, or the usual kind of judicial command. Acts or forbearances of a class are enjoined generally by a law and acts determined specifically are enjoined by an occasional command. Blackstone is wrong in thinking that laws can be distinguished from particular commands according as the direction is to persons generally (or a particular class of persons) or to a person or persons designated individually. Blackstone's definition, Austin points out, will not fit common usage of the terms precisely. Neither, of course, Austin recognizes, will his own, but the argument seems to be that his definitional measures will clear up confusion whereas Blackstone's will not.

Austin goes on to emphasize that he is within the field of definitional exercise rather than the provision of factual information when he explains the terms superior and inferior in relation to law. That laws emanate from superiors is an identical proposition or tautology. Superiority signifies might, not precedence or excellence. God's superiority is absolute, but human superiority only exists in certain aspects or characters in which persons find themselves, so that the member of a sovereign assembly in his character as a citizen is inferior to the judge.

Now Austin – startlingly in view of his sacrifices in the interests of tidiness thus far – tells us that there are objects improperly termed laws which are nevertheless properly within the province of jurisprudence, though they are not commands. In this category Austin includes authentic declaratory legislation, laws to repeal laws (permissions) and laws of imperfect obligation which lack sanctions imposed by the state, though they may have other kinds of sanction such as religious or moral. We have seen in the previous chapter that declaratory and repealing laws were important kinds of laws to Bentham because their operation was essential to the understanding of what was a complete law. But Austin treats them as not strictly law while at the same time apparently making a concession to Bentham by including them within jurisprudence.

Austin proceeds to include within laws some objects which may seem not imperative but are so. Some may think, he says, that there are laws merely creating rights which are not imperative. But while there are laws which merely create absolute duties, every law creating rights imposes a correlative duty, expressly or impliedly. Again some have thought that customary laws are not commands of the sovereign legislature, but either the spontaneous adoption of the subjects enforced by the judges or the creations of these judges. However, in truth, so long as custom is in the realm of spontaneous adoption it is only positive morality, but when enforced by the judges it becomes the will of the sovereign legislature either through the authority the sovereign has given the judge in that respect or by acquiescence in what he does. Abhorrence of judge-made laws springs from an inadequate conception of the nature of sovereign commands which may be tacit through refraining from countermanding what could be countermanded. Here Austin utilizes Bentham's notions of indirect commands of the sovereign constituted by judicial law-making to reach a conclusion opposite from Bentham's. Bentham thought judicial law-making was to be abhorred because it involved a usurpation of the power which should be properly exercised by the sovereign in a codified system, leaving the law at least in a hopelessly confused form because of the shortcomings of judicial legislation in point especially of design, expression, and accessibility. It would always be hopelessly incomplete law from every point of view.

At this point Austin concludes his first lecture.[2] The relation of his work in some of its aspects to that of his associates is already beginning to appear. The naming process which, for John Stuart Mill, was the first step in a logical attack on a field and involved empirical investigation as well, is proceeding apace, with Austin showing a strong self-consciousness about what he is doing. Some of what he is doing to Bentham's notions is also becoming clear, and some of that simply consists in adoption of them. Law as a command of the sovereign is substantially Bentham, though there is the difference that Bentham preferred the term mandate to command. Austin however developed an elaborate nomenclature to indicate just whose commands we are talking about at a given time and no doubt considered that he had disposed of the ambiguities about the word command in this respect which concerned Bentham. In another important matter, too, that of the analysis of customary law, he substantially utilizes Bentham's notions of the sovereign's adoption of judge-made law, even though the distinction between pre-adoption and susception by the sovereign is not adopted in terms, and the application of the two distinct notions to the situation of the judge is rather slurred.

In other matters, what Austin does is to take what Bentham regarded as the more typical cases, frame his definition so that it applies to them, and then to exclude the less typical and doubtful cases in a way that Bentham does not, even though sometimes Bentham himself may leave their position doubtful. It is in this way, for example, that Austin gets rid of laws offering rewards from the field of positive law. All that Bentham had said is that the legislator usually has to proceed by threatening a pain rather than by offering a pleasure. Similarly Bentham does not exclude international law though he finds that a sovereign's involvement in it through, for example, treaties is different from that in relation to ordinary mandates addressed to his own subjects.

More serious from Bentham's own point of view, perhaps, is Austin's procedure in relation to matter which he excludes from positive law but includes in jurisprudence. The declaratory laws which Austin gives as his first example are regarded by Bentham as always having a double purpose, imperative and as asserting the existence of the previous law. There is no reason why they should not be called laws from his point of view, even where the purpose is other than explanatory of a previous law – the type with which Austin is concerned – which for Bentham is certain to introduce additional imperative aspects. A further serious matter in relation to Bentham's work is Austin's insistence on confining laws in strictness to general commands. Bentham was at pains to stress that laws *de classibus* and *de singulis* had to be considered as complementary if the totality of the exercise of power in a State was to be understood and that the matter was especially relevant to the understanding of constitutional law. In both the above respects, Austin's glosses are not helpful to Bentham's object of seeing a 'real' law in its completeness as an object of experience, and thus from Bentham's point of view not helpful to reducing jurisprudence to scientific terms.

Although Austin follows Bentham in the physical form of his chapters and in some degree in the present chapter the Benthamite practice of bifurcating concepts, he does not follow Bentham's practice of concluding a chapter by reference to the utility of what has been carried out in it. Austin's general comments on the utility of jurisprudence were not to be published in his lifetime. Thus we do not have any disquisition at the end of this chapter on the utility or otherwise of the definitional exercise in the way Austin has carried it out. It is apparent that he wished to proceed logically. It is apparent that he wished to be clear. It seems that he did not wish to depart too radically from ordinary language in the way he made distinctions, though he does not tell us, as Bentham does, where or whether he feels that this involves him in compromise of a watertight scientific exposition. Broader questions of what purposes are served for the future of the science of jurisprudence by the severe restrictions he imposes because of his narrow definition of positive law are not tackled, though succeeding generations of students working to Austin's specifications certainly agonized over the question how far the greatest happiness of the greatest number was served by his severe restrictions on the science, as did scholars. It does not seem that Austin's object was to delimit the science by reference to the limits of what he wished to make his own field of specialization. The latter was wider than jurisprudence. He hoped to develop teaching – at law school – and publication, in aspects of what is usually classed as law but which he relegated to positive morality, though he was ultimately frustrated by lack of students and by the unmanageability of even the narrower task with the restrictions imposed by his own strength and standards. No doubt it would be unkind to suggest that the utility of the severe restrictions which Austin imposed in his immediate circumstances was that it gave him some degree of escape from immediate responsibilities.

But at least he is able to devote Lectures II to V, almost half of his published work, to matters which he had excluded from jurisprudence, by way of discussing their distinctions from it. Divine laws, he begins, are laws properly so called, impose religious duties, and have religious sanctions annexed. Revealed divine laws are disposed of in a page and Austin turns to discuss what is the index of unrevealed divine laws. Some claim, he says, that the index is a moral sense, practical reason, or common sense, or some such, while the opposing theory is that the index is the utility of actions, because God designs the happiness of his creatures. If, Austin sarcastically says, we are not fitted with 'that peculiar organ' which the moral-sense theories suppose we have, then, in spite of the difficulties which are raised about the practical implementation of the utility principle by people, whom he makes plain he considers obtuse and ill-intentioned, we must do our best with it. It is not as if we had to make calculations in respect of every act we do. We concern ourselves with acts of a class, develop theories about the tendencies of acts of a class which are true in practice as any true theory always is, and are thus guided by rules and maxims about which we have sentiments. Thus it is these sentiments which immediately guide us. Criticisms about us being calculating machines if we are utilitarians miss their mark. Of course, there are exceptional situations which require us to make specific calculations, so that there come to be exceptions to our rules by resort to the ultimate principle of utility. Under this head, Austin raises the question whether it is always right to support established government, claims that it is not in those exceptional cases where the actions of government fundamentally oppose utility, and condemns those supporting the British government in its war with the American colonies.

If there is a contrast, though not necessarily a contradiction, between Austin's account of the principle of utility and Bentham's own in the *Principles*, it is that Bentham develops the calculations which are involved in working with the principles at very great length, catalogues generally the pleasures and pains which are involved and deals with the factors which cause variations in the responsiveness of particular persons compared with others, and attacks the competing principles on theoretical grounds. Austin, instead, sneers briefly at this point at the competing principles and devotes much time to minimizing the detailed calculations required by emphasizing the extent to which there may be reliance on maxims and rules. To develop any such maxims and rules it would presumably still be necessary to make the calculations and it is in considering these calculations that Bentham himself develops more detailed notions that give content to what many may think is the empty frame of utility. But Austin leaves the frame empty and says nothing at this point of what would be required to develop the maxims – just that the fact that this may be done answers the objections of those who claim utility is unmanageable as a working doctrine.

It is in his account of what the working maxims would be like that the merest hint of German philosophical influence may be guessed at, though falling far short of the steeping of utilitarianism in German metaphysics which Carlyle thought he detected in Austin. Austin tells us that when we are collecting the tendency of an act, we must think of the class to which it belongs and the question then is: If acts of the *class* were *generally* done, or *generally* forborne or omitted, what would be the probable effect on the general happiness or good? This is obviously not Kant's categorical imperative calling on a person to act so that the principle of his conduct may become a universal rule. It aims rather at a universal rule which will be not merely possible of universal following, but the best of such possible rules once the independent criterion of utility is applied. But there is a relationship with Kant, and one not necessarily reached by a straight application of utility to the individual act which is after all what Benthamism strictly calls for.[3]

Austin begins his third lecture by explaining that he has not sought to expound the principle of utility in its various applications because he does not seek to treat of the science of legislation. Instead, he wishes to expound the idea of law. Austin does not explain here what he means by the science of legislation. But what he says is consistent with the proposition that he did not intend to deal with what Mill treats as a syllogistic exercise in applying the general principles of utility to specific fact situations, nor at least in that context, with the factual scientific questions which Mill saw arising in the process. Of course, Bentham himself would not have thought that precisely this was involved in any part of the science of law, censorial jurisprudence or otherwise for a variety of reasons including his emphasis on the special logic of the will and his contempt for the syllogism. Austin now says, continuing to concentrate on the question of the manageability of working with utility, that it is not necessary, when law and morality are what they ought to be, that all whom they bind should know the reasoning on which they have been reached. The results can be taken on trust, though a single mind could not compass all the reasons.

But Austin continues that ethics, and closely related sciences such as legislation, politics, and political economy, are not what they ought to be, because of the prominence of advocates rather than inquirers. The testimony of supposed experts cannot be trusted. In law the monstrous or crude productions of childish and imbecile intellect have been cherished and perpetuated. Nevertheless the leading principles of these sciences are gradually finding their way to the mass of the people and making them docile to the voice of reason. The broad or leading principles of the inestimable science of political economy may be mastered with moderate attention in a short period (John Mill's blushes for his father are not recorded) and would implant truths of ineffable moment in the multitude. It would teach them that want and labour spring from the niggardliness of nature, not the institution of property, that without capital the rewards of labour would be far scantier, and that capital is a creature of the beneficent institution of property. If the multitude wish for greater rewards, they may find in Mr Malthus's true principle of population the means which would give them comparative affluence. They will see that the solution to their ills lies in adjusting their numbers to the demands of labour instead of in breaking machinery and burning corn-ricks. Offences against property which are the usual result of poverty and prejudice will fall away and the fear of public disapprobation of such crimes will build up as understanding forms the public moral character. An enlightened people will be a better auxiliary to the judge than an army of policemen. This will follow even if the public does not understand the nicer points like the functions of paper money and the incidence of taxes.

Austin says he could equally show the advantages of the public understanding the leading principles of ethics, if he had time. Only the few could develop ethical science by observation and induction applied to the tendencies of actions on the basis of their utility, but their numbers could be recruited from the lower classes if their coarse and sordid pleasures were replaced through education with refined amusements and liberal curiosity, leading to expansion of the class whose opinion determines the success of books. (Unfortunately this did not happen soon enough for the first edition of *The Province of Jurisprudence Determined*.) But they should not read Dr Paley on *Moral and Political Philosophy*, for the sinister influence of the position he occupied cramped his generous affections and warped the rectitude of his understanding.[4] Paley was far too frightened of offending the narrow prejudices of such readership as he could then command, and consequently the book which Paley wrote was unworthy of the esteem in which Austin held the memory of Paley the man. With a properly educated leadership people would read Hobbes and Locke.

The future of positive law and morality therefore stands for Austin thus. The diffusion of ethical science will gradually remove the obstacles which retard its advancement and many of the defects and errors in existing law and morality will in time be corrected. Though the many must trust to authority for a number of subordinate truths, they are competent to examine the elements which are the groundwork of the science of ethics and infer the more momentous consequences. Ultimately, impartial and rational authority will emerge on which the uninstructed can rely.

What, therefore, Austin has done in his third lecture[5] is to concentrate on the theme of the perfectibility of man. This, as we have seen, was among his early influences. We have also noticed that Austin's optimism about this was apparently encouraging to Mill after his mental crisis. But, even if this material was likely to please one of Austin's audience, the time spent on it did nothing to advance the process to which Austin refers. Neither did his abdication of immediate responsibility for advancing the cause of morals and legislation by separating them as distinct sciences from what was centrally jurisprudence in a way foreign to Bentham's approach.

Nor does Austin's fourth lecture advance him in the constructive part of his task of elucidating jurisprudence, whether according to his own notions or any broader ones. The earlier part of it, after some repetition of the material of Lecture III, argues that it is no refutation of the validity of utility as an index to God's commands to say that an all good and wise Being would not leave us with an imperfect index. The refutation proves too much because it would apply to any index which can be put forward. So Austin proceeds for the remainder of the lecture to attack the 'moral sense' approach to ethics, upon which up till now he has only cast very general aspersions. His general approach to this kind of theory is Bentham's – that this kind of approach offers no index to what is right and wrong at all. The statement that something is justified by the moral sense does not offer a reason for the act being right. It is merely an *ipse dixit* to that effect – nonsense ethics as Bentham puts it.

Austin's own contribution to the controversy is to offer as an instructive illustration a child abandoned in the wilderness and growing up in estrangement from human society. He meets a man carrying a deer kill and knocks him on the head for it. He is then affected by remorse, compassion, and guilt. He then meets another man who attacks him and he kills him in self-defence, without remorse, but with compassion, and with a tranquil conscience (as the saying goes). If a justification is to be found for his differing reactions in the two cases, it has to be by reference to the independent criterion of utility, which offers reasons where conscience does not. The reasoning is that the first act is pernicious, the second is not. But the savage is not in a position to explain this distinction, which involves reference to notions of political society, supreme government, law, legal right, legal duty, and legal injury. The moral philosopher opposing utility is left in the position of the savage. Austin is here indicating by implication the connections of his own and Bentham's approach with that of Thomas Hobbes.

Austin goes on to refer to the absence of evidence that we have elementary moral feelings incapable of further explanation – 'instinctive' – so as to be ultimate justifications for action. In fact he finds that the reactions of different classes of people at different times differ in ways which the hypothesis of utility would lead one to expect.

Austin next refers to theories which offer a compound of 'moral sense' and utilitarian notions, though he considers that these are exposed to the same objections as the pure moral-sense theories with only slight adaptations. Insofar as they suppose that moral sense is a sufficient index to the rightness of actions where men agree in the matter, they are in the same position as any other moral-sense theory. Austin takes the classical distinction between *jus gentium* and *jus civile* — and the classical distinction between law natural and positive which he takes, dubiously, to be the same — as representing this compound view, as well as the distinction of offences into those which are *mala in se* and those which are *mala prohibita*. Therefore these distinctions are all subject to theoretical demolition.

For the rest of the lecture, Austin returns to defending the principle of utility against current objections. He has already engaged in this in Lecture II, but whereas he was there mainly concerned with objections to utility on the grounds of its alleged unmanageability, he is here concerned, firstly, to refute objections which confuse utility as a measure or index to what is right — the right way to regard it — with the view that the springs of action are always calculations of utility. Austin says that utilitarians do not claim that a man kisses his mistress for the common weal or that he should. Motives are not characterized as good or bad by utilitarians, it is the effects which are so classed and these may vary from time to time with the same motive. Austin is here merely seeking to present Bentham.

The second objection with which Austin deals is what he calls a misconception of a hypothesis concerning the origin of benevolence, which in the light of the misconception is styled the selfish system, and is then coupled with a mistaken supposition that the hypothesis as so misconceived is an ingredient in the theory of utility. The true position, according to Austin, is that philosophers like Hartley, whom utilitarians respect, suppose that benevolence is generated by self-regarding tendencies but do not for that reason deny the existence of benevolence. And in any case the theory of utility will hold good whether benevolence or sympathy be a simple or ultimate fact, or be engendered by the principle of association on self-regarding affections. Austin himself believes that if genuine benevolence or sympathy were not a portion of our nature, our motives to consult the general good would be more defective than they are. Bentham, Austin points out, assumes or supposes the existence of disinterested sympathy, and scarcely adverts to the hypothesis with regard to the origin of the feeling. Austin makes it plain when he is developing the opponents' view that it has to do with their understanding of the part that motives in trade play in Benthamites' accounts of economics. But Austin does not attempt to deal with the question how the existence of economic laws depending on the uniformity of selfish motives is to be reconciled with the view that benevolence exists and is important.[6]

The province of jurisprudence determined: the analysis of laws generally

In Lecture V Austin virtually begins again. The remaining two lectures will comprise much more than half of the *Province* and elaborate his scheme of laws more systematically. So he begins with a logical discourse. Resemblance between objects may either be resemblance in a narrower sense or resemblance merely by analogy. The former occurs where two objects have all the properties which place them in a class expressly or tacitly referred to. They are analogous when only one has all those properties and the other only some. In this case the latter is improperly called by the name of the class. The analogy may be strong because the object possesses many of the qualities common to the class in question or weak in possessing only a few. We may distinguish the latter by saying that the name of the class is only metaphorically or figuratively applied to it.

On this scheme, laws properly so called are, firstly, those set by God to men, secondly, those set by men to men as political superiors or in pursuance of legal rights, and, thirdly, laws set by men to men not in pursuance of legal rights. Laws improperly so called (but closely analogous) are opinions or sentiments held by men in regard to human conduct. Austin says he calls the first item among laws properly so called 'laws of God', the second item in laws properly so called 'positive law' and the third item in the first class – together with everything within the second class – 'positive morality'. (He does not say anything of the class, laws metaphorically so called, at this stage.) He explains that the reason for his scheme is that the second item among laws properly so called covers direct or circuitous commands of the sovereign person or body – the political superior.

Austin now proceeds to define jurisprudence as the science of positive law, considered without regard to its goodness or badness, no doubt recalling in his mind Bentham's strictures especially in his *Fragment on Government* and the *Comment on the Commentaries* on the prevalence of confusions of fact and desirability in what purport to be accounts of the actual law. Austin adds that there might be a closely allied science of positive morality, though in this field it is only international law which is systematically treated by writers. Again, this would involve treating the subject without regard to its goodness or badness. It would be distinct from the science of ethics which affects to determine the test of positive law and positive morality, the one which relates especially to positive law being specially titled the science of legislation.

Austin next engages in some recapitulation, offering in the process his definition of positive law and now promising further elaboration of it. Every positive law, or every law simply and strictly so called, is set by a sovereign person, or sovereign body of persons, to a member or members of the independent political society wherein that person or body is sovereign or supreme. Positive laws thus share with other laws properly so called the properties of being commands, emanating from a determinate rational being, and, with the implication of the word command, there is a sanction annexed. Those of the laws falling under positive morality which are commands, and therefore laws properly so called, are divided into those established by men not living under a state of government, those established by sovereign individuals otherwise than in a sovereign character because they are not directed to those in a state of subjection to them, and those set by subjects but not in pursuance of legal rights. In the third category Austin gives as examples laws set by parents to children and imperative laws set by masters to servants. But we may notice that Bentham said that if a cook be bid to dress a dinner, this is by the sovereign's orders (susception). There is thus clearly a departure from Bentham in the implications of indirect commanding by the sovereign drawn by Austin.

Austin now proceeds to the second class of rules of positive morality, which are laws improperly so called – laws set or imposed by general opinion. Among these some groups are named, for example, rules of honour, the law of fashion, and international law. These are laws only by analogy because they emanate from an indeterminate body and the sanctions are applied by indeterminate persons. Some specific person may nevertheless command what is called for by opinion, for example, one sovereign commanding another, and this will be a law proper.

Because of the importance of the distinction between determinate and indeterminate bodies of persons, Austin elaborates it. Determinate bodies are those to which people belong by reason of being specifically or individually determined, or to which they belong because the body comprises all those in a generic class. Or parts of the determinate body may be determined in one or other of those ways. An indeterminate body may be an indeterminate portion of a body determinate or certain, but a body or class of persons may also be indeterminate because it consists of persons of a vague generic character. A determinate body is capable of corporate conduct, but an indeterminate body is not because the several persons cannot be known and indicated completely and correctly. Thus it cannot command as a determinate body can. As to how a determinate body commands, Austin has said thus far only that it can act as a body by all or any proportion of its members, without saying, in the latter case, when the command is to be attributed to the body.

In order that a supreme government may possess stability, Austin says that the holders in succession must take by a given generic mode or modes. Instability in Rome resulted from the fact that an emperor did not succeed by a generic title. The title of any rebel, who might eject him, would not have been less legitimate or less constitutional than his. Positive law or morality did not point out who was to succeed. The same applies when positive law or morality does not point out a body in generic terms who is to be sovereign. Austin does not explain at this point why, if sovereignty is a matter of factual might or power, as he has told us, he feels entitled to use a string of expressions which imply that it can be determined by legal authority in some sense – either legal authority in the strict sense of positive law, or in some looser sense.

Austin next speaks of the influential character of those laws, improperly so called, which are set by general opinion, saying that he has forborne to rank sentiments of precisely determined parties under this head in deference to the established language which speaks of laws set by opinion as those which are so set by general opinion, a quite vague class. But his scheme, he says, could be adapted to embrace laws set by any opinion.

Sanctions annexed to positive laws may be emphatically styled legal, and also political, since they are enforced through the existence of a society political and independent. Sanctions attached to positive moral rules may be called moral sanctions, some being sanctions properly so called and others sanctions by an analogical extension of the term. Similarly, we have religious duties, legal duties, and moral duties, some of which last will be duties only by analogical extension of the term.

A right arises by imposition of a corresponding duty. If the corresponding duty is a creature of a law imperative, it is a right properly so called. If the duty is a creature of a law improperly so called, the right is so by an analogical extension of the term. Thus a right under positive law or the law of God is properly so called. If the right is conferred by a duty imposed by positive morality, whether the right is properly so called depends upon which of the two classes of rules of positive morality imposes the duty.

The bodies or aggregates of laws which may be styled the law of God, positive law, and positive morality sometimes coincide, sometimes do not coincide and sometimes conflict. Thus murder is universally forbidden by positive law, by positive morality and by the law of God as known through utility (coincidence). Lack of coincidence is illustrated by smuggling, which is forbidden by positive law, but not by the opinions of the unreflecting, nor even by the opinions of the reflecting where the impost is imposed for the absurd and mischievous purpose of protecting a domestic manufacture. Conflict occurs when something is enjoined by one set of laws but forbidden by another, as in the case of duelling in some nations of Europe. Conflict between positive law and religious and moral laws may make the imposition of the positive law nothing but a gratuitous vexation, something which an intending legislator might do well to heed. The reader may notice in the above that the James Mill influence is prominent in Austin's examples.

Austin takes some approaches to customary law as indicative of a failure to deal correctly with the situations of coincidence and lack of coincidence. Until recognized by the courts, customs are rules of positive morality only. When sanctioned by the courts, thus indirectly becoming commands of the sovereign, there is coincidence of positive law and positive morality. It is wrong to think of the customs, at this stage, as being positive laws by the institution of those who set up the customs. Here we may notice in passing that Austin is digging into one of the major hornets' nests of legal theory. It is not clear that his analysis is, at any rate, universally correct even on his own view of law. What if the courts have let it be known that they will recognize customs which are established to exist in particular ways, at least under certain conditions, and the sovereign has issued no counter-command despite this? It would seem that in such circumstances a custom which can be so established, and in fact meets the conditions, is positive law and positive morality by coincidence even before it individually comes before any court.

Austin gives even shorter shrift to the law of nature by claiming on the supposed authority of classical jurists – whose authority would in any case scarcely dispose of the matter in the light of its continuing vitality – that it is to be considered as part of the *jus gentium* – laws common to different nations, and further claiming that as such it is part of positive law by the creation of human sovereigns, independently of the fact that it may coincide with that laid down by God. Again, even on his own view, the same questions would arise as in relation to customary law where a particular official-dom in a legal system recognizes natural law as a 'source' of law in the way that some systems recognize custom as a source of law.

Austin goes on to appeal to the authority of Locke in his *Essay on Human Understanding* for the distinction which he has drawn between laws properly so called and laws by analogy. He quotes Locke to the effect that law may be divided into divine law, civil law, and law of opinion or reputation. By the first, Locke says, we judge whether actions are sins or duties, by the second whether criminal or innocent, and by the third whether virtues or vices. The first set gives the test of true moral rectitude, the second of criminality and the third of credit or discredit, of actions. Locke's main point, in the very extensive passages which Austin quotes, is that morality of actions is a matter of relations to tests rather than innate qualities. But Locke's analysis of classes of rules does not have the complexity of Austin's.

In the final part of the main text of Lecture V, Austin deals with meta-phorical and figurative laws. These are of numerous kinds, but have for Austin the common feature that no character in them can be likened to a sanction or duty, though they do have a remote analogy to other laws in that, whereas other laws tend to produce regularity of conduct, we tend to speak of laws wherever we observe a uniform order of events or of coexisting phe-nomena. In the case of a deist this remote analogy is strengthened by the supposition that uniform modes of behaviour of anything are attributable to the will of God, but in the case of the atheist this reinforcement of the analogy is lacking. Apart from the behaviour of inanimate things or irra-tional animals a uniformity may arise from rules set by a man for himself, which also lack sanctions, or from rules of art which practitioners are advised to observe, which again lack sanctions.

The importance of the above disquisition, Austin says, is that merely figurative laws may become confused with others. Thus he accuses Ulpian of confusing laws governing animals with certain human laws regarded as arising from elementary instincts. This he attributes to the fact that Ulpian fails to distinguish causes of the human laws, the instincts, from the relevant human laws themselves – the *jus naturale*. Austin here repeats his view that *jus naturale* as used by classical writers is thought of as the *jus gentium* – universally accepted rules – explained as being the result of innate moral instinct or sense. He now does refer also to the natural law of the moderns, and says it ought to be thrown out of jurisprudence, along with the classical notions, because of its dependence on nonsense about moral sense. This is, of course, a further repetition of a Bentham point. Austin proceeds to discover confusions of different kinds of laws, through misuse of the idea of what is natural, in Montesquieu and claims that this sin is universal in Blackstone and in Hooker's *Ecclesiastical Polity*.

Bentham would have agreed with all this, but Austin signifies his independence by disagreeing with Bentham on one aspect of his own treatment of this matter. He complains of Bentham speaking of physical or natural sanctions in addition to religious, legal and moral ones. Austin sees Bentham's view of a natural sanction as an evil naturally produced by the conduct whereon it is consequent, reaching the suffering party without the intervention of a law. An example is burning one's house through failure to extinguish a light. Austin dislikes this use of the term sanction. Such sanctions are not suffered through failing to comply with the desires of rational beings, and their inclusion within the general notion of sanctions deprives the term of its specific application.

Austin concludes by saying that declaratory laws, laws repealing laws, and laws of imperfect obligation, are signs of pleasure or displeasure proceeding from law makers. Because of the narrowness of Austin's definitions of the imperatives he classes as laws, he considers that this analogy is only remote and they ought strictly to be classed as laws only by metaphor. But he proposes to include these within jurisprudence for convenience. We have already remarked on this uncharacteristic untidiness in Austin, in the context of his previous explanation of these phenomena, where the explanation of his exclusion of them from positive law appears to differ in detail from the present.

Austin appends to Lecture V[7] a lengthy note[8] on prevailing tendencies to confuse what is and what ought to be in law and morality. He gives this well-worn Bentham theme a colour of his own by discussing it in terms of his scheme of classification of laws. On his basis, the confusions are likely to be, and are found to be when one comes to giving examples, both between positive law as it stands and positive law as it would be if in accordance with the demands of utility, and positive morality as it stands and positive morality as it would be if in accordance with the demands of utility. The former confusion reflects itself in the proposition that human laws are invalid if they conflict with the divine laws whereas the truth is that they are only subject to criticism. They do not cease to exist as positive laws in the way the confused view would have us believe. Blackstone is one who makes the mistake of supposing that a positive law is not binding if it conflicts with the divine law. Austin claims that an exception, demurrer, or plea founded on the law of God was never heard in a Court of Justice.

However, the reader may attribute this last claim to Austin's ignorance of facts. It depends on what the system in question treats as sources and we have already suggested on this matter that his own theory could be understood in a way which would take account of this. In other words, one may feel that Austin was mistaken in thinking that even his own theory involved that such a plea could not be raised or even upheld. Perhaps Austin was too busy putting his theory in order to notice what the English Court of Common Pleas had done in *Bird* v. *Holbrook***** four years before he published his book.

Austin points out that the confusion of positive morality with morality as it ought to be is instanced in Paley and likewise in writers on international law, which Austin consistently treats as positive morality. They confuse the rules which obtain with their own vague notions of what they ought to be, and von Martens is seen by Austin as the first writer to seize on the important distinction between the two. Then Austin looks at Roman lawyers as men who have managed to commit the two major kinds of mistakes possible here both at once, in the first sentence of the Institutes of Justinian and elsewhere. In the course of this he says that when we talk of law and equity in this context as opposed to each other, we mean to express mere dislike of law.

Austin next attacks Lord Mansfield for his reasoning in what is in fact *Pillans* v. *Van Mierop*.** The criticism appears to be to the effect that the judge is there to enforce the law and the law was distinct yet his Lordship assumed he was there to enforce morality, which was a mistake. On the other hand Austin immediately goes on to say that it is desirable for judges to legislate in some circumstances because of the negligence and incapacity of the legislator.

Austin's statement here of both the actuality and desirability of judicial legislation is important, because his theory is maligned if it is suggested, as it occasionally has been, that he believed that in any legal system the decisions necessarily flow logically from general principles. Neither Bentham nor Austin ever believed anything of the kind. Although they were both from an early period described as 'analytical' jurists this was for reasons we explore

---

* (1828) 4 Bing. 628. In holding that an action on the case was maintainable for setting a spring gun, without notice, which injured the plaintiff, Best, C.J. said (at 641):

It has been argued that the law does not compel every line of conduct which humanity or religion may require; but there is no act which Christianity forbids, that the law will not reach: if it were otherwise, Christianity would not be, as it has always been held to be, part of the law of England.

** (1765) 3 Burr. 1663. In his *History and Sources of the Common Law: Tort and Contract* (London, 1949), C.H.S. Fifoot sees this case as one of Lord Mansfield's two major assaults on the doctrine of consideration. In this assault he sought to destroy the status of consideration, requiring recompense for a promise, as an essential and independent element in the action of Assumpsit – simple contract – and to reduce it to the level of evidence (*ibid* 408). The doctrine of consideration was at this stage 200 years old, but, in Fifoot's opinion, was not so firmly defined as to preclude fresh examination (*ibid* 406). But the challenge to orthodoxy was repelled in *Rann* v. *Hughes* ((1778) 4 Brown 27; 7 T.R. 350) where Lord Mansfield's decision in accordance with the principle adopted in the earlier case was reversed by the Court of Exchequer Chamber and the reversal upheld in the House of Lords.

at the beginning of a later chapter. It was not because they believed the content of any existing legal system could be deduced logically from a few general principles. Austin, however, distinguishes his position importantly from Bentham's when he says: 'Notwithstanding my great admiration for Mr Bentham, I cannot but think that, instead of blaming judges for having legislated, he should blame them for the timid narrow and piecemeal manner in which they have legislated.'

This difference sprang from a good deal more than a disposition on Austin's part to a show of courtesy to the judges which Bentham was far from showing at any time, either in his earlier work or in later ones like the *Rationale of Judicial Evidence*. To Bentham the manifold deficiencies of judicial legislation rendered its continuance intolerable and comprehensive codification was therefore of the utmost urgency and the matter towards which energies should be constantly directed and about which they should be organized, including in particular those of the jurist. For his part, Austin undoubtedly thought Bentham lacked realism in these aspects. We shall see that Austin came to dwell in the later part of his work on the unsatisfactory conditions for codification in his time, most particularly having regard to the deficiencies of those to whom the tasks would have to be entrusted. We shall equally see that Austin attempted to show how judicial legislation could be represented in intelligible principles by logical analysis as it was made, and that this would permit more modest exercises in codification from time to time. Whatever might be said about Bentham's unrealism in his enthusiasm for general codification, we shall see that there is unhappily no doubt about Austin's unrealism in his view of the character of judicial legislation, upon which he based his view of prospects of codification.

It will be observed that Austin constantly raises in the present note the distinctions between positive law and positive morality as they are on the one hand and positive law and positive morality as they ought to be on the other – that is, as they would be if each of them met the demands of utility. This is important common ground between Austin and Bentham as far as it goes, and Austin's references in this context do not appear to throw any further light on what differences may have existed between them concerning how questions of what 'ought to be' are to be understood.

The province of jurisprudence determined: the analysis of positive law

Austin defines positive law in his sixth lecture thus: Every positive law is set by a sovereign person, or a sovereign body of persons, to a member or members of the independent political society wherein that person or body is sovereign or supreme. If a determinate human superior, not in a habit of obedience to a like superior, receive habitual obedience from the bulk of a given society, that determinate superior is sovereign in that society and that society is political and independent. But to refer to the independence of the society, Austin adds, is really only a way of expressing the independence of the superior.

Austin proceeds to insist on some features of his definition. There is no habit of obedience to an occupying army where its commands are spasmodic and transient and the ordinary government then remains sovereign. The same is true of a feeble state which now and again submits to the demands of some more powerful state or alliance. Austin further insists on his point that it must be the bulk which has the habit of obedience to one and the same superior, so that internal strife where there is a balance of forces will prevent there being at any rate one political society and perhaps any at all, leaving a state of anarchy. If the superior himself obeys a determinate human superior, it is the latter which is the sovereign.

A political society is contrasted with a natural one where there is intercourse within the community but not subjection to a sovereign. Thus independent political societies live in a state of nature with one another to the extent that the sovereign of each is independent of the other and international law, regulating their relations, is not positive law. Austin says that, for precision, we must regard international law as obtaining strictly between sovereigns. This is another instance of an Austinian definition taking its stand on precision without regard to utility. There is, of course, a powerful view that the human misery caused by declining to regard individual people as the subject of international law is enormous, and consequently a widespread refusal to accept this Austinian restriction.

Austin next explains that there are some societies which will not fall under the heads independent natural, independent political, or subordinate political. These consist of members in subjection to a political superior considered as private persons, for example, a society of parents and children. These are not political societies. He next explains that the marks he has given of an independent political society themselves admit of degree, and the determination whether to apply the expression to cases near the extremes of the definition will cause difficulty. These difficulties cause consequential ones for the application of the positive moral rules comprising international law, for example determining when a revolting group becomes sovereign and is therefore to be treated as a subject of international law. Austin then proceeds to add a further requirement, conceded to be fallible, to his definition of an independent political society, namely, that it must not fall short of a substantial number. But this need not be applied to a subordinate political society within an independent political society. Austin points out then that his definitions of sovereignty and independent political society involve being more precise than what Bentham, Hobbes, Grotius and von Martens achieved in this respect.

Austin then proceeds to draw an implication of his definition of independent political society which has been justly criticized, especially by Professor Hart, as taking simplification to extremes of hopeless unrealism. Austin says that an independent political society is divisible into two portions, the portion which is sovereign and supreme, and the portion which is subject. The existence of a sovereign body consisting of the whole community, Austin says, is not impossible but so extremely improbable that it can be left out of account. Thus every sovereign is either a monarchy (one) or an aristocracy (a number). The tests of distinguishing aristocracies in strictness from oligarchies and democracies on the basis of proportionate numbers in government are too fallible for the distinctions to be adopted. The distinction of heterogeneous aristocracies, on the basis of the modes in which the sovereign powers are shared between portions, has also failed to be systematically worked out, though some have been broadly classed as limited monarchies. This expression causes obscurity. A limited monarch is not a monarch in the proper sense of the term, that is, a sovereign constituted by one person. The use of the expression often depends on no more than accidents of labelling which trouble the peace of mankind.

It is always necessary for the sovereign body to delegate powers. Thus in the United Kingdom the commons, within the sovereign body, exercise the whole of their sovereign powers through elected representatives during their term. If the commons were the whole of the sovereign body not a single sovereign power would be exercised directly. But the commons might delegate the powers subject to trusts, though Austin appears to suggest they do not in fact do so. They render themselves liable to such things as their delegates during their terms lengthening their own terms, or transferring their powers elsewhere in combination with the king and peers, at any rate as far as positive law goes. What trust there is exists under positive morality.

So that part of constitutional law which relates to the duties of the representative towards the electoral body is positive morality merely. Nor is this extraordinary. For all constitutional law, Austin promises to show in any country is, as against the sovereign, positive morality merely, and much of it even as against parties who are subject or subordinate to the sovereign. If a trust imposed on the general delegates were enforced by legal sanctions, the general delegates would be able to abrogate them because they enjoy the legislative function. To escape this inconvenience, the positive law binding the delegates in the matter would have to be made by the electoral body itself, or, if it were only part of the sovereign, by itself in conjunction with the other components in the sovereign body. Then it could not be abrogated by the delegates. In New York, for example, the ordinary legislature is controlled by this kind of extraordinary legislature.

The reader's attention should be called at this stage, in advance of looking at the subsequent history of Austinian theory, to the fact that there are two of the major sensitive points of Austinian theory involved here. Firstly, the relegation of the bulk of constitutional law to positive morality prevents the distinction between constitutional law and constitutional convention being drawn in the manner in which modern constitutional writers commonly draw it. Secondly, Austin summarily disposes for the time being of the phenomena of rigid constitutions, where there are checks and balances between the organs of government under the control of a constitution alterable only by a special constitution-making body, by identifying the sovereign as this body, even though it acts only rarely. This scarcely squares with his theory that the sovereign must be habitually obeyed to qualify as such.

On the first point Austin clearly regarded it as one of his major functions to draw distinctions in such a clear way that the peace of mankind should not be troubled because those who have to deal with legal problems do not understand the issues with which they are faced. We have seen above that this is what he stressed when speaking of what he considered the confusing notion of a limited monarchy. But he did not contribute to this objective by amalgamating, as positive morality, some constitutional conventions which may be observed as a matter of political practice and for which observation there is a spread of official community support, but which the courts do not commit themselves to support, with other rules which, although they relate to the fundamental workings of government, nevertheless the courts do commit themselves to support even if they might also recognize that their decisions could be overturned by a legislative or other power with higher authority. Failure to recognize this distinction is Austin's offence against clarity to which we referred first in the preceding paragraph, and its practical consequences are seen, among numerous examples, in the confused and angry arguments relating to the Australian constitutional crisis in 1975 when the Governor General dissolved Parliament.

This first feature of Austinian theory in the present context is related to the second feature in it which we mentioned as a sensitive point, for both are attempts to work out the implications of an identification of law with sovereign commands. A theory which identifies law with the commands of a body habitually exercising power will not explain the features of any constitutional system where habitual commitment, by the judiciary in particular, cannot be plausibly supposed to be given such a body because there is none which will satisfy the conditions. Hence Austin's inconsistency. The conditions under which authority is accorded to rules require very much more complex explanation and especially in relation to rules which have somehow become 'entrenched' – continue to be accorded authority though they were not made by any body habitually operating, or still habitually operating, in the country in question – and may continue to be accorded this authority despite attempts to alter them by the legislature accorded most authority in the country in question. This situation, along with others equally complex, has become familiar in former British colonies.

Austin passes to the distinction between legislative and executive (or administrative) powers of government, which, he says, does not correspond with the distinction between supreme and subordinate powers. Legislative sovereign powers and executive sovereign powers do not belong in any society to distinct parties. Of all the larger divisions of political powers, the division of those powers into supreme and subordinate powers is perhaps the only precise one. The former are the total of those political powers actually belonging to the sovereign, while the subordinate ones are the portion of the former delegated to political subordinates, which may, however, include the persons who share in the supreme powers. All the individuals or aggregates composing a sovereign number are subject to the supreme body of which they are component parts. It may even happen that a sovereign in one community shares the sovereignty in another community and is thus in a state of subjection in the latter. In that case he has two characters which are practically distinct, by reason of which there is no inconsistency between his being supreme in one and subordinate in another, in the same way as parts of a domestic sovereign are sovereign and subject when acting in different capacities.

Here again we must warn the reader that this is one of the sensitive points in Austin, going to the whole question whether the determination of supreme authority can be a mattter of fact as Austin supposes it can. The argument here is that a distinction between capacities or characters can only intelligibly be a matter of rule, and that the present is a revealing inconsistency in Austin pointing to the conclusion that the determination of authority must generally be a matter of rule.

Austin proceeds to consider the matter of sovereignty in federal unions. Ordinarily in a federal union he asserts that the sovereignty lies in the several united governments forming one aggregate body of which the federal government is only a delegate. By that aggregate body, the powers of the general government are conferred and determined and by that aggregate body its powers may be revoked, abridged or enlarged. Thus he believes that the government of the United States is merely a delegate of the united states' governments. His main argument for this is that it is the only account which can be given consistently with his theory of sovereignty, but of course the reaction of many to this extraordinary conclusion has been: so much the worse for Austin's theory of sovereignty.

Austin distinguishes a federal union, or composite state, from a system of federated states. A system of federated states is not essentially different from a number of independent states connected by an ordinary alliance. The only vague difference is in the intention of permanence. The legal effect is only through the laws fashioned on the agreements by the different states.

Austin now turns to the limits of sovereign power, which he says is incapable of legal limitation. That would be a contradiction. Any limitations which a sovereign imposes on himself or his successors may be abrogated at pleasure. It can only be a rule of positive morality to the successors and to the sovereign himself only law by metaphor. Thus to call an act of the sovereign unconstitutional because the sovereign has expressly adopted a principle in conflict with the act, or has habitually observed that principle, even if the principle is generally approved, does not mean that the act is in conflict with positive law. In a more specialized meaning, to say that an act is unconstitutional means that it conflicts with positive constitutional law. This cannot, however, apply to an act of the sovereign, which can only be unconstitutional in the former sense.

On the other hand, any constituent part of a sovereign body may be legally bound by positive laws of which the sovereign aggregate is the author, or by laws immediately proceeding from judges or subordinate legislatures. But in fact or practice they are commonly free wholly or partially from such restraints, though remaining subject to restraints of positive morality. If, however, some legally irresponsible part of the aggregate, like the British king, abused its powers by purporting to act for the whole, its command would not be legally binding and an agent who tried to carry out that mandate might render himself amenable to positive law. Such freedom as there is from positive law for parts of the sovereign aggregate is usually only given in a public capacity, but in the case of the English king is rendered both in a public and private capacity. It should not, however, be inferred from this that the king is the sovereign. He could be made legally responsible by Act of Parliament, his commands beyond the constitutional limits of his authority would have no legal force, and he habitually obeys the sovereign of which he is a constituent member.

The fact that the sovereign power is incapable of legal limitation means for Austin that political liberty is a matter of the liberty which is in fact left to a citizenry by the sovereign – even though the sovereign is legally free to abridge it – based on obligations deriving support from positive morality and the law of God. Political or civil liberty is in any case not more worthy of eulogy than political or legal restraint, even though ignorant and bawling fanatics stun you with their pother about liberty. Government exists not for liberty but for the common weal, and the degree of liberty appropriate is subject to considerations of its utility. Utility will require not only the conferring of rights, involving political liberties, but also the imposition of absolute duties on subjects, involving no correlative rights for subjects and hence no political liberties for subjects. Where liberties do exist under law, they are rarely independent of rights, for liberties would be useless unless they were protected.

It is not sensible, in Austin's view, to use the term despotic, as a term of blame, of a government, and the term free, as a term of praise, of a government, on the basis that the latter leaves more of political liberty to its subjects than the former. The allocation of blame or praise should depend on the utility or otherwise of the freedoms and restraints which each gives. Probably, those who make the distinction into free and despotic governments as a matter of praise and blame are suggesting that popular governments conduce more to the common weal than those where power is in the hands of the relatively few, because of the greater identity of interest between governments and citizens in the former case. But Austin says he has no direct concern with the merits or demerits of such arguments. He mentions them only to clarify the point that the arguments are not related to the question of legal sovereignty when they are properly understood.

What is perhaps revealing here is the consideration that if Austin was only concerned to show that the various issues he raises do not go to legal sovereignty, there was no need to commit himself to the proposition that the object of government was utility. This goes for him to what it ought to do rather than its legal status. It was, however, safe for him with his audience of Benthamites to commit himself to utility, just as it was safe for him in an earlier lecture to express views about political economy deriving from the notions of James Mill, Ricardo and Malthus, so illiberal that Charles Dickens would have prescribed a whole battery of Christmas spirits for Austin's Scrooge. But it was not safe in that company for Austin to express the anti-democratic views he had expressed to Mill in private and, according to Sarah Austin, also to Jeremy Bentham.

Austin attributes quarrels with the proposition that sovereign power cannot be limited, to confusion of the power of one component of a sovereign body (for example, the English king) with the power of the whole sovereign body, and says that the error is remarkable because the lack of legal limitation follows from the nature of sovereign power. He goes on to appeal to the authority of political writers to the same effect, to Sidney and to Thomas Hobbes. Austin takes this proposition to be the fundamental one of Hobbes's treatise, criticizing Hobbes only because he inculcates too firmly the duty of obedience to established government and because he ascribes the origin of sovereignty and political society to a fictitious agreement. Austin denies that Hobbes's defence of monarchical government makes him a defender of tyranny. The principal cause of tyranny in Austin's view is the failure of the multitude to understand the political sciences, and Hobbes was a great propagator of them and hence a foe of tyranny. With an enlightened community able to press its views, Austin says that the form of government is a matter of indifference. He agrees that the form of government is very important when the populace is not so enlightened, but does not say what in that case it should be.

Austin continues that a sovereign government has no legal rights against its own subjects. A legal right requires three parties, a sovereign government, the person on whom it is conferred, and the person subject to it. Everyone having a right acquires it by the power or might of another who would have to be the sovereign. So the notion that the sovereign can be in possession of a right involves a contradiction. Austin here appends a footnote about rights in relation to might. He says that my ability to move about may be called might or power, though my ability to move without hindrance from you may be properly called a right if the ability is owed to a law imposing a duty. This may throw some light on the fact that both Bentham and Austin sometimes seem to use 'power' as equivalent to what, later, Hohfeld was to call a privilege, something merely permitted by law, and distinguished from a right to do acts which are protected in the sense that interference by others will be a breach of duty. For Hohfeld, a power is different from a privilege, since the existence of the former means that the person having it, by the act which is empowered, changes the legal positions of others. Austin here seems to think of the exercise of freedom to move about as involving the use of a *physical* power. Unfortunately, the Benthamite terminology appears at times to lead Benthamites to confuse a power in this mere physical sense with a power in Hohfeld's sense, though it cannot be suggested that Austin is guilty of this confusion in this passage. It does appear to be prominent in some of Bentham's treatment of constitutional law.

Austin goes on to say that a sovereign can have divine or moral rights against its subjects, and since the test of true morality is utility which is the index to Divine commands, any true moral right of the sovereign is a Divine right. Thus the British government, for example, had no right to tax the American colonies because it was inexpedient for the colonists and the British alike.

Austin's next point is that it cannot be inferred, from the fact that a sovereign appears before a tribunal of its own making, that it has legal rights against its subjects or legal duties to them. To suppose that it is under duties would be inconsistent with its sovereignty because it would place it under subjection to the tribunal it had established by delegation and it could always defeat the claim if it wished by abolishing the law under which the claim was made. It merely submits to the claims made as if they were legal rights, and the procedure followed often recognizes that the claims are met as a matter of grace or favour. A sovereign may have a legal right against subjects of another government where it is acquired from the other government, since here there is no inconsistency with the theory of sovereignty.*

Austin next proceeds to the origin or causes of the habitual obedience of subjects on which the existence and exercise of sovereignty depends for him, in other words to the origins of political society, a matter which will involve him in problems of general political theory for the remainder of the lecture. We have heard all we are going to hear about the application of the theory of sovereignty to specific legal phenomena. The analysis of the matter now to

---

* Bentham's position in relation to duties of the sovereign was that they arose under a different kind of law from the others with which he was concerned since they could only be enforced by moral or religious sanctions, but he considered it useful for the sovereign to lay them down for himself, and he refrained from categorizing them under a heading which might appear to give them an inferior status, as Austin did (*Laws*, 64 – 71). The sovereign in Bentham's theory is the supreme power. He viewed powers as generally involving rights, though the converse was not true since the person with a right might have to rely on the powers of others (see, e.g., *Principles*, 205 – 6, footnote e 2). The footnote cited is one of the places in which Bentham argues that notions like right and duty cannot be defined in the ordinary way, and is related to a note in the *Fragment on Government*, Chapter V para. 6, explaining the sort of definition of them possible as 'paraphrasis'. This has been regarded as connected with the points made by modern linguistic philosophers about the variety of functions of language. Austin appears, as we see later in this chapter, to accept this verbally, but makes nothing of it in his detailed work. Neither does Mill, in his account of legal relations such as debtor and creditor which we mentioned in the previous chapter, claiming that legal relations can be reduced to states of consciousness, and this attitude is likely to have influenced Austin.

be considered can only be important to Austin's jurisprudence insofar as it may serve to justify theoretically belief in the existence of sovereigns — that is, go to show that this phenomenon exists by enabling us to understand why. But Austin nevertheless begins with the proper end of government, and answers that it is the greatest happiness of mankind, while freely confessing that this question belongs to ethics rather than jurisprudence as he conceives it. If the populace were properly enlightened, the cause of habitual obedience to sovereign government would be its utility and would only continue while it served those purposes. But since every society is inadequately instructed, the habitual obedience to government which is rendered by the bulk of the community is partly the consequence of custom — the persistence of habits formed in the past — and partly the consequence of prejudices in favour of the kind of government which exists or the persons involved.

But Austin claims nevertheless that habitual obedience to government arises in part from the perception of one kind of utilitarian consideration, namely the preference for government as such over anarchy, especially having regard to the deficiencies of rules of positive morality in regulating a society. This one is the only cause of habitual obedience common to all societies and therefore the only one which Austin sees a general disquisition like his own as properly embracing. Other causes are matters of particular history. The general cause goes both to the origin and permanence of governments.

Austin now considers the view that, because government depends on the consent of the governed, therefore the people are the fountain of sovereign power in some sense. But all that the premise on which this conclusion is based really means, he says, is that people are determined by some motives or other to obey the government and if they ceased to do so, it would cease to exist. It cannot be taken to mean that the people prefer the established government to any other, because this leaves out of account the evils they would have to undergo by attempting to substitute another. Nor can we infer that because the bulk of the community do not wish to have the established government continue, it ought not to continue, for the dislike of the government may be due to the inadequate instruction of the multitude in matters required to determine the utility of the government.

The fact that a people freely submits to established government is not inconsistent with their motive being that they could not withhold consent unless, perhaps, they resisted to the death. Hence the proposition that those consenting to be governed enter into a promise to obey the sovereign at the outset of the establishment of government is grossly incorrect. We have seen that Austin has already complained of this point in the theory of the admired Thomas Hobbes, whom he is generally choosing to follow. After pausing to say that the duties of the people to the sovereign are imposed by religion, morals and law, and the duties of the sovereign to the people by religion and morals, Austin proceeds to criticize the hypothesis that government is founded on an original covenant or contract, or fundamental civil pact.

The first plank of the social contract theory as Austin sees it is that the future members of a political society about to be created resolve to unite themselves, at the same time specifying the paramount purpose of the union. This may be the advancement of human happiness or it may be, for example, the eternal principles of right or justice, which Austin guesses is general utility darkly conceived and expressed. Then the members jointly determine the constitution of the government. Then the process is completed by promises of obedience given by the subjects and accepted by the sovereign, and promises to govern given by the sovereign and accepted by the subjects. The pacts at the three stages may be called *pactum unionis, pactum constitutionis,* and *pactum subjectionis*. But for Austin the first two are only introductory resolves, and the last only a convention. Otherwise it could not be sensibly supposed to bind the successor subjects and sovereigns from time to time.

Austin says that the accounts of particular writers may vary from the above model, but they do not for that reason escape the force of Austin's ensuing strictures. The first of these is that the hypothesis is unnecessary for the purpose of accounting for duties of subjects already accounted for by religion, morality, and law, and of the sovereign accounted for by religion and morality; and it is inadequate in any case to account for what it seeks to explain. But all Austin really seems to do in developing this latter point is to demonstrate that the obligations supposed to arise under the social contract theory are inconsistent with the implications of Austin's theory, and his strictures are not likely to convince anyone who does not accept it. Austin's elaboration merely involves traversing familiar material.

Thus Austin says that every convention which obliges legally derives its legal efficacy from a positive law. The sovereign, however, could not be bound by his own law if he made one proceeding from the pact and if the subjects were so bound the legal binding quality would proceed from the law and not the pact. Any religious obligations on anyone deriving from the pact would be annexed by the law of God itself, but the pact could not affect the laws of God, laying down the proper end of government, by itself laying down a different one. If it laid down the same end, it would be superfluous. And even if the pact somehow bound the original covenanters religiously, these religious obligations could not extend to their successors. In this respect, religious obligations are not like those which may be transmissible under positive law. Finally, such moral opinions of the subjects about the end of government as might bind the sovereign and subjects to keep the pact under the dictates of positive morality, would have existed prior to the pact and do not arise out of it. There would in any case be insufficient unanimity about what the end required in particular cases for there to be much control by this means over the government's specific actions. And even if subordinate ends were closely specified in the pact as well, their real effect would depend on the influence these had on subsequent opinions. Their force again would not derive from the pact itself. The only case in which moral duties of the sovereign could be generated by the pact would be where the subjects attributed some mysterious force to the supposed promises of the sovereign themselves.

In the circumstances where duties raised by positive morality might be generated by the pact, the pact would be useless or pernicious. If it merely affected people to accept the ultimate end pronounced, it would have little effect on attitudes to concrete actions for reasons specified above. If it specified more particular means to the end, it would be useless if it did not affect popular opinions. If it did it would probably be pernicious by giving an arbitrary force in people's minds to what was in the pact, substituting the barbarism of a primitive age for what might later be dictated by enlightenment through diffusion of sound political science.

Austin then puts a different criticism from the one dependent on the acceptance by the reader of analysis in terms of his own definitions. This is that the pretence of the existence of the pact is a fiction approaching an impossibility. Here, again, however, the argument will only have force in a limited fashion. Many social contract theorists do not pretend that the pact is anything but a fiction. Its hypothesis is supposed to have a usefulness for clarifying political and ethical issues despite this.

After explaining the essentials of a convention under legal systems, Austin begins to develop this branch of his critique by saying that the promise of the sovereign would have to be accepted by the subjects with understanding of its import. But the ignorant or weaker portion of the community could not do so, whatever signs they gave. There is, moreover, no evidence that anything of the kind which has to be supposed has ever happened. In the Anglo-American States those who determined the constitution were a mere fraction of the whole. Most constitutions, in any case, grow through the work of a long series of authors and are not the product of an instant plan. The opinions which support them grow too. Promises by particular sovereigns on accession have little resemblance to the supposed original compact. It is not an answer to say the convention may be tacit, for genuine conventions, whether express or tacit, must be signified. Significations are lacking, and could not have been given with understanding. Origins of government such as violent conquest would exclude any inference of a tacit agreement.

Austin now adverts to adherents to social contract theories who do not pretend there ever was a social contract. He thinks they tend to waver between saying that, although there was no express pact, there was a tacit one, and saying that the supposition is required if the government is to be rightful, lawful, or just. Austin has already disposed of the first suggestion; he disposes of the second merely by saying that, if that is so, no government can ever be lawful because in fact there was no original compact. But we must comment that this twists the sense in which the 'supposition' is made by theories which make it as a fictional hypothesis to test ethical propositions. Austin's final remark concerning the social contract theory is that it may have been suggested by a false belief that duties are necessarily connected with conventions. This belief is inconsistent with Austin's theory of the way duties arise and he says so.

Austin continues with a subject he regards as connected with that of the origins of government – the distinction between governments *de jure*, governments *de facto*, and governments *de jure* and *de facto*. A government *de jure* is a rightful government supplanted or displaced, a *de facto* government one which has established itself but is not rightful. The word 'lawful' is sometimes used as well as rightful, but an established sovereign government can be neither legal nor illegal. It cannot be illegal under positive law when the supposed law is that of a disestablished government. The disestablished sovereign itself cannot be a lawful government when it has lost power. In terms of positive law, the distinction of sovereign governments into lawful and unlawful is without meaning. This distinction may, however, be drawn in terms of positive morality and in particular in terms of the positive morality obtaining between states. Equally, it may be drawn in terms of the law of God.

Austin is thus again drawing out the implications of his definitions and now suddenly repeats his definition of positive law as a preliminary to some final warnings about it. Mill could not dissuade him from going back to the beginning even in what he published. Generally, Austin now says, the implication of his theory of positive law is that it binds only members of the subject community. Anything else would seem to be inconsistent with the definition. But the definition, Austin adds, is imperfect because a stranger to the community is bound if he can be affected by the sanction, and this is not really inconsistent with the sovereignty of the stranger's own sovereign because the duty is not imposed on the sovereign but on the subject. The sanction is not executed against the foreign government or within its territory unless with its permission or authority. Austin concludes that his definition of positive law is slightly too narrow and hence his definition of jurisprudence slightly too narrow. But he believes that he has defined positive law and jurisprudence as accurately as can be done in general terms and that what anomalous cases there are will have to be developed in the body of the course to which the *Province* is the introductory part. We may comment that Austin at least learned this procedure from Bentham, who would halt his analysis at some point in the *Principles* or *Laws* and promise more detail in the work to which they were both introductory. They both left the body of the work in incomplete manuscript, which was scarcely surprising in view of the extent of their ambitions to be both comprehensive and detailed.

Austin concludes with a further warning about his definition of law. He has not attempted to determine who are the members constituting the political society over which a sovereign is superior. We have commented on this already in passing. Austin now says that membership may be in numerous modes, but to explain them all would be to go into the detail of the subject and anticipate. Austin does say enough, however, about what is involved in a 'mode' to make it clear that here, right at the end of the *Province*, we have another sensitive point in the theory.

Austin says that membership is fixed in different ways under different systems and cites the French Code. The difficulty for Austin is obvious. Sovereignty is defined by reference to superiority over an independent society. An independent society is treated as an aggregate of members. But membership is apparently capable of definition by law, leading to the inference for later writers that sovereignty itself cannot be treated otherwise than as a matter of rule.

For good measure, Austin now concludes the *Province* by saying that, when we consider that the sovereign cannot be bound legally we must consider him in two characters. We have already noticed that Austin's conception of characters has been seen as involving him in the same kind of difficulty as his notion of modes. Here the distinction of characters with which Austin is concerned is that between the sovereign's character as chief of its own society and its character as the subject of a foreign community. As being generally or partially a subject of a foreign government, the sovereign can have legal rights, Austin tells us. The argument against Austin here, as already noticed, is that the distinctions between capacities itself can only be established by rule, that it is a legal, not a factual, conception.[9]

Austin's 'main course' lectures: legal positions of persons

Austin himself considered that the part of his lectures which he published as the *Province* was the more interesting. In the light of the sketch of it we have presented, the reader may have a sinking feeling about what is coming when we move on. But it is possible that Austin was wrong. Now we see a much more human Austin, thinking as he goes along rather than polishing the finished product, correcting himself when he feels he has gone wrong, puzzling in an overt fashion over some problems, struggling manfully with the task of holding manifold threads together. By any criteria, it is all, moreover, important: important for the new light it throws on Austin's continuing themes, important for the new ones it introduces, especially for those which emerge in later nineteenth-century legal works at a time when the classic text-books on individual branches of the substantive law were being written, as well as for the future of jurisprudence itself.

The lectures which occupy the remainder of Volume 1 of the Campbell *Austin* of 1885 are headed generally 'Analysis of Pervading Notions'. But they are perhaps no more or less pervasive than much of what follows. The central theme is the rights and duties of persons in relation to other very general notions involved in Austin's notion of law. This is the field which Kocourek has called Jural Relations, and Hohfeld has called Fundamental Legal Conceptions. But perhaps a simpler expression is the legal positions of persons. These relations are only one complex set among legal relations anyhow, as we have already sought to explain.

We have observed that, in general, Austin in the *Province* tends to restrict himself, among the variety of legal positions which later writers have discerned, to discussion of rights and duties. Occasionally he seems to distinguish a liberty or permission from both, and calls a liberty a power. In the present pages we learn that he was frankly puzzled about whether he should recognize a liberty as something distinct from a right. In a fragment following one lecture, Austin says that liberty and right are synonymous because the liberty of acting according to one's will would be altogether illusory if it were not protected from obstruction.[10] But he makes it clear that he is uneasy about the relation of this proposition to Bentham's division of laws, which he wishes to accept, into those obligatory and those permissive. He further displays uneasiness about the implications of what he has said for privileges, which he treats as exemptions for some persons from general obligatory laws. Hohfeld, on the other hand, generalized the notion of a privilege to cover anything which involves an absence of legal restraint on a person's action, but does not involve others in a duty to refrain from interference. Despite Austin's feeling that a privilege is an illusory advantage to its possessor, there are such things in existing legal systems.

In this part of his work Austin appears to object to the term 'power' as confusing. A right is sometimes called a power, he says, but the power involved is really that of the State. A right may sometimes be called a power, he thinks, in the sense that a man has a power over something when he can deal with it free from interferences by others. But in this sense the term power would be practically confined to rights to forbearances by others.[11]

On a distinct matter Austin appears in this part of his work finally to convict himself of circularity in his definition of law. It will be recalled that he allows the matter of a 'capacity' or 'character' in which the sovereign acts to enter into the identification of a command of the sovereign. He tells us now that to have a character means to be invested with rights or to be subject to obligations.[12] Austin's identification of sovereign commands is thus apparently dependent on us being able to identify the law already before we are able to use the identifying test.

In one very important respect, at least to the present writer, Austin's treatment of legal positions is superior to that of many of those who followed him. This superiority lies in his determined empiricism. One important feature of the definition of law as commands of the sovereign is that it at least purports to present law as something that happens. In the terminology of later writers, it aims to present law as a process. The command theory was, we have seen, immediately derived by Austin from Bentham, and Austin was surely right in a sense, at least about this part of Bentham's theory, when he said that Bentham belonged to the historical school – in spite of the annoyance this statement caused the historical school.[13] A process is in a broad sense a history, and the Benthamites sought to concentrate on things that have histories as objects of knowledge. In this they were in one respect more historical than those members of the historical school who believed that there were fundamental factors controlling history which did not have histories themselves – metaphysical realities sometimes presented as Idea and sometimes as Matter.

When Austin supports the traditional division of persons into natural persons and legal or fictitious persons, he comments that we are all the time in fact dealing with physical persons, but by ascribing rights and duties to feigned legal persons, we are frequently able to abridge our descriptions of them.[14] Austin points out that some legal persons are considered as aggregates of rights and duties, but insists that this is just a way of talking for convenience. The truths being described are relations of physical occurrences, including mental ones.

For Austin, duty, from which he scarcely distinguishes obligation, is a more pervasive phenomenon than right. There is a duty involved in every legal command, for to speak of a person having a duty means that that person is exposed to a sanction. But if the duty is absolute there is no correlative right. There is only a correlative right when the command is of a nature which imposes the duty towards a determinate person who is enabled to exact an act or forbearance from the obligee. Obligees might be determinate persons, (in the case of rights described as *in personam*) or might be persons generally (in the case of rights described as *in rem*).

Austin warns that from a remote aspect all duties are to persons generally, because the utilitarian object of their imposition is the general happiness. Hence distinctions between Public and Private Law on the ground of the different interests protected is wrong. Public law so called is in fact, says Austin, to be identified as part of the law of persons. It deals with those with a political 'status' – given special rights and duties under the law as part of government. Nor can civil and criminal law be distinguished, he says, on the grounds of the interests concerned. The true distinction lies in whether the application of the sanction is to be at the discretion of a determinate injured person (the person with the right) or at the discretion of the State.[15]

At this point, Austin is already getting into difficulties because of the number of threads he is seeking to trace. If he had followed Bentham's advice given in the *Principles*, he would have concentrated specially on one kind of inquiry in jurisprudence: the working out of what legal provisions, or at least kinds of legal provisions, lead to the greatest happiness of the greatest number. We have suggested that there were influences working on Austin, particularly the example provided by James Mill's admired *Elements*, which would have suggested to Austin that a proper scientific approach would rather be to concentrate on the characteristics of the workings of laws in general, good or bad, wherever they might be found, and to discuss the characteristics of good and bad laws at convenient points, just as Mill discusses what were good and bad economic policies at convenient points, though with some systematic basis for determining convenient points.

But if Austin was to adhere to this approach consistently, he could not make the assumption that the object of laws with which he was concerned would always be the general happiness. Bentham made this assumption for his special practical purposes because he was addressing himself to legislators and the only kind of legislator he wanted to talk to was the legislator who made his object the furtherance of utility. Austin with his different framework should consistently have proceeded on the basis that he was likely to find bad laws, the object of which was not the utilitarian one. On this basis he would have had at least to put his argument for the impossibility of distinguishing public and private law, or civil and criminal law, by reference to the kinds of interests involved, rather differently. As it is, Bentham might with some justice have accused Austin of Blackstone's cardinal error of confusing the 'is' and the 'ought' of law.

If, however, we can ignore Austin's attempt to reconcile Roman and English law as he found it with an analysis of what a legal system ought to be like along Benthamite lines, we find in the part of Austin's work under discussion a treatment of one topic in particular which represents a model of what the scientific approach of the Mills calls for, and a cameo of the scientific Austin at his very best. It also appears to have been highly influential in the context which existed when Sarah Austin rescued this part of her husband's work from oblivion in ways which we explain at the conclusion of the next chapter. The topic in question is the treatment of the notion of 'injury'.

Austin proceeds to the notion of injury from the notion of duty. Every legal duty is a duty to do (or forbear from) an outward act or acts and flows from the command of the sovereign. To omit (or forbear from) the act which the command enjoins, or to do the act which the command prohibits, is a wrong or *injury*.[16] One terminology, therefore, for speaking of what the sovereign commands or prohibits is by speaking of what he makes an injury. Here what it is vital to recall is that the sovereign by commanding operates on the human mind by setting up a prospective pain, the chance of which arises whenever a command is breached. For the enquiry into how this is to be effectively and economically done, the first essential for the enquirer is a philosophy of the human mind. So we come to Austin's psychology.

In this field Austin does not always find Bentham himself helpful, and occasionally says so when referring to particular points. There had been substantial developments in this field for the Benthamites since Bentham was treating this subject in his major works some half a century before Austin delivered his lectures. At the time when James Mill studied in Edinburgh, Dugald Stewart was professor of philosophy, and he was succeeded in 1810 by Thomas Brown. Mill retained his interest in philosophy and he and the Benthamites generally found Brown's essay on causation a landmark. In it one of Brown's major points was that the conception of 'power' confuses causation theory. Thus, for example, when we are saying that the occurrence of a loadstone is an invariable antecedent to iron being attracted, we invent something in the loadstone called its 'power' of doing this, though in fact to say that the loadstone has the power of attracting the iron adds absolutely nothing to what we have already said. Brown applied this to sequences of mental phenomena as well as to sequences of physical phenomena. In psychology, the use often made of the notion of 'will' corresponded to the use made of the notion of power in relation to physical phenomena. In the sequence of causal relations between mental phenomena, and mental phenomena and physical phenomena, there was no mysterious 'will' in some which represented a special power of control over others in the sequence.[17] These notions featured in the last two chapters of James Mill's *Analysis of the Phenomena of the Human Mind*, to which he turned in 1822, and of which John Stuart Mill was to produce an edition with criticisms in 1869.[18]

If the reader doubts Hart's claims that one of Austin's benefits to posterity was that he was a model of clarity in putting important positions, let him first read James Mill's final chapters and then read Austin's account of these matters in the part of his work under discussion. He tells us that our desires of those bodily movements which immediately follow them are the only objects which can be styled volitions, which we may if we like call acts of will – this is a compromise with popular language – but the bodily changes referred to are what are to be strictly called acts. Austin thus rejects Bentham's distinction between internal and external acts, and insists that we confine 'acts' to the bodily changes even though the word 'acts' is often taken, confusingly, to include consequences of the bodily motions. The act is wished for in a volition and immediately follows as a consequence of the volition. It is both 'willed' and intended – intended in the sense of expected. The consequences may be intended in the same meaning of the word intention, but they are not 'willed' in the sense of being the next in causal sequence from a volition.

There are desires which are not volitions because they do not consummate themselves immediately without the intervention of means as a volition does. Consequences of an act may be the object of such a desire in the sense that they are the final end of it or because they are themselves the means to a final end. In either case they are both wished and intended. But intended consequences extend to those which are expected to follow from an act even if they do not subserve the end – are not wished. Austin is here always speaking of the psychological notions important in relation to acts. A forbearance is intended – I go, for example, somewhere else when I have an appointment or avoid an act because of aversion to the consequences – but not 'willed': not the immediate consequence of a volition. A forbearance is contrasted with an omission, which is not doing without expectation of not doing. An omission involves in this sense inadvertence.

Injuries, in the legal sense which Austin has explained, may in some circumstances be 'willed' and in some circumstances intended. If the breach of duty is a forbearance, then, for Austin, it is intended but not willed. Injurious omissions are negligence. Negligence is to be contrasted with heedlessness, involving breaking a negative duty (a duty not to act) by committing an act. Negligence is omitting an act and breaking a positive duty. Rashness is contrasted with both, for it is accompanied by advertence to a mischievous consequence, yet the act is done because the consequence is considered certain not to happen. For Austin, where the act is done though it is thought the consequence might happen, it is intended. Attempting to distinguish, by different notions, degrees of expectation in the person's mind of the consequence is to Austin an invitation to lack of precision and he rejects it. In speaking of negligence and heedlessness, Austin assumes that the party should properly have adverted to the consequence, though in fact he did not, and in speaking of rashness should properly have thought that the consequence might happen though in fact he did not. This is because Austin is thinking in the context of what he would regard as a proper legal system, which would not ordinarily set up pains (sanctions) except where they would operate upon the minds of the citizen so as to further the utilitarian object. In other words, what would now be called establishing absolute liability is senseless. Austin makes some rather desperate attempts to convince himself that instances of absolute liability he finds in English law are not really there, and does not always succeed in convincing himself, with some resultant inconsistencies in what he says – for example, about the liability of the common carrier, and about absolute liabilities arising *ex contractu*.[19]

Austin continues his account of psychological phenomena by considering intentions to act or forbear in the future, which he analyses as a desire coupled with beliefs, but in which the desire does not consummate itself in the way that a volition does because of its different character. Austin diverts here to say something of the intention of the legislator, the testator, and contracting parties. His account is brief and in terms of his psychological theory.[20] He says nothing here of how the intention is to be understood by a judge, and this reticence is proper at this point in terms of a scientific approach. Interpretation is not merely a matter of finding something in the psychological events which cause a response by an interpreter, but goes also to the character of the response.

Austin proceeds to consider the ways in which sanctions can be made to operate in the light of his psychology and here he shows the influence of the long-standing interest of the Benthamites in the associationist psychology for which they revered Hartley. By setting up a sanction the legislator may influence the way the desires operate. But he cannot immediately destroy the desire to commit an offence, only influence other desires to operate against it. However, the desire to commit the offence may be destroyed gradually by the mind's habitual couplings of ideas. The desire to commit the offence, if weaker than the desire to avoid the sanction, comes to be regarded as the cause of probable evil (the sanction) and the aversion for the consequence comes to be transferred in the mind to that cause. A disinterested love of justice and hatred of injustice may develop which are none the less real because they originated in interested motives.

Austin considers civil sanctions and criminal sanctions to operate in much the same way, to secure obedience to law, though this may be achieved in the short term by redress to the injured parties. He extends his notion of a sanction further to cases in which the law annuls a transaction. Thus he places annulment of a marriage under the heading of a vicarious punishment, in which the major pain falls on the bastardized issue, and observance of the conditions of marriage is thereby fostered because the parties will wish to avoid the pains to the issue, from sympathy with them.[21]

In the demonstration of Austin's acceptance of James Mill's psychology in relation to the matter of the will, which is provided by the part of Austin's work above discussed, we have already indicated, at the conclusion of our treatment of Bentham's influence, that we see significance not only for Austin's theory of the way law works with sanctions, but for his general method in jurisprudence. At least a natural outcome was that social sciences, including jurisprudence, were not to be expounded in terms of a special logic of the will, but according to the logical method of the sciences generally with minor adaptations, as John Stuart Mill said. This was not inconsistent with the social science serving the corresponding art in John Stuart Mill's view. Rather it made the science better able to serve that art when called upon, and the art had constantly to call upon the science in Mill's view, as we have seen. The science provided understanding both of existing laws and ideal laws.

Austin's 'main course' lectures: sources of law

In this part of Austin's work his difficulties of organization continued and grew worse, for the same reasons as in his previous section, with some new ones. Fundamentally, the problem was the enormous canvas on which he had set himself to work − involving the utilization of all available knowledge which affected the social sciences and law in particular. The previous section had called for an excursion into psychology and Austin had his position on the psychological issues cut and dried. But the present seemed to him to call for an extensive examination of logic. He could not work with John Mill's *System of Logic* in the way he had worked with James Mill's *Analysis of the Phenomena of the Human Mind*, for the first-mentioned work was more than a decade away. Austin's main development of logic in connection with the present section of his work appears in a very elaborate separate note called *Excursus on Analogy*[22] which is obviously work in progress. Towards the end of it, Austin says of logic:

> I incline to think that the important part is not syllogism. But terms, propositions, definitions, divisions (abstracted from all particular matter) are all-important. . . . From my friend John Mill, who is a metaphysician, I expect that these, and analogical reasoning and induction, abstracted from the particular matter (which are the really practical parts), will

receive that light which none but a philosopher can give.[23]

There were other difficulties of exposition. He was prepared to assume that his listeners were familiar with English law, but not with Roman law, and in the result the exposition became unbalanced in terms of the respective efforts devoted to explaining the Roman sources and explaining the English sources. He felt also that he must explain the Roman constitutional structure at some length – and with some difficulty – as a preliminary to using Roman law terms to his class, and when he came to consider natural law and equity as sources of law, he felt he must explain the activity of the Roman praetors at some length, and here also encountered occasional distracting problems. We must confine ourselves here to examining his main jurisprudential themes.

Austin makes two broad classifications of sources. The first is into written and unwritten law. Claiming support from Roman usage, he asserts that written law means law immediately emanating from the sovereign and unwritten law that which does not immediately so emanate, but is expressly or tacitly authorized. So under the English system statutes are written law. Delegated legislation comes under the heading of unwritten law as does judicial legislation, though the last would be classed as written law if made by the sovereign in the judicial mode. Austin considers the distinction of modes more important than the distinction by reference to the immediacy or otherwise of the sovereign's authority. Legislation may be in the direct mode – the ordinary imperative mode – or in the indirect (oblique) mode. In the former case, the proper purpose of the immediate author or authors of it is the establishment of the law. In the oblique mode the existing law is professedly applied by interpretation or construction, but in fact a new rule is applied which then passes into law by becoming a precedent. Such is judicial legislation, and Austin takes the opportunity here to disagree again with Bentham's proposition that judicial legislation is undesirable.[24]

Apart from classifying sources of law, in the sense of authoritative sources as opposed to literary sources which he distinguishes, Austin devotes substantial space to discussing what particular phenomena which have been claimed to be sources can properly so qualify. Here his general procedure is to examine whether a prescription emanating from the particular claimed source meets his own definition of law or whether it does not, that is, whether it is either an express or tacit command of the sovereign. Hence his conclusions will not appeal to those who have different criteria for recognition of the presence of law. Austin's only general kind of argument against those with different approaches is to say that they get into confusion if they ignore his clear line of distinction. Sometimes, no doubt, he demonstrates that they do get into confusions, but whether this is because they do not accept his definition often seems to be less clearly made out.

Matters might have been improved if Austin had not demonstrated some arbitrariness in applying his definition. Thus, as an individual example, he distinguishes himself from some other positivist thinkers by refusing to recognize rules made by the parties to private transactions, for example, contracts and conveyances as law. His expressed reason is simply that only public persons make law.[25] This is put forward simply dogmatically and does not seem to be necessarily connected with his general definition of law, whatever may be said for or against it.

The arbitrariness appears to move to a more general level when we come to his arguments for judicial precedents being properly regarded as law. Austin says that the general reasons or principles of a decision are its *ratio decidendi*. Though not a rule in form, it is tantamount to a general command proceeding from the sovereign. For since it is known that the general reason of a decision on a particular or specific case shall govern decisions on future resembling cases, the subjects receive from the sovereign (on the occasion of such decision) an expression or intimation of the sovereign will, that they shape their conduct to the reason or principle of the case.[26] Austin does not, of course, mean that the sovereign actually does anything on the occasion in question. It is what Bentham called adoption by susception in the *Laws*. But Austin adheres here to the expression 'tacit' adoption, which Bentham used in the *Fragment on Government*.

If Austin was prepared to apply this argument to judicial precedent, it is difficult to understand why he was not equally prepared to apply it to other alleged sources of law, the claims of which he summarily rejects. Thus Austin, while recognizing among 'unwritten' law the laws established by subordinate legislatures and those arising under judicial precedent, classes custom as always only positive morality until a custom is recognized by a decision in the judicial mode which makes a precedent, or by the sovereign or some subordinate legislature in legislation in the ordinary imperative mode. However, if a given legal system has either in legislation in the imperative mode or in legislation in the judicial mode prescribed conditions under which customs are to be recognized, it should follow on Austin's own reasoning that a particular custom is law under those conditions before the specific custom has been recognized in either mode or even though it never comes to be so recognized at all. It would, of course, be a matter for examination of each system whether the conditions under the system were specified sufficiently for the sovereign's hypothesized approval to have something known to operate upon. But the question of whether customs are law, and when, could not be disposed of on a general basis in the negative in the way that Austin disposes of the question.[27]

It may equally be argued that Austin would have been led to different conclusions about the position under his theory of other alleged sources of law than custom, if he had been prepared to generalize the form of argument which he used in relation to judicial precedent. We have seen that he categorized the whole of international law as positive morality on the basis that this is where it fell under the system of definition and classification which he formulated at the beginning of the *Province*. But if he had been prepared to investigate whether a particular sovereign with whom he was concerned recognized the system of international law generally, or whether numbers of them did, he might have been led to a much more standard view of the basis of authority of international law than the snap conclusion he made that it could be nothing other than positive morality or, at its best, utility or the laws of God. He might have come down on the side of the particular hypothesis that international law derives its status as law through recognition by the individual municipal system, as distinct from the universal hypothesis of recognition in a basic norm of the entire international system, both of which the later positivist Kelsen regards as tenable logically.

The same may be said of Austin's summary disposal of numbers of other alleged sources of law. He makes the same analysis of law laid down by private lawyers, or by jurisconsults not occupying public positions and purporting to exercise public functions, as he does of customs. The practices of conveyancers, or the writings of jurists, are not law until that magic moment when the particular practice or the particular principle asserted, is passed into law by official recognition in the imperative or judicial mode.[28] Again, if Austin had been prepared to generalize the argument he applied to precedent, it would have been a matter for investigation under a particular system whether it was known beforehand that the authorities would act under given conditions on materials from a particular source, and if the answer was in the affirmative, materials from that source under those conditions could be treated as law before the particular material arose for decision at least where the principles of recognition are known to be those acted on by the courts.

From a Benthamite viewpoint, Austin had more solid reasons for his refusal to recognize natural law as a possible source of law under any system. On Jeremy Bentham's approach, the simple conclusion that natural law cannot be recognized as law follows from the consideration that there is nothing to recognize. The purported 'discovery' of a proposition of natural law is no discovery at all because no fixed criteria are being applied. The attaching of the label is a mere *ipse dixit* of the propounder of the proposition, falsely offering the attachment of the label as a reason for the making of the proposition.

Austin advances little beyond this as a matter of general theorizing on the subject, as distinct from going into especially the Roman history of the notion in jurisprudence and its derivation from Greek sources. He does say, however, that some of the laws which obtain as positive laws in all communities would obtain in any community, although it were a natural society and living in the savage condition. Austin's reason for this proposition is that there are political communities which are scarcely descended from the savage state, and it is probable that some of their laws rest on grounds of utility which are strictly universal and also strikingly obvious. He goes on to say, however, that the distinction which might be drawn between those positive laws in a political community which are natural, as belonging to this class, and other positive laws, is apparently nearly useless.[29]

Austin does not elaborate his conclusion but the reader who has examined some natural law exposition may sympathize with Austin to the extent of thinking at least that some arguments based on this kind of distinction are grossly overdrawn. The most obvious ground of utility which can be appealed to as requiring a particular measure universally is that it is essential to the survival of any community. But the arguments which are made to establish this kind of connection are sometimes tenuous, and rendered less convincing by shifts in the meaning of the expression 'survival of the community' as the argument proceeds. One finds oneself continually asking whenever the expression is used: 'survival as what?'

Austin's treatment of equity is annexed to his treatment of natural law. In many of its more general meanings he finds the term attended with such vagueness that it is not a useful conception: a species of interpretation, impartiality incumbent on judges, judicial decisions not determined by rules, good principles of direct or judicial legislation, the cheerful performance of imperfect duties, positive morality, or good principles of deontology. From the sporadic occurrence of these general notions in the thinking of officials or others, Austin distinguishes the situation where equity is part of the positive law of a political community, whether administered by separate tribunals, as he conceived the position to be in the England of his time, or administered by the same tribunals as administer other parts of that law, as he conceived the position to be under the Roman system. Austin considers that the position of equity as part of the law is often concealed by fictional thinking, and he has something to say about fictions generally. But he tends to put down the resort to fictions as often due to what he calls imbecility. Bentham, on the whole, made his greatest public impact when he was at his most personally vitriolic, and Austin occasionally indulges in these displays, perhaps in an effort to make an impact on the class. But the heat did not generate light, and the emergence of brilliant general hypotheses concerning the general relations of fictions to equity, and of both to legislation had to await, fortunately not very long, the appearance of Sir Henry Maine. Austin found equity in his time to have solidified in England into ordinary rules of law, offering no special problems about source. What was classed as equity was partly legislation and partly judicial precedent.[30]

If Austin had been taxed with the inconsistency which the present writer has suggested exists, between his treatment of judicial precedent and his treatment of other alleged sources of law which have not in his view received the seal of sovereign approval, whether as equity or some other part of positive law, there can scarcely be any doubt what his answer on his general approach would have been. It is a matter of what is determinate and what is not. Austin would fairly clearly have said that even where the sovereign does appear on his tests to have given his approval to something, the something is not law unless it is determinate. But the question which then arises is: Why did he think that a rule supposed to exist under judicial precedent has, or at least commonly has, a determinacy which what emerges from the other sources considered, lacks?

There is no doubt he did think that the rule emerging from even a single decision was determinate or, what was the same thing to him, could be rendered determinate by logical analysis. This emerges, for example, in his arguments in support of the possibility and desirability of codifying the English legal system of his time. It was possible to codify the English legal system as it existed – and prior to giving it the kind of tremendous overhaul which Bentham's utilitarian principle required and which was increasingly being regarded as impracticable because too formidable – because in Austin's view the principles of the common law *could* be extracted from the decided cases and worked into a general code with the materials already enacted in the imperative mode.[31]

The story of why Austin believed that the principle of a precedent is determinate, or at least believed it most of the time, is the story of his struggles with logic to which we referred at the beginning of this section. Lacking assistance, or at least sufficient assistance, from Benthamite sources, Austin began his analysis of the *ratio decidendi* of a case, with the guidance offered by his German reading in Thibaut and Mühlenbruch. The rule to be extracted from a case or cases must be gathered from the grounds or reasons of the decision or decisions. One arrives at the general principle by induction or abstraction from the specific peculiarities of the case. Because the terms of the judicial decision are unlikely to have been scrupulously measured, it is not right to give effect to its terms in the way that one would give effect to the clear terms of a statute. They probably tally imperfectly with the reasons upon which the decision is founded. It is therefore the reasons of the decision which are to be followed, whereas in the case of a statute with clear terms it is those terms which are to be followed. The general terms which a judge uses are impertinent and ought to have no authority unless provoked naturally by his judicial decision on the very case before him. Further, as the proper purpose of the judge is the decision of the specific case, any general proposition which does not concern it (what is ordinarily called an *obiter dictum*) is unauthoritative. Austin says that the process of arriving at the *ratio decidendi* involves removing the specific peculiarities of a case and the reasons suggested to the judge by its specific peculiarities.[32]

All this might not in itself be sufficient to indicate that what comes out at the end of this process is a determinate principle, but Austin further says that the principle of the case is confined to the species to which it belongs, presumably meaning that the principle is to the effect that cases of the species to which the case belongs are to carry the legal consequences which the case before the court was determined to have. For this he relies, not specifically on the Germans, but on what was said by Sir Samuel Romilly and what was said in *Read v. Brookman*.[33] By referring to the case, Austin does not seem to be saying that each system has its own authoritative rules for determining the *ratio decidendi*. The general assumption throughout appears to be that it depends on general considerations which one might expect to be utility – and there is a faint hint of this in the above as will be seen – or logic, which appears to be the more general assumption in the lectures in question and the long notes on logical issues.[34]

The determination of the species of the case would only give us a determinate rule if anything at all that exists including a law case belongs only to one species, which thus gives us the breadth of the principle in the case. It might seem that Austin began his long *Excursus on Analogy*, which he evidently found himself unable to incorporate into the lecture, with this idea at least at the back of his mind. Austin says at that point that things have generic differences and specific differences, the one kind of difference between it and other things being common to it and other things in its genus – the broader class to which it belongs – and the other kind of difference being between it and other things being common to it and other things in the species. At this stage he further seems to suggest that the term analogy applies between things which have common generic features. But later he abandons this at least for the time being, and equally has by now abandoned any suggestion that things belong necessarily to single species. He now says also that we fix the species to which a thing belongs 'for the purpose in hand'. We may comment that this would seem to mean, in relation to the problem of determining the *ratio decidendi* of a case, that we fix the species of the case by reference to the reason behind the decision. In that case logical reasoning about species can give us no assistance in determining the reason – which is, according to Austin, what is authoritative about a case. The argument for saying that the authority of the reason gives us a determinate rule is left in the air.[35] But the more general drive of Austin's treatment of this present topic seems to be along the lines that we fix as its species, for the present purpose, the narrowest species to which a case belongs, after abstracting its individual peculiarities.

The notion that a thing has an *infima species* – that there is a category to which it belongs which is the lowest (literally) or narrowest category to which it belongs – is accepted by John Stuart Mill. It also appears in Bentham as the narrowest description of a particular offence, so that the total of all such descriptions are the *monads* of which the legal system is composed. But for Bentham these are made by the legislator, whereas to suppose that the facts of a case have a narrowest category under which they can be subsumed and which would enable us to identify its principle logically is a different proposition altogether. The present writer confesses that he cannot accept the notion either that there is a natural lowest species of a thing, or that the individual peculiarities of a thing can be separated off from a thing's class characteristics in some way. The infinite complexity of things precludes us from arriving at a narrowest class, while at the same time its characteristics are always class characteristics rather than individual ones and the uniqueness of the thing lies in their patterning. A truly individual characteristic would be unrecognizable.

Although Austin falls in one place, perhaps by inadvertence, into saying that case law is inherently uncertain, he will not have it that the fact that what is law under judiciary law induces a degree of uncertainty compared with statute law where the terms are authoritative, gives judiciary law a greater degree of desirable flexibility than statute law. He will not accept the argument based on the famous statement of Lord Mansfield that case law is in a position to 'work itself pure' over a period while statute law is not. He poses logical dilemmas for the historical jurists who considered that a code will petrify the law while under a case system it will continue to develop. Either judiciary law is law or it is not. If it is law at all − which presumably means, as generally for Austin, determinate law − it is no more in a position to develop than statute law is.[36] This seems more like special pleading than logic.

While Austin devotes a great deal of time in different places to one of the problems involved in determining the authority of a case in establishing a precedent, the determination of its *ratio decidendi*, he disposes very briefly of the problem of what he calls the validity of the rule in a case. By this he means the problem of determining which cases carry weight as precedents, so that their *rationes*, once they are ascertained, are law. He says he is not aware of any test of this matter, and asks whether it is the number of decisions with which the case is aligned, the *elegantia* of the rule laid down, or the reputation of the judge who decided it.[37] Austin does not suggest that there might be different tests from system to system. Yet this is, again, what might have been suggested to Austin by his notion that it is the capability of the sovereign being aware of the conditions under which a rule is treated as law which justifies us in saying that his *imprimatur* has been given to it.

Austin does give considerable space to the question of what happens when a court is faced with what would now be called a case of first impression. Here it has no rule established as law to follow and judicial legislation is required. Here there can be no question of it appealing to an authoritative source for a rule which covers the case, even though in one place Austin hesitates, curiously, about whether this is true, indicating his tentativeness in logical matters.[38] Generally, however, his view is that there are here causes rather than authoritative sources of the rule which the court comes to adopt. Under the heading of suggestive causes, he places custom and usage, the consequence or analogy of custom and usage, judges' notions of what ought to be law whatever the standard used, the opinions and practices of lawyers, statutes which are used as a basis of judicial legislation under a pretence of interpretation, and foreign law or positive international morality. Austin thinks, with a brief flirtation with historical jurisprudence, that the natural or customary order of development is, first, rules of positive morality, the adoption and enforcement of those rules by the tribunals, addition of other rules by consequence or analogy, then judges introducing new rules they think ought to be law, then legislation proper following a similar development to judicial legislation, and, finally, mutual reactions of legislation proper and judicial legislation.[39]

It will be seen that in the course of the above exposition, and in fact also elsewhere, Austin felt called upon to discuss what amounted to interpretation of legislation, in a proper sense of the word, and what amounted to judicial legislation under the guise of interpretation of a statute. Although Austin criticized Bentham for his generally disapproving attitude to judicial legislation, he followed Bentham in disapproving judicial departure from the clear words of a statute. The literal meaning of a statute ought to be given effect by the courts in Austin's view because the words were weighed, and Austin assumes virtually by definition that the intended meaning of the legislator is what must be law. It is only if there is doubt about the wording that the *ratio legis*, the purpose of the statute, is properly taken into account.[40] Spurious interpretation – restrictive or extensive interpretation – occurs where the words, though clear, do not give effect properly to the purpose, and the judge interprets by reference to the general purpose rather than the specific intention of the words. The objection to this with Austin is that it lays all statute law at the arbitrary disposition of the tribunals.[41]

There is, however, a different situation where judicial legislation is properly required, which Austin calls the situation where there is a competition of opposite analogies. This is where either two statutory rules exist, or two common law rules exist, neither of which covers the case but both of which offer analogies and which point, on this basis, in opposite directions. Austin does not suggest that the competing analogy type of case is the only one where the judge may frame new law by analogy, but it is the most difficult, just because of the competition of analogies. In a note on interpretation, distinct from his lectures, Austin suggests that competition of opposite analogies arises in some special ways for statute law in the process of its *application* because of vagueness of expression of the terms in which two statutory rules are expressed, or because, although they are clear, they in fact conflict. But these cases are distinct from the one already described, where it is a problem of how the judge is to *legislate*, either on the analogy of statutes or judicial rules.[42]

The concluding section on the competition of opposite analogies which is involved in judicial legislation proper is described by the editor as 'wanting' from Austin's 'Note on Interpretation'. This is quite possibly no accident. Austin may have deferred detailed treatment of it until he had written his 'Excursus on Analogy' which immediately follows in Campbell's *Austin*. This is the general logical note to which we have already referred. Starting with analogy, Austin in this note finished by saying something on virtually every major problem in logic, but without throwing any particular light on how a judge might properly proceed with a problem of competing opposite analogies. It is hard to suppose that Austin thought he could find a solution to the problem for the judge purely on logical grounds. If there were such a

solution, then the proper conclusion would be that the judge was not legis-
lating at all. There would be a determinate result to the case in the existing
authoritative materials. But by assuming at the outset that judicial legislation is called for, Austin assumes that it is not so. In fact, the excursus
appears to throw little light on the way in which the problem of competing
opposite analogies is to be attacked.

Austin's treatment of sources of law concludes with his treatment of
codification partly in what is incorporated in his lectures, partly in his notes
on the subject included at the end of the Campbell second volume, and
partly in his essay on Codification and Law Reform at the end of the work.[43]
The first remarkable feature of this section is the extent to which Austin
insists that judge-made law is determinate in an effort to persuade his
listeners that codification of the existing law is practical, and does not have
to await its general reorganization on the basis of utility. This is probably a
response to attacks on Bentham's lack of realism in this respect. It seems to
be a strategic move. The final essay makes unhappy reading, for it seems to
reflect loss of confidence in the ability of the legal profession to produce
those capable of codifying. The study of general jurisprudence tends, says
Austin, to form men with the talent required, which can only be acquired by
scientific study, and the want of such learning is the greatest difficulty in the
way of codification. Mere practitioners can never perceive the legal system
as a whole and the relations of its parts, and for innovation they need a
general knowledge of the moral sciences as well as the details of the system.
Codification is a question of time and place. In the abstract a complete code
is better than a mixture of statute and judiciary law. But, in the concrete, are
there men, then and there, competent to produce a code that will, on the
whole, more than compensate the evil that must necessarily attend the
change? To this question, Austin gives no answer for the England of his time
as he lays down his pen.

In retrospect, this section of Austin's work is, in its detail, a story of valiant
pioneering attacks on important problems, of some pregnant suggestions,
and of missed opportunities. We have indicated that the subsequent history
might have been different if he had been prepared to generalize his notion
that the tacit approval of the sovereign is to be regarded as given to what
rules he would find accepted among the judiciary for the recognition of what
comes from precedents. If he had regarded this last as the important
question to be asked in relation to *any* alleged source of law, the transparent
fiction of Bentham that the reason it is important is that it can then be
inferred that the sovereign approves of the practice, might have been dis-
pensed with altogether, and the whole test for the identification of law reap-
praised. The same approach might then have been applied to those rules
which Austin treats as emanating immediately from the sovereign, leading
to the view that there, too, it is their recognition by accepted rule, rather
than the power of their promulgator as such which qualifies the mandates as
law. Once this step is taken, the fact that Austin had to talk at times of 'capa-

cities' and 'characters' of the sovereign in some legal sense becomes capable of explanation. This would at least have been a much more defensible view, though it would have posed the problem for Austin of how the rules could be identified in a way which would measure up to the requirements of his empiricism and at the same time distinguish these rules from positive morality. While subsequent analytical jurists have moved from Austin along the lines we have indicated, we believe that the consequential problems which Austin would have seen are real problems and that they have not been satisfactorily solved.

Austin's 'main course' lectures: the map of a legal system

This part of Austin's work is the one in which the materials are most scattered and incomplete. These are the lectures headed 'Law: Purposes and Subjects', but 'purposes' are discussed incidentally and certainly not on any plan which Bentham would have considered was required to relate legal provisions to the requirements of utility. The subjects covered carry out only a small part of what Austin indicated to be his intentions. He proposed that he would deal with the law of things and the law of persons as his major division – the law of things first. Within the law of things itself, his major division was to be into primary rights, with primary relative duties, sanctioning rights with relative sanctioning duties, and absolute sanctioning duties. Delicts or injuries, which Austin regarded as the causes of sanctioning rights and duties arising, were to be included within the account of sanctioning rights and duties. Austin's next division was of primary rights into *jura in rem* and *jura in personam*, which he had explained in the previous section.

Austin proposed to deal with primary rights under four main headings: rights *in rem* simply, rights *in personam* simply, less complex combinations of rights *in rem* and rights *in personam*, and more complex combinations of rights *in rem* and rights *in personam*. Unfortunately, Austin was unable to complete even the first of these four main tasks, still less to begin the tasks, beyond those four, concerned with sanctioning rights and duties. Sarah Austin says that the last lecture he ever gave at London was on 26 June, 1832, though we have noticed that there is some conflict among the authorities about this. The lecture she so identifies is the beginning of Austin's detailed consideration of titles, the events by which rights *in rem* are acquired or lost, and it consists of very brief notes of what he intended to say on that matter. Sarah has added some fragments from Austin's loose papers on the law of contracts, quasi-contracts and quasi-delicts, which Austin intended to deal with under his next heading of simple *jura in personam*. They only amount to a few pages of jottings.

The information concerning Austin's map of the legal system which is provided by his lectures, is supplemented by his Outline of the Course,[44] and by various Tables which he issued to his students – or intended to issue in some cases: Sarah Austin rescued material from the printer – and by notes to the Tables in question.[45] But the Tables do not include Austin's own map of the legal system. They are Austin's interpretation of the arrangement of the Institutes of Justinian, first as Austin understood it to be in the minds of the Roman lawyers themselves and then as it stood in the minds of later Civilians – latter day interpreters of Roman law. In any case, Austin considered this arrangement was founded on historical principles. The other tables show Blackstone's arrangement, and Bentham's arrangement as interpreted by Dumont in the *Traités*, of both of which Austin was critical. The most useful material outside the lectures themselves concerning Austin's unfinished work is to be found in the Outline, which he published along with the *Province*, in order to show the relation of that work to the rest of his course. It is published at the beginning of the Campbell *Austin*.

From the various materials, Austin's structure of the legal system appears as follows. The most general division of the law, into the law of persons and the law of things, is justified by the consideration that if we had to express the modifications of the law affecting special classes of persons whenever we were dealing with any department of the law, there would be much unnecessary repetition. Therefore, it is a matter of economy of exposition to deal with the general law first and then deal with special modifications affecting particular classes. The reason for the order of treatment is that the latter is naturally unintelligible without the former, while the former is perfectly intelligible without the latter. The term 'law of things' is misleading but convenient. What it really means is the law minus the law of persons, so that it is really only the law of persons which needs positively to be defined.

The special rights, duties and capacities marking the status or condition of some persons, reside in the person as a member of a class, with regard specially to that class, and are so considerable in number that they give a conspicuous character to the individual or extensively influence his relations with other members of society. The classes in question are not to be thought of as classes which persons can enter or leave at will, so we do not include, for example, persons entering into contracts as a class. Status does not inhere in a person, it is nothing more than a complex of his rights and duties.[46]

Austin considers that from the point of view of commodiousness in exposition of the law, there may be some argument for detaching other branches as well as the law of persons from the general account represented by the law of things. But he rejects the view that we ought to detach the law of actions. That ought to be distributed under the law of things and the law of persons.[47] Similarly, he rejects the view that we ought to have a special category for public law, giving rise to a distinction between public law and private law. Insofar as some public persons have a special status under the law, this is already catered for by detaching the law of persons, which includes a treatment of political conditions. The sovereign is, of course, to be excluded from any accounts of rights and duties because he does not have any position under the law which he makes, so that constitutional law, so called, affecting him is only positive morality. For the rest, tests of what may be public law are too vague to base a division of law under a rational system. There can be no division on the ground of ultimate purpose, because the ultimate utilitarian purpose of any rational law is the happiness of the public generally.[48]

Within the law of things, Austin began, as we have noticed, with simple rights *in rem*, distinguished from rights *in personam* by the compass of the corresponding duty. This means that for him rights which exist against persons generally are rights *in rem* as distinct from rights *in personam* existing against specific persons. Therefore, there does not have to be a thing involved in a right *in rem*, despite the derivation of the term literally. The subject of the right may indeed be a thing, but it may be a person as in the case of a man's rights concerning his own body, or there may be no physical subject of the right at all.[49]

Within simple rights *in rem*, the major distinction which Austin makes is between property and *servitus*. While not pretending that all his definitions in this respect correspond precisely with usage anywhere, Austin gives the following definition of property as opposed to *servitus* or easement. Property is any right which gives to the entitled party an indefinite power or liberty of disposing of the subject. The extent of the right is limited only by the rights of other persons. Modes of property differ from one another by reason of variations in the rights of others limiting the proprietary right, the most extensive mode sometimes having the term dominion applied to it. The various modes of property cannot be precisely defined, but need to be capable of precise distinction from one another under any system.[50]

Servitus is contrasted in that where a person has a servitude over a subject he may apply it only to a given purpose or purposes, as distinct from indefinite purposes limited only by the rights of others. Generally, servitudes are over subjects in which others have a right of property. A servitude is a *jus in re aliena*. Austin is unsure how he should classify what he calls a negative servitude, a mere right that another should not put the subject to a given use, as distinct from a positive right to use it for a given purpose. A real servitude resides in a party as owner of land against a party as owner of other land, so that there is dominant and servient land. A personal servitude resides in a person separate from his capacity as owner of any land. Austin suggests that a term for the latter would be 'in gross'.[51]

Austin turns to distinguishing rights *in rem* in point of duration. A right of indefinite duration, as commonly understood, has to be thought of as inhering in the party himself, and in his successors of a given character or characters for an indefinite period. A right of indefinite duration has to be distinguished from a right of absolute property where there are powers of alienation as well as enjoyment. Absolute property is usually taken to involve indefinite user, unlimited duration, and alienability by the owner from every possible successor.[52]

Rights *in rem* can be for Austin present (or vested) or future or contingent. The right if in existence at all is always a present right, even if not coupled with present enjoyment, so strictly speaking the term vested is superfluous. All that can be contrasted with an existing right is a chance or possibility of a right. In Austin's view, a chance of a right may be called a contingent right where some of the complex of facts necessary to bring a right into existence (the investitive facts) have occurred, but not as yet others, which may or may not occur. In Austin's view, the term contingent right may be properly extended to the situation where the investitive fact which has not yet occurred is an expression of will by the person whose right may be brought into existence by that expression.

Austin calls investitive facts, which bring the rights into existence, 'titles', as also those events through which those rights cease to exist. Among the titles which exist in every system and are therefore matter for general jurisprudence are occupancy, acquisition by labour, accession, accession combined with labour, alienation, and praescription.[53]

Before Austin could consider these in detail, his strength failed. He was able only to give a few preliminary lectures about titles in general. He pointed out that a law is itself a fact – a command – and sometimes titles arise by immediate operation of law. But he thought this term, contrary to the usual usage, was only appropriate where the command conferred the title by its terms on a specific individual, as when a special Act of Parliament was passed for him. While all titles are logically complex, Austin distinguished a simple title from a complex title, on the basis of whether it was necessary to distinguish some of the investitive facts from others for the purpose in hand, in which case the title is complex. Austin points out that people refer to a title as arising by operation of law when the complex of facts does not include the act of the party himself. But he will not have it that this is logical. Neither is the usage in which something is said to arise by law because it is a consequence annexed to a transaction otherwise than through the acts of parties. It is at this point that Austin's fully written-out lectures end.[54]

It appears from his outline that Austin would have proceeded next to consider possession as giving title, that is, unauthorized or adverse possession. This gives rise to a right of possession, which Austin distinguishes from the title itself. It is the right acquired through the title. A biographer of Austin has selected the drawing of this distinction by Austin as an example of his distastefully laboured exposition. But it was an important distinction for Austin to draw in the light of his general exposition and he drew it perfectly clearly. Austin continues that the adverse possessor's title gives him this right against all but the person to whose rights the possession is adverse, but he may acquire a right against that person too by praescription. So praescription is another title. At this stage the original adverse possessor has dominion. Austin then proposed to go into these matters in more detail, referring to English and Roman law.[55]

Austin next intended to proceed to simple rights *in personam*, having now completed simple rights *in rem*. Here he intended to deal with contract and quasi-contract. Under the third of the four divisions of primary rights – comparatively simple combinations of rights *in rem* and rights *in personam* – he intended to deal with such matters as a conveyance with a covenant for title, a mortgage, and a sale completed by delivery with a warranty for title or soundness. In his fourth department he intended to deal with complex combinations: such universities of rights and duties as arise by universal succession. Austin explained that universal successors include the executor or administrator of a testate or intestate estate and the general assignee of a bankrupt or insolvent, as well as, with respect to certain matters, heirs to, and devisees of, real estate. In all these cases, Austin explained, it was true in his time that large collections of rights and obligations passed all at once from one person to another by reason of their kinds or sorts, rather than specifically. There is a right *in rem* relating to the aggregate, even if the individual rights are *in personam*. Universities of rights might be divided into those which come from the living and from the dead and Austin proposed to go into detail about each with reference to English and Roman law.[56]

Austin proposed, after dealing with some testamentary matters not logically within *universitates juris*, to proceed to Sanctioning Rights and Duties, dealing first with rights and duties arising from civil injuries and then duties and other consequences arising from crimes. He thought rights arising from civil injuries were generally *in personam*. But they could be distinguished into those which arose from rights *in rem* and those arising from rights *in personam*, and then subdivided according to the immediate purposes which the rights and duties arising from the delicts were calculated to accomplish. Firstly, the user of an infringed right *in rem* might have rights of action to restore his right, or a right by self-help to restore his right, the exercise of which self-help might then have to be justified in court. Secondly, all that could be achieved for a violated right *in rem* in many instances would be satisfaction, pecuniary or other. Thirdly, in some cases restoration and satisfaction might be combined. Fourthly, an incipient or impending offence might be prevented by appropriate order.

Austin next proposed to deal with rights arising from civil delicts which are infringements of rights *in personam*. It is under this head that he deals with rights arising out of breach of contract and quasi-contractual obligations, to specific performance of the contract, injunction against its breach, liens for money owed or labour done, and rights to satisfaction in lieu of or in addition to specific performance.

As an appendage to the rights arising from delicts generally Austin proposed to deal with the modes in which they were exercised, that is, to deal with the law of civil procedure, divided into what is required for the pursuit of rights of action and the raising of defences; the functions of judges and other ministers of justice, pleading, judicial evidence, judgments, and appeals. Austin proposed to deal with judgments as causes of ulterior rights, and those judgments which are mere solemnities attached to conveyances or contracts in non-contentious proceedings.[57]

Austin next proceeded to the plan of his lectures on duties, and other consequences, arising from crimes. Here Austin repeated what he had said elsewhere that these are absolute duties with no corresponding rights because there is no determinable person to whom the duty is to be observed or the person does not have rights, in other words, is the sovereign. Under the present heading, though he did not consider it logical, Austin proposed not only to deal with absolute sanctioning duties, as his plan required, but absolute primary duties because it was commodious to deal with them here. After dealing with absolute primary duties he said he would classify crimes, whether they were breaches of primary absolute or primary relative duties, then he would touch on the duties arising out of crimes and notice the consequences of crimes in punishments. Finally he would deal with the modes wherein crimes were pursued to punishment − criminal procedure.[58]

All the above part of Austin's map of a legal system relates to the first of his two major departments of the law, the law of things. The remainder is concerned with the law of persons, and is divided into private conditions, political conditions, and anomalous or miscellaneous conditions. Under each of his divisions and subdivisions Austin proposed to consider the special legal consequences attaching to the condition and the facts which invested or divested them.

Austin proposed to divide private conditions into domestic and professional. Under the first would come Husband and Wife, Parent and Child, Master and Slave, Master and Servant, and the various Persons who were thought to require special protection and restraint under the law. Professional conditions were to be reviewed in a similar manner, but Austin did not elaborate.

Under political conditions he proposed to deal with subordinate political superiors: judges and ministers of justice, defence officials, revenue officials, educational officials, welfare officials, and public works officials. Under anomalous or miscellaneous conditions, he proposed to deal with aliens, persons under incapacities by reason of religion and persons under incapacity by reason of crimes.

Austin concluded his sketch of the law of persons with a note in which he said that his subdivisions of treatment of each condition would follow his arrangement of the law of things. The major division would be primary and sanctioning rights, each subdivided then into rights *in rem* and rights *in personam* and combinations thereof, with continual reference at all points to the principles expounded in the law of things.[59]

After saying that he would conclude with a brief account of the principles of positive morality which recent writers styled the positive law of nations or positive international law, Austin concluded his outline with a plea for leniency from the reader: 'But, until I shall have traversed my ground again and again, it will abound with faults which I fairly style inevitable, and for which I confidently claim a large and liberal construction.'[60] Perhaps this is one instance in which Austin did not quite precisely state his meaning. If what Austin really wanted was a large and liberal construction of his faults, what has happened in the century and a half since he wrote those words would, on the whole, have justified his confidence. It is his virtues which have been subjected to restrictive interpretation.

For our part, we do not propose to niggle about the details of Austin's map. It is a powerful – and influential – map, drawn in strong lines and probably with a good deal more knowledge of the details of the law that might be inferred from the fact that it does not always fit the English system. Austin knew it did not, and said so in places, and probably knew it did not in places where he had no space to say so. In any case, more important for general jurisprudence than the details of his map, are the general principles on which it is founded, and the explanations Austin gave in the course of constructing it of why he did one thing and not another. It is because of the issues which Austin thus raised that an argument can be made that the pages of this section are the most important he wrote, at any rate for general jurisprudence, even though they were written at a time when student interest was dissolving, his health bad, and his future grim.

What is most striking about the general principles upon which Austin's map is founded is obviously the prominence given to rights. This is remarkable in the light, firstly, of the fact that, among the two legal positions on which Austin has concentrated in an earlier section, rights are less pervasive for him than duties. Rights only exist when the framing of a legal rule is such that a determinate person is accorded a discretion whether or not to seek the application of a sanction in some particular interest. Duties on the other hand are involved wherever there is a law at all. If it is of a character which calls into existence a right, then there is a relative duty. If it is not, there is an absolute duty. The fact that Austin proceeded on the basis of rights meant that he covers relative duties at the same time as he discusses rights, because whenever he talks about A's right against B, we are to understand from him that statements about B's correlative duty to A are implied. But when Austin comes to crimes, he has suddenly to switch to duties, and although he conceives this only to require him to talk about the absolute duties which arise out of crimes, he tells us that he will talk about absolute primary duties there, in effect because they have not fitted into his scheme anywhere else.

If we ask why Austin did this, the answer is probably that he found that this was what the writers who presented him with models for his map did. If he had gone against the grain in this respect, he would have had a hopeless task in his limited time because he would have got so little help. He was under very great pressure and the thing that probably most impressed him about this approach was that it seemed to be the only one which workably produced a systematic account of law – that it was proven. He began his visit to Germany with contemptuous remarks about the work of the civilian jurists and he ended by describing them as models of arrangement. The necessity for producing the map for his classes was coming closer and in fact it appears he could not meet the deadline.

The departure from what was emphasized by Benthamite theory, the cutting edge of the law on those subject to it, was considerable. If the law was to be organized in terms of legal positions of persons at all, primary attention ought surely to have been concentrated on the legal position which is always implicated with the existence of a sanction in Austin's view — the duty. But more important was Austin's procedure in working out his map of the legal system in terms of the legal positions of persons at all. This meant that, although for Austin law was defined as the command of the sovereign, the sovereign does not figure in the account of the law except incidentally. He has no legal position for Austin. What might be thought of as duties to the Crown are called by Austin absolute duties, not requiring a correlative right, and Austin says that if we think of the Crown as having rights we have to realize that this is just an artificial way of talking for convenience. But he felt bound to do some of this himself when he was talking about the reservation of 'rights' to the Crown in relation to real property. It is arguable that his whole account of the feudal elements in the English system of real property is distorted because of his treatment of the sovereign as outside the system of rights and duties. It seems that, although Austin was writing in the nineteenth century, he found it much easier to talk about copyholds than he did about the standard kind of tenure in free and common socage — just because the former involved the consideration of the holder's relationship to a mesne lord who was not generally the sovereign.[61] How he could have dealt with questions of eminent domain under American law one does not know.

But the problems raised for the development of a Benthamite theory of law by an organization of law in terms of legal positions went much further than the mere fact that things got dealt with in a curious order, with some things being expounded in odd places because there was nowhere else they could conveniently go, or even the fact that some very important things got left out altogether. The most important thing that happened to Jeremy Bentham as he faded and died was that one fundamental question which he posed for himself at the end of the *Principles*, and struggled to work back to in the *Laws*, was not solved, but obscured. That question was: What is a complete law?

To answer this question, Bentham conceived that one had to look at the way in which a legal rule is structured, having regard to the purposes of the law, and the manner in which the means adopted for the achievement of the purposes affect its design. Bentham conceded that the exposition of the rules of a system would not trace an individual legal rule through all its terms in full because this would lead to repetition in the exposition, but the exposition had to make clear what was being done in this respect.

For Bentham, a complete law was a real law. Although Bentham described his difficulties as 'metaphysical', one does not need to suppose that he was using any special notion of reality when he said this. If a law was not complete in a given system, this did not mean that there was no reality of any kind, but that it could not be described as a real command, and had to be filled out somehow before it could operate as one. But it appears from the *Laws* that he did think that before there could be a scientific analysis of the real commands comprising a legal system, focus had to be achieved on each individual command in terms narrow enough for us to avoid including, under one command, prescriptions which provided different consequences for different offences. It will be recalled that single commands, thus envisaged, were called by Bentham monads, a term of the philosopher Leibniz. This notion places Bentham in a stream coming from the ancient Greeks concerning what is required for scientific examination of any material. The scientific examination is seen as following the organization of miniscule elements in the reality.

By shifting attention in his map from offences to rights, Austin suggested, though he certainly did not intend to be understood thus, a quite different way in which the legal system could be looked at as a scientific organization of miniscule elements. The miniscule elements would be individual positions of particular persons in relation to other particular persons concerning particular matters. The miniscule elements might then be organized, in some metaphorical sense, 'under' legal rules. Austin himself certainly did not intend to be understood as meaning that this would be a satisfactory scientific organization. He is very loose about his use of the singular and plural when he is talking about legal positions. Sometimes he will talk about very complex situations as *a* right *in rem*, for example, and then make it clear that the right could, if we liked to talk that way, be broken down into a number of rights. He regarded singularity or plurality of rights as only a matter anyway of degree and he was conscious of the fact that much of what he was doing in his organization was based upon convenience of exposition and not upon science or logic, as he, a Benthamite, would understand the situation.[62] However much he criticized Bentham in detail, his view of law was fundamentally Bentham's. It would not, on Bentham's basis, be right to regard law as made up of relations of persons to the fact that a sanction was threatened by the sovereign having issued a command to that person or another person.

Austin justified his major distinction between primary rights and sanctioning rights on the basis of clearness and compactness. He conceded it was not 'logical', by which he meant that the description of a primary right is not complete without reference to a sanctioning right.[63] This is a recognition of Bentham's point that to get to a complete law we must have a complete description of the sanction threatened and the procedure. But although to speak of a person having a primary right is not a description on this basis of his relationship to a real command, Austin feels that he is justified in talking as if it were so.

It is the same for Austin with the question whether we are talking about collections of legal positions as if they could exist apart from the people who are in the legal position. Of course they cannot do so. But it is convenient to talk very often as if it were so, as in the case of talking of universities of rights and duties.[64] In fact, in elaborating his map, Austin finds himself talking constantly as if rights and duties were entities which could exist apart from the persons, even though all the time he is making it clear that what he is talking about is relations between happenings, including the happening of sovereign commands.

Austin further emphasized that this last is his view of law by attacking particular ways of talking about legal positions which involved the setting up of occult qualities in people or things − like the will in psychology which he mentioned again at one point in this section. He attacks the notions that we are necessarily talking about real things in dealing with the law of things at all, that there is necessarily any thing involved when we are talking of rights *in rem*, that we can have incorporeal things, that when we speak of a person having a status we are speaking of a quality in him rather than merely his relations to commands in respect of a variety of matters, and that when we talk of a real servitude we mean that the servitude is a thing.

Austin did not go any further in justifying the misleading language of legal writers so far as he adopted it, or even in justifying talking as if things were true when they are not, except by a few dogmatic statements about the requirements of clarity, convenience, compactness, or commodiousness. Here, as often, he did not extend his arguments to the question of the utility or disutility of what he was bound to regard as very fundamental fictions in legal thinking. But these would be continuing questions.

Incidentally, in the present section, Austin said some things which would provide hints for expounding legal positions by reference to more numerous notions than those of right and duty. We have seen that Austin had himself defined right and duty in a previous section, and was a little puzzled concerning whether he should add what was later to be called a privilege − the situation where A is legally permitted to do X as against B if he can, but, if B interferes with A's performance of X, this does not give A a ground of legal complaint against B. Austin, we have seen, was reluctant to envisage that this situation was sensible. But when he came down in the present section to the matter of the distinction between property and *servitus*, he distinguished them on the ground that a person with property has an indefinite power or liberty of using or disposing of the object limited only by the rights of other persons. This implied the existence of an area where it was at least suggested that the owner would have liberties to act and the party who had rights outside that area would have no right to complain within it.[65] Hohfeld was to call the liberty a privilege and the correlative legal position of the other party a no-right, for which a less awkward term is perhaps an exposure.

In the course of discussing the law of persons in the present section, Austin said things which suggested the existence of a further group of legal positions. The particular matter which he was here considering was the definition of a person's condition or status as a capacity or faculty. Austin proceeded to give a definition of capacity in his usual empirical fashion — as a relationship of certain events to a command. A person is capable of a given right, or is capable of a given duty, if, on the happening of a given event, the law would invest the person with (that is, the fact of the relevant command having occurred would imply) that given right, or would impose on the person that given duty. A person was to be considered incapable of a given right or duty, if, on the happening of the given event, the law would not invest him with the given right, or would not impose on him the given duty. Austin added that a capacity or incapacity to incur or become subject to a duty, certainly sounds harshly. Consulting mere propriety of speech, he said, he would rather style it a liability to a duty, or exemption from a duty. But he did not propose to use these terms, but rather to stick to speaking only of capacity and incapacity for the sake of brevity. Austin finished by objecting to the definition of status in terms of capacity, his first major objection being that there are capacities which are common to all persons, and, secondly, there are many conditions which consist mainly, not of capacities, but of incapacities.[66]

Here was the broad hint. Capacity was a general kind of relation of persons to the law and so inferentially was incapacity. Thus, if we abandoned brevity, we could get a capacity (Hohfeld called it a power) in one person (A) to act to change the legal position of another person (B) in manner X. B would correlatively be under a liability (and that is what Hohfeld called it) to have his legal position changed in manner X. Then, if we turn our attention to the incapacity situation and look first at the position of the person in the position of advantage we may say that A has an immunity from having his legal position changed in manner X by B, to which correlates B's disability as to changing A's legal position in manner X. At this point, in right correlating with duty, privilege with no-right (or exposure), power with liability, and immunity with disability, we have, completed, the eight fundamental legal conceptions of Wesley Hohfeld, his building-blocks of the law.

The practical use to which Hohfeld turned his legal conceptions was particularly in exposing inconsistencies and confusions in the law arising out of mistaking one legal conception for another, or just being vague about it, especially in discussions of the relations of law and equity. But Austin, as we have indicated, had a much broader purpose: to see the discussions of legal positions as discussions of the relations between things that happen, to see the law and its relations as processes and relations of processes. One great object of the theory of law is to see how talk about the technicalities of law can be seen as, or become, talk about what happens, like the talk of any other science, so that it can be examined in one world with other sciences. People have found keys to jurisprudence in many different places but the empirical representations of legal positions is surely one of them. Lawyers talk much, in and out of court, about legal positions, if only because their talk is client-oriented. Austin, partly by a side wind when criticizing a definition, made a substantial and influential contribution to the enquiry into the real meaning of this often highly technical talk.

Austin on the uses of the study of jurisprudence

The essay with the above title was compiled by Sarah Austin from the matter of Austin's introductory lectures. These were not published with the *Province* and Sarah Austin thought them inappropriate to precede the *Province* in the full publication of Austin's Lectures. The essay therefore appears in the Campbell *Austin* as an appendix[67] and is also appended to Hart's edition of the *Province*.[68]

In it, Austin defines the subject of jurisprudence as positive law, so that particular jurisprudence deals with the law of a particular country systematically, and general jurisprudence the principles, notions and distinctions common to the various systems. The science of the principles common to mature systems is contrasted both with particular jurisprudence and with the science of legislation. The science of legislation deals with the utility of the principles of systems, while general jurisprudence is for the most part not concerned with their goodness or badness.

Of the principles, notions, and distinctions in question, some might be esteemed necessary, because we could not conceive coherently a system of law existing in a refined community without them. The first class of Austin's examples of these are the notions of Duty, Right, Liberty, Injury, Punishment and Redress; and their relations to one another, to Law, Sovereignty and Independent Political Society. Another kind of example lies in the distinction between written and unwritten law. A third is the distinction between rights *in rem* and rights *in personam*, a fourth the distinction of property into dominion and more restricted rights, a fifth the distinction of obligations into those arising from contract, those from injury, and those arising from neither, and a final one is the distinction between civil and criminal injuries. Austin cannot imagine a system of law in a refined community without these things and without additional implications. Other principles, notions, and distinctions are not necessary in that sense but will be found everywhere because they rest on very general considerations of utility, such as the distinction between the law of persons and the law of things. These, too, are within the subject of general jurisprudence.[69]

A preliminary task is to determine accurately the meaning of leading terms: Law, Right, Obligation, Injury, Sanction, Person, Thing, Act, Forbearance. Unfortunately, these terms are extremely complex, and writers have shrouded them in obscurity. By a careful analysis of leading terms law can be detached from morals, written from unwritten law, and the science of jurisprudence from the science of legislation. It is, however, impossible to consider jurisprudence quite apart from legislation, since considerations of expediency which lead to the establishment of laws must be adverted to in explaining their origin and mechanism. But the jurisprudence professor should not insert his own opinions of goodness or badness under pretence of assigning causes.[70]

When proceeding with the general principles common to different systems it is necessary to illustrate by example, especially from the Roman and English systems. The great value of Roman law is in the Roman writers' command of their system. The study of the Roman law is not necessary in the sense of Aristotelian logic, but it bears the same relation to law and morals as scholastic logic bears to philosophy. The similarity of English to Roman law in many respects is not to be attributed in great degree to derivation of English law from the Roman, but shows how much developed systems of law have in common with others.[71]

A student of English law, by studying general jurisprudence, might perceive the various relations of its various parts, the dependence of its minuter rules on its general principles, and the subordination of such of these principles as are less general and extensive to such of them as are more general and run through the whole of its structure. This study would in no way disqualify the student for practice, it would qualify for practice by enabling the student to see the rationale of practice. The Prussians appreciated this, and in the Prussian Universities little or no attention was given to the actual law, only to general principles of law and to the historical bases of their system. An English student would be readily able to understand foreign systems if he understood the general principles of legal systems, and this would help him to understand the defects and merits of his own.

The training of a theoretico-practical lawyer should consist of the study of law and the sciences related to law, with a knowledge of classical languages essential to the understanding of the moral sciences, and a knowledge of logic, for there must be an understanding of the nature of terms and the process of reasoning. Study of the rationale of law exercised the mind in the process of deduction from given hypotheses. The process of inference founded on analogy – the basis of all just inferences with regard to matter of fact and existence – was cultivated by law. Analogical inference was involved in its application, in the processes by which existing law is built out, in analogical inferences from considerations of expediency on which law is founded, and in the principles of judicial evidence.[72]

It will be observed from the above account that certain notions come into it at two different points, for example, Law, Right, Injury and Sanction (or Punishment and Redress). They are, firstly, necessary notions and, secondly, they are involved in the clarification of leading terms. Bentham had said that general expository jurisprudence would deal with the general terms of legal systems and so Austin is following him in this. Bentham had added that general expository jurisprudence would be largely confined to this. But in his view that these notions will necessarily be found in legal systems, Austin is demonstrating his interest in the search for necessary truths about legal systems which would enable expository jurisprudence to measure up to the ideals of a science which he had absorbed from the Mills.

It is noteworthy that the account which Austin gives of necessary truths in his *Excursus on Analogy* is closely related to that to which we have called attention in Mill's *System of Logic*. Mill, we have seen, thought that an object might be necessarily associated with another as a *proprium* of it, and Austin advances the same idea. A necessary truth, says Austin, is what is true of objects in a class by reason of their having that wherein they are analogous: a necessary efflux of that; a something without which the object cannot be conceived as having that. Such a truth is a *proprium*, or property of the object strictly so called.

Admittedly, Austin is here dealing with only one kind of *proprium* from Mill's point of view, the kind which could be shown necessarily to attach to an object by way of demonstration, and Austin says nothing at this point of Mill's other kind of *proprium*, something which necessarily attaches to an object by way of causation. Yet Austin clearly thought that questions of the causes of legal phenomena fall within the field of the expository science of law. In his account of the uses of jurisprudence we have seen that Austin warns against the professor of expository jurisprudence inserting his own opinions of the goodness or badness of laws when attacking the task of assigning causes. We have also seen that Austin attempted himself to give an account of causes of judicial decisions in cases where the matter before the court was not determined by a governing rule.

We see Austin's warning against the investigator of causes of decision allowing his account to be coloured by his views of what ought to happen as a valid one. They are two different inquiries and any confusion can only obscure the truth for the scientific inquirer and obscure the situation with which a reformer is confronted from him, with sacrifice of clear-headedness in his reforming efforts. There was no disagreement between Bentham and any of his associates about this.

At the same time we must repeat in the present context the concessions to Austin's critics which we made earlier. If the performance in the science was to measure up to the aspirations of it as the Mills envisaged a social science, the search in practice for causal principles especially had to be unremitting and the aspiration to find them kept steadily in view. Austin was too ready in practice simply to compare provisions he found and too ready to speak as if the search for common principles in laws was a major objective in itself, in a way that Bentham's contrast of expository jurisprudence with censorial jurisprudence suggested that it was. Austin in his discussion of the uses of jurisprudence contrasts the expository science with the legislative *science*, as if they were independent. This obscures the importance of a general science of causal relations to the corresponding art along the lines that John Stuart Mill explained the matter at the end of his *System of Logic*. The service of *the* science to the art, as we saw it was explained by Mill, is that the art relies constantly on the science in the working out of its own objectives. Austin grasped this best when he was discussing the mutual influences of law-making and human psychology as presented by James Mill. But there is an unfortunate contrast between this and some other parts of his work.

4

Austin: conservative or reformer?

Austin's political writings

It will be recalled from the first chapter that Austin produced four articles and one pamphlet in the course of his life: 'Disposition of Property by Will – Primogeniture' in 1824,[1] 'Joint Stock Companies' in 1826,[2] 'List on the Principles of the German Customs Union' in 1842,[3] 'Centralization' in 1847,[4] and the pamphlet *A Plea for the Constitution* in 1859.[5] They would make all told but a slim volume. Yet Eira Ruben[6] claims that it is only with their assistance that a comprehensive view of Austin's thought, especially affecting his legal theory, can be obtained. Ruben argues that the intentions lying concealed behind Austin's scientific approach to jurisprudence are the defence of the middle classes against the aristocracy and the labouring classes, and that his claim to scientific rigour is ideological.[7]

Nevertheless, a considerable part of the material to which Ruben calls attention does no more than reinforce conclusions already emerging from the material so far canvassed in the present work. The reader will not be surprised to learn in the light of the previous chapter that, in 'Joint Stock Companies', Austin extols the virtues of economic freedom, stresses the discipline exerted by natural economic sanctions, and pleads for the removal of legal restraints on joint stock companies, partnerships, and lenders.[8] Nor will the reader be surprised to discover that in Austin's review of List's work he advocates free trade between countries, even to the point where Austin claims that the interests of humanity would be more promoted by general freedom of commerce than by a speedy extinction of slavery.[9]

Much of what Ruben produces from Austin's article about primogeniture is as little startling. Austin attacks Burke, praises the French Revolution for its benefits to the French people, and claims that it would be just to take up arms against the enemies of utility.[10] Ruben claims that these are strange views for anyone familiar with Austin's legal theory.[11] Yet Austin argues the same points in relation to the American Revolution in his lectures on jurisprudence and elaborates them there at greater length than in the article under discussion.[12] It is the same with the passage to which Ruben refers in which Austin attacks reliance on the wisdom of our ancestors, stressing the importance of keeping abreast of the wisdom of modern times.[13] This is a reappearance of Austin's theme concerning the perfectibility of man – also prominent in his lectures on jurisprudence.[14]

Ruben produces some statements in the article about primogeniture to show that Austin was at this time still professing to be a democrat,[15] a stance which we have noticed he did not take by the time of the delivery of his lectures, displaying instead pointed reticence about the matter. His references to the desirability of real representation of the masses in the article about primogeniture are not altogether unequivocal either. They are open to the interpretation that a democracy of the 'middling' classes is all the democracy England needs in her circumstances.[16] Ruben demonstrates that, by 1859, Austin had abandoned caution and said publicly what he had said privately to Mill many years earlier, that democracy of the masses was unnecessary to the furtherance of the public welfare, and Austin added plainly that it was undesirable.[17]

Ruben finds the theme of Austin's article about centralization to be that the most effective legal order, that is, the legal order that is best at enforcing the ends it pursues, is a legal order which is necessarily based on a stable morality and which can best defeat the ends of socialism. Such a legal order would have no room for the concept of civil liberty, because a commanding public opinion would not permit the infringement of useful liberty. The legal order cannot be limited. To limit the central authority, Ruben represents Austin as arguing, would detract from its sovereignty and thus impair the stability of government.[18] Ruben complains that we here have two inconsistent kinds of argument for centralization, one based on logical considerations about the nature of law, the other an empirical argument that unless you have unrestricted sovereignty, bad consequences follow. If the first argument is correct, Ruben points out, the second is redundant, if the second is relevant the first must be false.[19]

To suppose, however, that Austin got himself caught on the horns of the dilemma on which Ruben seeks to impale him is to flatter the degree of tightness of organization of Austin's article on centralization. Ruben calls it a development of Austin's theory of sovereignty, but this is flattery for the same reason. Much of the matter in it is the same matter as in Lecture VI of the *Province*, including the matters we have mentioned above from Ruben's account but presented in a much less connected way in the course of the discussion of the books which Austin is reviewing. In the result, what we are to understand about the relationship between sovereignty and centralization emerges with less than Austin's customary clarity.

But what Austin seems to wish us to understand is that, though sovereignty implies that there is a body whose express or tacit commands are carried out by all public institutions in the community, nevertheless the notion of a tacit command – acquiescence by the sovereign in what is done – has to be understood broadly enough to accommodate situations where the sovereign acquiesces through sluggishness or inefficiency in much that he is not wholly happy to approve. A proper ideal of government is to strengthen the hierarchical administrative chain so that what the sovereign acquiesces in comes to correspond with what he wholeheartedly approves. This is centralization. It does not mean that there may not be an appropriate amount of devolution of authority, which will vary with the circumstances. Austin makes it clear that ideally the final test of what is appropriate will always be utility – the happiness of the community. But, in conditions of advanced civilization, the happiness of the community is likely to be best served by large-scale units in which the devolution of authority is carefully controlled, however extensive that devolution may be.

In all this, there is a mixture of kinds of propositions. Austin's definitions of law and sovereignty are frequently resorted to for the purpose of showing that those with whom he is contending catch themselves in inconsistencies in what they say. Scientific generalities about what can be expected to follow from given conditions are advanced to support arguments concerning what should be done to advance objectives which Austin supposes to be comprehended within the general objective of the greatest happiness of the greatest number. In itself, there does not seem to be any objection to this in principle, from the point of view of what we have understood to be Austin's notions of the science of jurisprudence and its uses for the art of legislation. What does have to be said in criticism of him is that the article is an object lesson in the unsystematic way in which these various kinds of propositions are likely to be brought up if a writer makes the development of the science his exclusive object in the first instance as Austin did, without having a system of constant reference to the uses of the scientific principles being discussed for the art. Bentham made a practice of doing this virtually at the end of each chapter of his work. Austin's comments about the uses of his scientific jurisprudential principles in his lectures were only in very general terms by way of introduction, and, for the rest, as often as they happened to occur to him.

From Ruben's general standpoint, however, this is no mere deficiency of technique. For her, Austin was just not interested in reform, but rather in defending the status quo so far as it served the interest of the middle classes, and this is seen to come out in his minor works to an extent which it does not in his lectures on jurisprudence.[20] However, it is certainly not true that Austin's view of the desirability of leadership by the middle classes in the community fails to emerge in his lectures. Austin's account in Lecture III of the *Province* makes it abundantly clear that he regards education of the masses as calculated to reconcile them to their economic position in relation to the middle classes, to prevent their efforts to destroy capital equipment, and to induce them to support the institution of property. Austin there makes it equally clear that the labouring classes can be expected always to have to take numbers of matters springing from education on trust from the leisured classes, even though they may in a modest way be recruited to the leisured classes or at least participate more in the educated activities of the leisured classes.

These things are no doubt further stressed in Austin's pamphlet, *A Plea for the Constitution*, in the last year of his life. But the emphasis on desirability of leadership by the leisured middle class with its more refined tastes and better educated approach to the business of government was no new departure. The major difference was in Austin's progressively melancholic attitude to the prospects for general enlightenment which we have seen attested by Sarah's correspondence.

Ruben nevertheless sees this pamphlet to be finally giving Austin's game away. The *Plea* provides the clearest evidence that Austin 'collapses his notion of what the law is into his notion of what the law ought to be'. Austin, Ruben claims, finally rejects utilitarianism there and adopts traditionalism as a justification for a coercive legal order.[21] Ruben, however, develops her interpretations of Austin's minor works to this culminating point by using, at least at key points, a method of construing what Austin says to which we believe objection can legitimately be taken. She re-defines what Austin says and builds on her re-definitions. Ruben charges Austin with confusing empirical propositions about sovereignty with definitional ones about it. We have said that Austin cannot be easily convicted of this charge, especially in the light of the discursiveness of Austin's exposition. But Ruben's exposition is a model of conciseness and coherence. We believe she succeeds in confusing questions of definition and empirical questions about Austin, where Austin failed to achieve the same result in discussing sovereignty.

Thus, in discussing 'Primogeniture', Ruben quotes Austin's statement that 'so far therefore as happiness is the effect of wealth, those institutions and customs are most to be praised, which most conciliate augmentation in the quantity of wealth with equality in the distribution of it. These ends are conciliated in the middle class in England as far as they can be.'[22] Ruben immediately says: 'The way the principle [utility] is constructed − happiness means augmentation in wealth and equality in distribution − means that it is geared to satisfy the aims of the middle classes.'[23]

This 'gearing', however, is accomplished not by Austin but by Ruben, by her re-definition of what Austin says to exclude Austin's qualification. Certainly Austin does not say that happiness in general means wealth. If Ruben is to prove that that is what Austin really meant, which is what she purports to do, this can only be done by the production of empirical evidence from Austin's work pointing to his meaning being something different from what he said. But, as it is, Ruben's re-definition substitutes for evidence.

Ruben goes on to quote Austin's approval of the sentiments of the middle class in the matter of even-handed distribution of property against the primogeniture principle of descent favoured by the aristocracy, the former principle in Austin's view militating against the happiness of the many.[24] Ruben now re-defines Austin's defence of the sentiments of the middle class in this respect to mean simply defence of the middle class itself: 'the defence of the people has turned out to mean the defence of the middle classes against the vestiges of aristocratic power.'[25] Certainly Ruben produces empirical evidence to the effect that Austin generally comes to the conclusion that what conduces to the happiness of the middle classes conduces to the happiness of the community generally. But Austin produces arguments for this, whatever may be thought of them. To suspect the arguments is one thing, to re-define Austin as *meaning*, by the good of the community, the good of the middle classes is to substitute an indefensible short cut for what needs to be demonstrated through empirical examination of Austin's work.

When she turns to introduce her discussion of *A Plea for the Constitution*, Ruben quotes Austin to this effect: 'It may be presumed from the possession of property acquired by industry, that the possessor is endowed with energy and perseverance as well as with fore-thought and care for the public interests.'[26] The same re-definition as Ruben has made in discussing 'Primogeniture' follows in her own very next sentence: 'We now have a clear explanation of what Austin means by "the general good of the country" or "the public interest"; he means the interests of the propertied classes; that is, the preservation and protection of private property in their hands.'[27] Our comment on this must be the same as our comment on Ruben's previous exercise, which this one duplicates.

Ruben says roundly that Austin rejects utility, both at the beginning of Ruben's treatment of the *Plea*[28] and in Ruben's final conclusion to her article.[29] So Ruben bases her claim that Austin wished to amalgamate the law that is with the law that ought to be, on Austin's alleged rejection of utility in favour of tradition. Yet, in between times, Ruben explains Austin's position in the *Plea* thus:

> The importance of Austin's final rejection of utilitarianism and espousal of traditionalism in connection with an understanding of his legal theory cannot be sufficiently stressed. I am not saying that traditionalism and utilitarianism are two incompatible doctrines. What I am interested in is the way in which they are reconciled. The reason it is possible to reconcile them, seems to me, to be due to the characteristics of utilitarianism itself. Utility is such a vague and vacuous notion that there is no difficulty in saying that prescriptivism is for the good of the people. But Austin is led to reject utilitarianism, that is the utilitarianism of his youth with its potential radical overtones. He saw a contradiction between *that* principle and traditionalism, because of what he read into the principle of utility.[30]

So now we learn that, in saying baldly that Austin ultimately rejected utility, and saying it in more than one place, Ruben has been varying our re-definitional diet by re-defining her own definitions of Austin's views. It turns out that Austin did not purport to reject utility, but rather a particular version of it, while continuing to maintain his own version. In this, as in other respects, what Ruben claims to be a vital point about Austin emerging from his minor works, is not so startling in the light of what he said in his lectures on jurisprudence. Austin makes the point in his exposition of utility in the early lectures,[31] that direct calculations of utility as a regular matter would be impracticable. We have generally to act on maxims and we develop sentiments about the maxims themselves. He is now applying this to principles of the constitution, claiming that a general sentiment of constitutionalism in the conditions of his own time was valuable for the furtherance of the aims of utilitarianism as he understood them.

In sum, we do not for ourselves see Austin as proceeding from a middle-class conservative bias to mere rationalizations of this bias in the presentation of his economic, political, and legal theories. He did not simply identify, as a matter of language, the achievement of the commercial interests of the middle class with the achievement of the greatest happiness of the greatest number in society. Nor did he, on any similar basis, identify the reign of law with rule by the middle classes. We do not find for ourselves any suggestion in Austin that the sovereignty which he thought associated with law could only exist if there were rule by the middle classes, or a group with any special character, or that the continuance of a legal system was bound up with the preservation of the status quo whatever it happened to be.

On the other hand, it is plain that Austin reached some conclusions which are reactionary when measured by present-day standards. The source of some of these was the economics which came to him through James Mill, the influence of which we have observed both in his jurisprudence as well as in his political writings where they are so much stressed by Ruben. The heavy emphasis which this economics placed on the importance of the automatic operation of market forces untrammelled by governmental interference for the maximization of the general wealth, and particularly the key position of the economic entrepreneur allowed to pursue his own wealth in the optimum functioning of economic processes, powerfully appealed to Austin. The apparent tight logic with which the theory was advanced convinced him, and it was long after Austin's time that the kinds of false assumptions which lay concealed in the theory were exposed.

The direct influence of this economic theory is seen in the advocacy of *laissez faire* in some of Austin's political writings and appears with the same kind of influence interstitially in his lectures on jurisprudence. The economic theory when combined with further premises also had an indirect influence on Austin's general political stance, again visible prominently in Austin's political writings and interstitially in his lectures on jurisprudence. Commercial success, having regard to Austin's acceptance of Mill's theory of the way the economy worked, was to him evidence of skill and intelligence, and the achievement of wealth by the skilled and intelligent gave leisure to pursue educational activities natural to such persons. These fostered an interest in matters of general welfare and fitted them for the government of the country.

The sharp difference between the Mills and Austin in their attitudes towards democracy does not appear to spring from differences about the above matters. It was rather that the Mills saw the labouring classes as supporters of middle-class leadership under favourable conditions of mass education and under the same conditions as monitors of the performance of the middle classes furthering the general welfare in government. While

Austin, as we have seen, theoretically maintained that the prospects for education were unlimited in the light of the pliability of human nature, he became increasingly pessimistic about immediate prospects. He was therefore, as we have also seen, repeatedly drawn into sharp though courteous conflict with John Stuart Mill in his later years concerning extensions of democracy in particular times and places.

For ourselves, we see Austin's conservatism, in the sense in which we have explained it, as deriving from the above theoretical sources and not from his view of law, which in any case in its more fundamental aspects he shared with Bentham and the Mills. It is true that Austin definitionally made painful sanctions the exclusive instrument of the lawmaker in a way that Bentham did not, and that this suggests a view of law as a corrector of aberrational conduct which is inconsistent with a view of law as a re-distributor of wealth in the interests of social reform. But it would be unrealistic to see this kind of substantive significance in this difference between Austin and Bentham. Their economics was sufficiently alike for neither of them to have wished to see their definitions of law emphasizing a role of the legislator which would have seemed to them antithetical to the achievement of the general welfare through the free operation of economic forces against a background of respect for property.

No doubt the arguments have to be pushed further back, and the issues relating to Austin's conservatism multiplied, if, firstly, we are to obtain a balanced picture of the springs of his thinking about reaction and reform, secondly, of the extent to which his practical influence was reactionary or reformatory under the conditions of the times in which it was operative, and, thirdly, of how far there continues to be theoretical value in Austin's work for our own times. In the remaining sections of this chapter we look at each of these matters in turn.

Austin's motivations

Ruben considers that Austin's motivations are referable, for practical purposes exclusively, to the interests, in a narrow sense, of the economic class with which Austin unquestionably identified himself. Other factors, from the narrowest personality factors to the broadest cultural factors, are ignored. So are such class factors influencing Austin as are referable to divisions of classes in society according to other values than the economic, which an investigator might think important for a comprehensive view.

We may begin an attempt to answer the question of the motivations behind Austin's leading ideas by recalling the immediate sources of them. His general notions of juristic science, which Ruben stigmatizes as ideological – presumably in the sense descriptive of a theory which pretends to be, in Ruben's expression, 'value free'[32] but whose real purpose and purport is to support special values – Austin derived from a mixture of sources. His aspiration was to produce a science of the kind exemplified by Ricardo's economic theory as summarized by James Mill, though in practice this was modified, and in some degree the objective obscured, by Austin's attempt to relate Mill's notions of a science to Bentham's notion of an 'expository juris pudence' which would be distinct from a 'censorial jurisprudence'.

Having regard to what Austin wrote in his diary before leaving the army,[33] Austin's motivations might seem at that stage to have been predominantly an ambition to belong to the intellectual elite in society, rather than the social elite or an economic elite. Nevertheless, against the background of the times on which we commented in our initial reference to this matter, it is likely that ambitions to join these other elites were associated with his desire to join the first. Bentham and James Mill were not averse to social contacts with the aristocracy as attested by their partiality at different times for the aristocracy's women.[34] On the other hand it is plain that their social ambitions were very much secondary to their other objectives. The aristocracy was consistently attacked, and Austin took his share in this throughout his life. This is not to say that Austin's attacks on the aristocracy, to some of which Ruben draws attention, did not acquire an extra cutting edge of aggressiveness because of his disappointment and bitterness about his lack of intellectual, social and financial success.

Yet it seems to do far less than justice to any of the group under discussion to attribute overwhelming importance to their class associations of whatever kind as stimulating the general character of their scientific interests in finding the order in reality. They were constantly fascinated by the search for truth, as well as goodness, in social fields on a comprehensive scale, and the degree of interest in the products of that fascination 150 years later attest this. It was Austin's misfortune, however, that the insecurity feelings which affected his treatment of any matter turned his fascination with subject matters of his inquiries into obsessiveness. He had the greatest difficulty in getting off a subject once he had begun it. He told Sarah so early in their association.[35] When he came to prepare and deliver his lectures this characteristic became a major obstruction to the effectiveness of his work.

He began his analysis with the definition of law, for reasons stemming from the James Mill approach to science.[36] He naturally adopted Bentham's definition of law for this purpose though that was not where Bentham began. For with Bentham the question became important only in connection with the mechanisms as opposed to the substantive objectives of an ideal code. It was with this latter matter that Bentham was fundamentally concerned, and it was with it he began.[37]

Austin, having begun in his different way, and being imbued with a determination to tie every piece of relevant material he saw tidily into his definition of law, became obsessed with it. He drove his class distracted by his failure to proceed from it, and by his reversions to matters of untidiness in his treatment of it which disturbed him.[38] In later articles, whenever any aspect of sovereignty became incidentally relevant, he would skid back to the subject like a broken record. We do not agree with Ruben that Austin thought that any sort of question could be solved in terms of the theory of sovereignty. But it is easy enough to see how the effects of this personality factor in Austin contrived to induce that impression.

While Austin's exposition of sovereignty as the notion central to law was, as we have seen,[39] facilitated by the centrally important matters on which he could follow Bentham, we have also noted the damaging effects of Austin's obsessive anxiety to adopt sharp cut-off points in relation to his definition of positive law.[40] This left major matters, of importance to legal scholars, either clearly within the definition or relegated to some category outside it, when Bentham thought it unnecessary to commit himself. The exclusions which resulted were undesirably narrowing to the focus of interest of any lawyer who took Austin's definition as an index to what was appropriately of concern to the lawyer.

The most serious of these exclusions, in the order in which they arise in Austin's exposition rather than their order of importance, were, firstly, the exclusion of offers of rewards by community decision makers from the field of positive law.[41] The second was the exclusion of particular commands from the field. This latter had severely limiting effects on the extent to which it was possible strictly within Austin's theory to examine the total exercise of authority in the State which was to Bentham central to an understanding of the operation of legal machinery.[42] In fact Austin made no attempt to deal with Bentham's problem of what was even formally involved in a complete expression of a legislative command. Thus, thirdly, Austin excluded from law – but chose to include within jurisprudence by way of indicating his growing desperation with his pinning-down operation – declaratory and repealing laws. These were among those important to Bentham in connection with the matter of the completeness of a law.[43]

In a fourth category of Austin's exclusions from positive law are his relegation of constitutional laws directed by a sovereign to himself or future sovereigns – and international law – to positive morality.[44] Bentham pointed out the limitations of the kinds of sanctions which operated in these instances, but at the same time stressed the extent to which regularity in these matters could be expected in the light of those which remained.

In sum, we see Austin as consumed by a desire to be in the forefront of the intellectual elite, but fascinated by what he was doing to the point where his motivations at least quickly became broad cultural interests. But these were distorted in their execution particularly by personality factors. The same personality factors, we indicated at the beginning of the second chapter, would have reinforced the appeal to him of a stress on the coercive aspects of law which he found embodied in Bentham's definition. It is in his adoption of this kind of definition of law that Ruben finds the cat of Austin's motivation in the interest of the dominant middle class escaping dramatically from the bag. If this is so, Bentham is implicated, too. Indeed Bentham's presentation of the community as a power structure dominated from above is carried a good deal further than in Austin's presentation, because

Bentham considered that tacit approval by the sovereign gave legal force to multitudes of private transactions. Austin, on the other hand, concentrated on employing this idea in relation to the orders of public decision making bodies.[45]

But neither of them identified might in general, or the might of the established order in particular, with right. Bentham attacked confusions between the law that is and the law that ought to be not only in general terms, but specifically and repeatedly, in particular against Blackstone, precisely on the basis that this feature of Blackstone's work was indicative of Blackstone's complacency about the established order. There can be no question but that in Bentham's hands the theory of sovereignty and his use of it to identify the actual as opposed to the ideal law was designed to function and did function in just the opposite way to the manner in which Ruben claims it was designed to function and did function in Austin's hands.

The point may nevertheless be argued that by Austin's time the following of Bentham's theory in this respect and Bentham's application of it against the aristocracy could be and was used by Austin to defend what was by now the dominant middle class in the continuance of its power. But in fact Austin was writing against the background of a transitional power situation in the community. In attacking primogeniture, for example, he was attacking an established institution and it would be anachronistic to treat this as displaying conservative motives because such an attack would have that aspect now.

More plausible points can be made about the motivations behind Austin's account of how tacit approval by the sovereign of law-making by the judiciary functioned. Bentham classed judicial law-making within customary law and saw it as having the general appalling deficiencies of customary law in its operation – hopeless lack of definition and inaccessibility. While Austin followed Bentham in seeing some judicial practices in interpreting legislation as involving usurpations of power, and attacked some judicial attempts to develop the common law for the same reason, he believed, in contradistinction from Bentham, that judicial legislation could achieve a high degree of definition of the common law. Hence, for Austin, tacit sovereign approval could be operating on well-formed judge-made laws. We have said that we think that the logical considerations Austin applied to judgments, in his efforts to establish how this was so, are simply wrong.[46] But we should not be disposed to attack the genuineness of his motivations. His attitude to the character of judicial legislation was, however, one of a set of considerations which we see influencing – sincerely – Austin's attitude to what a political catch-phrase of the present day designates 'the pace of change'. Personality factors, no doubt, influenced this attitude. To say that he was a less sanguine personality than Bentham is very much of an understatement.

Austin makes it clear when he is discussing codification that he regards judicial legislation as paving the way for codification in a manner which Bentham's contempt for judicial methods led Bentham to discount.[47] But acute legal observers of unquestioned integrity of our own age, even possessing the sanguine temperament which Austin lacked, have taken the same view as Austin. Karl Llewellyn did, basing himself on a variety of considerations about the way the common law develops, under the best conditions, which are a good deal more convincing than Austin's logical considerations.*

In Austin's case, the wish to see codification more modestly and cautiously approached than Bentham envisaged, was reinforced by Austin's pessimism about the degree of skill which was available to achieve codification on a broad basis, and Austin's pessimism about the manageability of producing sound solutions to problems by a direct appeal to utility in the absence of developed rules of practice tested by some kind and degree of experience. But all this is not to say that his ambitions for codification did not go beyond those of people surrounding him, as witness his frustration with the lack of breadth of outlook in his colleagues on the Criminal Law Commission and his collapse into one of his illnesses at being prevented from proceeding to the codification task in Malta.[48]

The largest ground of suspicion of Austin's motivations will no doubt always remain: Whatever he thought about the fundamental importance of the science which occupied his attention, why did he announce, from the beginning, his intention of stopping in his jurisprudence course at the science of positive law without proceeding to a systematic treatment of what he was himself prepared to call the science of legislation? We believe he was right, in terms of what a scientific point of view itself requires, to give the former priority, for reasons which appealed to the Mills and influenced Austin. We have equally made it clear that we do not believe that the science he gave priority, in the sense that the Mills conceived it, can properly be described as relating to the law that is rather than the law that ought to be. It was concerned with principles that apply to any law actual or ideal, and we have said that some criticism misunderstands this.[49] We have conceded that Bentham's distinction, misleading from this aspect, between expository and censorial jurisprudence may have led Austin into what was in some respects an unfortunate choice of material, involving exposition of contents of laws to a degree unnecessary to the scientific purpose.[50] For the rest, Austin's excuse for not proceeding systematically to the art or science of legislation must be shortness of time and recurrent illness. These are probably reasonable excuses, but not for some historians. They will continue to regard Austin as the man who defended the law in force because he liked it and shut himself off from reform. This probably says as much about the vaunted verdict of history as it does about Austin.

---

* William Twining, *Karl Llewellyn and the Realist Movement* (London, 1973) Chapters 10 to 12 and Appendix E, demonstrate Llewellyn's appreciation of the complex relations between case law and legislation. But what we have in mind particularly here is the facilitation by the Grand Style of judicial handling of cases and arrival at rules which 'make sense on their face' (*ibid.* 252) and can therefore serve as a basis for legislation.

The practical consequences of Austin's work

If Ruben's thesis about Austin's work is sound, it might be expected that Austin's effects could only be in slowing legal change. And since Austin's biggest effort in this respect was to prevent the advance of democracy in the United Kingdom, we might seem to have to come to the conclusion in that case that he was singularly ineffective. But this has not been the traditional view of Austin, which is that he has had a degree of influence on practical legal developments which is exceptional for any legal theorist.[51]

This is one instance in which the traditional view appears to be correct. It is not possible here to trace the influences in detail, and this is by no means a matter only of the limitations of our space. We can only observe correlations between features of the later law and Austinian ideas which were part of the education of those conducting legal affairs at relevant times, and sometimes professions of Austinian allegiance by these administrators. These correlations provide some basis for inferences of Austinian influence.

A useful starting point is the influence of Bentham and Austin on colonial constitution making. In some degree, the legal institutions of British colonies could be left to grow by piecemeal legislation and by judicial development, the initial base being provided in some cases by Blackstone's principle that Englishmen take with them to an unsettled country so much of the general law of England, in force at the time of settlement, as is suitable to their condition. Some matters might also be left to the Crown prerogative. But, as a matter of elementary efficiency, major matters of government had to be dealt with at the outset by British legislation, which had to be progressively altered as the development of the colony was thought to reach a stage where more advanced features of the British system became suitable for introduction. Fundamental constitutional documents were called for, on a kind of crash programme basis, exhibiting in confined space features of British government which had grown in their homeland over a long period, and some of which it had never been found necessary to put into legislative form.

To a degree, constitutional codification was demanded, and here was a field for application of Benthamite and Austinian principles about what was required for a proper constitutional structure. The fundamental lesson which appeared to be acted upon, moreover, was the one which we take to be the lesson of Austin's maligned article about Centralization, though it could be gathered from other Benthamite and Austinian sources as well: ultimately, the laws inevitably derive their force from the sovereign in some way, but that legal system will be the most efficient in which the chain of authority is clear and controlled, however much or little devolution of authority it may exhibit.

We must confine ourselves to an illustration from a single country of how the Benthamite and Austinian influences worked in this direction in practice. In the constitutional history of Australia up to the twentieth century there were two critical periods. The first was the period of the promulgation of the early fundamental constitutional documents of the colony of New South Wales, for many years comprising much of eastern Australia. The second was the period of promulgation of the Constitution of the Commonwealth of Australia. In both activities there was a specially prominent architect of the legislation. The first was Sir Francis Forbes, first Chief Justice of the Supreme Court of New South Wales. He was too early to be an Austinian. A Benthamite he was.[52] The second was Sir Samuel Griffith, first Chief Justice of the High Court of Australia. A later Chief Justice described his mind as representing the thoughts and learning of the Austinian age.[53]

Forbes, while in England, drafted the Imperial Act 4 Geo. IV c. 96, the New South Wales Act, under which the Charter of Justice was issued, and later advised on 9 Geo. IV c. 83, the New South Wales Courts Act. Griffith has been described as masterminding the 1891 Draft Bill on the Constitution, which became practically *the* Constitution[54] – the last section of the Commonwealth of Australia Constitution Act, 1900. The assumption behind all these documents was the unrestricted sovereignty of the United Kingdom Parliament and the necessity for devolving authority locally in ways that were as systematically organized as they were complex in the degree of devolution which they involved.

The Benthamite and Austinian notions of what a legal system was like served the kind of purpose we have been considering because they called attention to what was involved in a legal system being efficient when authority was concentrated at the apex of the system. The assumption that authority must always be so concentrated was suitable to encouraging efficient development so long as the assumption itself suited the requirements of particular times and places. But since the assumption was wrong, and legal systems need not in fact always be like that, this part of their theory ceased to command acceptance when it outlived its usefulness. This happened when circumstances called for authority to be recognized within a system, or within legally connected systems, on a divided basis, both in relation to the authority accorded to bodies and to principles. Events such as the passage of the United Kingdom Statute of Westminster, 1931[55] – purporting to be a charter of independence for the Dominions, but with certain exceptions, as much for preserving certain existing Imperial legislation as for reserving some authority to the Imperial Parliament – were the rocks upon which the specific Benthamite and Austinian theories of law and sovereignty foundered.

The pressures for crash programmed legislative activity in the colonies, while most urgent in matters of constitution making, extended far beyond that area to other fields of both public and private law. Leaders of English legal thought were pressed into the tasks of introducing English law in parts of the Empire. These pressures brought legal thinkers of other casts of thought into cooperation with those of Benthamite and Austinian persuasion, in some cases against their own professions. Sir Frederick Pollock, the

Oxford Professor of Jurisprudence, said, like a good historical jurist, that he was convinced that no legislative provision could handle a legal problem as successfully as a well constructed judgment in the same sense.[56] But in India what he found himself doing was seeking to put English principles of common law into legislative form, and this reacted upon what was done in England itself.* Sir James Fitzjames Stephen was to remark, moreover, that, in any activity that required classification, the historical jurists found themselves using Austinian notions, because historical jurisprudence did not of itself generate classificatory notions.[57]

There was thus a high degree of Austinian influence interacting with other influences in various ways. The great Indian criminal code of 1860 is associated principally with the name of the historian Lord Macaulay, a critic at times of the Benthamites. But it was the dedicated Austinian Sir Samuel Griffith, in his activities as a Queensland Minister of the Crown, who introduced a code based on Macaulay's code into the State of Queensland, as well as a defamation code similarly based. With further extensions in the course of time, codes based on the Macaulay code now stretch across the globe from Bangladesh through Western Australia to Queensland.

It is noticeable that, especially in England itself where the development owes some stimulation to the activities of English jurists in the colonies, the kind of limited activities in codification which took place in civil areas followed the modest kind of development which Austin, rather than Bentham, anticipated. This is seen not only in the limitations on their scope but, in the fact that their bases were normally principles developed by the courts. Illustrations are provided particularly in commercial areas, of which statutes concerning partnership and sale of goods are typical examples.

There are a number of parallels between the ways in which Benthamite and Austinian influences seem to have worked in the fields of constitution making and limited codifications of other branches of law, on the one hand, and the ways in which those same influences appear to have worked in common law developments on the other. The period of the late nineteenth century and early twentieth century was the period of the writing of the classical English text-books in the fields particularly of what had been the personal actions at common law, before the introduction of the Judicature System in 1875 theoretically abolishing forms of action – principally tort and contract. Texts in Criminal Law and Property have a longer history. Prominent among the classical text writers in the newer fields were Sir Frederick Pollock and Sir John Salmond.**

---

* Between 1882 and 1886 Pollock prepared a draft of a Civil Wrongs Bill in India which, however, was not passed into law. In England he drafted the Partnership Act, 1890. See 'In Memoriam – Sir Frederick Pollock' (1937) 53 *L.Q. Rev.*, 151, 156.
** The first edition of Sir Frederick Pollock's *Principles of Contract* was published in 1876 and the first edition of Pollock's *Law of Torts* in 1882. The former had reached 10 editions by Pollock's death in 1937 and the latter 13. Salmond's *Law of Torts* was first published in 1907 and had reached six editions by the time of the author's death in 1924. His work on the *Law of*

Pollock was hostile to Austin's approach generally, condemned it as a form of natural law approach, and even regarded it as dead and buried by his time.[58] As indicated above, he was himself sympathetic to features of the historical jurists' approach, and wrote about English legal history especially in cooperation with the legal historian F.W. Maitland. Nevertheless, his approach to writing in the field of personal obligations was to seek to discover broad principles, and, especially in the field of tort, to find these general principles in general liability wherever damage was caused to one person by the fault of another. Salmond was instead disposed in the field of tort to limit liability to those areas wherein it had been historically recognized. But in those areas where liability was to be recognized, he insisted, like Pollock, that a condition of it was the fault of the prospective defendant in the sense of intent or negligence. What differences there were between the two writers became less significant because of the broad basis on which liability in the area of the tort of negligence, which Salmond treated as a specific area of liability with a historical basis, was to develop.

It is arguable that the insistence on the general dependence of liability on fault in the area of civil injuries was one of those areas where Pollock was influenced by Benthamite and Austinian notions in spite of himself. The specific form which Salmond's arguments for the dependence of liability on fault took is even more suggestive of Austinian influence − as is the arrangement of his general work in jurisprudence which calls for consideration in our next chapter. Salmond emphasized the deterrent effect on a prospective defendant of having to pay for harm caused by his fault, and saw this as a good reason for not allowing the loss to lie on the one who suffered it and shifting it on to the shoulders of him who caused it, despite the administrative costs in doing this through processes of litigation.

In this kind of argument, the strategies of the law are seen to be similar in the field of civil injuries to its strategies in the field of criminal liability. The size of the sanction on the defendant is measured by what will compensate the plaintiff, but it operates nevertheless as a punitive sanction and this is what justifies its imposition.* This is in line with the Benthamite notion that the law operates on human nature, and that the nature of law and the nature of human nature, taken together, impose on the legislator the strategy of directing the laws to attaching deterrents to particular actions. But this cannot operate sensibly unless the deterrents are confined to actions of the defendant which could be expected to be influenced for the better by the

---

Contracts was incomplete at his death and editions were published with posthumous co-authors, at first P.H. Winfield and then James Williams, in 1927 and 1945.
* Salmond wrote (see, e.g., *Salmond on Torts* (6th edn, London, 1924), 12):
    Pecuniary compensation is not in itself the ultimate object or a sufficient justification of legal liability. It is simply the instrument by which the law fulfils its purposes of penal coercion. . . . Reason demands that a loss shall lie where it falls, unless some good purpose is to be served by changing its incidence; and in general the only purpose so served is that of punishment for wrongful intent or negligence.

existence of the deterrent. This is why Austin, as we have seen, devotes considerable time to classifying various psychological attitudes of a defendant.[59]

A view like Salmond's was more readily derived from Austin's work than it could have been from Bentham's, even if Bentham's specific treatment of the relation between the civil and the criminal law had not been buried in the manuscript of the *Laws* and hence unavailable to Salmond. Austin never got round to considering the relationship between civil and criminal sanctions in detail, and thus left it to be supposed that the civil sanction of damages operated in the same way as a criminal sanction in fundamentals, which Salmond supposes it does. Bentham, on the other hand, regards the right which is vindicated in a civil proceeding as generally only inchoate: what crystallizes the right is the individual judgment. Thereafter sanctions operate for the enforcement of the judgment which are of a penal character.[60] It would have been less easy on Bentham's basis to draw the simple conclusion that the mere prospect of civil liability operates as a deterrent in the way that the prospect of criminal liability does and that this is its major function.

The works of Pollock and Salmond both achieved authoritativeness in their authors' lifetimes, and editions were published after their deaths, still continuing in Salmond's case. Thus they served as channels for the operation of the ideas we have been discussing upon the law, though no doubt there was an independent influence upon the judiciary in the days when Austin was an important part of legal education. It must be conceded that much of Austin's classificatory system of mental attitudes never took root in English law itself. Before his work gained general currency through Sarah Austin's efforts, it had been settled that the law had, as a practical matter, to define negligence in an 'objective' fashion, at first as failure to behave like an ordinary, prudent man,[61] and then as failure to behave like a reasonable man.[62] These notions were developed in a way which restricted inquiry into the defendant's individual capacity to respond to the sanctions on his conduct set up by the civil law.

Yet, insofar as the law in its analysis of negligence itself departed from the subtleties of Austin's analysis of the account that needed to be made of human psychology so that sanctions for proper behaviour could be designed to operate economically and efficiently, this was at first on the basis that, though the object was to secure responsible behaviour of the citizen, concessions had to be made to practicality in legal administration. The need for concessions to practical considerations was a point that Bentham had stressed when discussing the operation of sanctions in the *Principles*.[63] The same balance of considerations entered into the law which developed about the circumstances in which, for purposes of the tort of negligence, the law would impose on the prospective defendant the obligation to refrain from negligent behaviour − in what circumstances he would be held to be under a duty of care. Lord Atkin's famous principle determining this in *Donoghue* v. *Stevenson* makes it clear that the objective is that the sanctions in this branch of the law should operate to achieve morally responsible behaviour of the citizen – though without going to the length of adopting utility as the standard of moral behaviour – and carefully specifying that the law's operation must subject the ways in which the objective is implemented to considerations of practical administration.[64]

As had happened in the area of constitution making, so in the area at present under discussion – and for the same kind of reason – the Benthamite and Austin theories, as general theories, outgrew their usefulness. Just as the theory that efficient constitution making *must* be based on devolution of power from a sovereign body turned out to be untrue, so did the theory that the only basis for efficient operation of the law upon citizens was for the correction of citizens' conduct as it affected the community on a moral basis, whether the morality involved was taken to be utility or whatever. Under social and legal conditions as they developed, the operation of this strategy was seen to produce thoroughly unjust results, by whatever acceptable principles the justness of those results were tested. Other strategies for decision makers were seen to be feasible and supportable, for example, the compensation of accident victims by making tort liability a vehicle of spreading the liability over the enterprise regarded as responsible for causing the accident irrespective of the fault of anyone involved, or, again, imposing the responsibility for compensation upon a government welfare system and disposing of tort liability in the area altogether. Which of these equally possible strategies is appropriate, or what mixture of them, are the major issues affecting accident compensation at the present time.*

Even now, attention to what is involved in the Benthamite and Austinian approaches to common law matters continues to be useful for clarifying what are the issues in matters like accident compensation. It is common in academic writings to contrast the 'foreseeability' approach, as Lord Atkin's approach to the determination of whether there is a duty of care is likely to be called, with a 'policy' approach, which is seen as something different in a way not always explained. Then the 'policy' approach is advocated as the only sensible one. This may impress judges who pride themselves on their progressiveness, like Lord Denning.** Others may be repelled by the word as introducing notions foreign to the common law, while still other judges may adopt compromises such as saying, in the area at present under discussion, that Lord Atkin's is the general approach to be taken, but gives way sometimes to considerations of policy.***

* The present writer has briefly compared and contrasted the major features of the individual liability (Salmond-type), enterprise liability, and welfare approaches in Morison, Sharwood, Phegan and Sappideen, *Cases on Torts* (5th edn, Sydney, 1981), 21–39.
** See, e.g., Lord Denning's declaration in *Dutton* v. *Bognor Regis UDC* [1972] 1 Q.B. 373, 397, as elsewhere, that the foreseeability approach to negligence is outdated and nowadays judges direct themselves to questions of policy.
*** See, for example, the treatment by the Court of Appeal of the fourth party proceedings in *Lambert* v. *Lewis* [1980] 2 W.L.R. 299 and the judgment of Megarry, V.C., in *Ross* v. *Caunters* [1979] 3 W.L.R. 605.

All this is well calculated to confuse the issues. If a policy is understood as a strategy for the achievement of a legislative end, Lord Atkin's principle is a policy, and, as he explained it, the kind of strategy that Austin and Bentham would have taken to be imposed on the legal administrator, if he was to act efficiently, by the character of law and human nature. In this they were wrong: other policies are feasible and may under given conditions be better adapted to acceptable ends. Lord Denning's appeals to policy in this area most often appear to be appeals to the notions involved in enterprise liability. But the presentation of the issue as between something which is no policy and something which is just policy does no service to a clear-sighted approach to the merits of the different policies.

Once the issues are clarified in the way suggested by our argument, it might still appear that the substantive values we might now wish to support were ill served by Austinian theory. In an area like accident compensation, it can well be claimed that the making of liability dependent on fault serves the interests of the entrepreneurs by restricting the circumstances in which they are called upon to pay for the damage caused by their enterprises whereas they ought always to pay for it − on a basis of absolute liability. In the same way it might be argued that the kind of influence which Austinian theory had on the development of constitution making in the colonies served the interests of British imperialism, and principally the middle classes through this.

Analogies can be observed between developments of the common law in England, in which we have discerned Austinian influence, and activities of the courts in the United States of America. Some early American twentieth-century decisions in particular contain ideas similar to Austin's notion that it is integral to the idea of law as it has evolved in developed systems that the strategy of the legislator is to apply a corrective to conduct which is in some sense wrongful, and not to redistribute property from one person to another where there had been no fault in the person from whom the property was taken. We noticed, when dealing with Austin's psychology in chapter 3, pp. 95−6 that Austin makes some rather desperate attempts to convince himself that instances of 'absolute' or 'strict' liability independent of fault which he encounters in English law are not really there. We suggested that this was because he imagines that in a proper legal system, the legislator does not ordinarily impose the painful sanctions, which are his exclusive instrument for Austin, except for the purpose of compelling the citizen to modify aberrant conduct toward the moral objective of contributing to the achievement of the greatest happiness of the greatest number. Some early twentieth-century American decisions, subsequently departed from, held workers' compensation legislation invalid because its mode of operation was seen to be inconsistent with constitutional provisions forbidding deprivation of property except by due process of law. It was said that to take the employer's money to compensate a workman for injuries arising out of a risk inherent in the employment, however careful the employer had been, reflected a theory, not merely new in the American system of jurisprudence, but plainly antagonistic to the basic idea of that jurisprudence.

At the present time, when Austin's limited views of the strategies appropriately available to law makers to achieve social control and development are discounted in America as elsewhere, there is to be found in some American writing a similar mode of analysis of legislative strategies to what we have noticed in current English judicial and text writing. The strategy which Austin regarded as virtually imposed by the character of law is contrasted with other strategies by calling those other strategies 'policy'. It is said, for example, that when a court is faced with a case of first impression, it may determine liability either on the basis of the unreasonableness of the defendant's conduct, or upon the basis of policy considerations, whichever is appropriate to the circumstances. We feel, as in the case of English developments, that this is a confusing way of posing the issues. Whatever may be thought of the Austinian approach to the objectives of legislation on substantive grounds in particular circumstances, it is surely entitled to be dignified by the name of a policy.

We do not suggest that the development in the United States was influenced specifically by Austin. At the time when the cases we have just mentioned were decided, J.C. Gray had only just begun to engage upon his task, to which we refer in the next chapter, of discovering the importance of Austin for Americans. Rather the American cases reflect ways of thinking which operated upon Austin himself to produce the relevant aspects of his own thinking. The economic theory which influenced Austin appealed in a society undergoing particularly rapid economic development in which the entrepreneurial functions were performed largely by private enterprise. These entrepreneurial activities were offered encouragement if legal interference with them was restricted to the basis suggested by Austin's approach to be that appropriate to the task of the legislator. There was, however, as little substance to claims in the American decisions to which we have referred that legal liability had been dependent upon fault in the United States over a long period as there was in Austin's similar analysis of English law. The 'moral' theory of liability under the law developed in the United States as the nineteenth century developed, as it did in England. This emphasizes the point that, if Austin's attitudes to matters of substance in the law are to be called conservative, it is from the point of view of our own time that this is so rather than from the point of view of his own, when the developments to which we have just referred were still in prospect.

It is undeniable that Austin's views in the present context are to be considered reactionary at the present time. It was, moreover, his misfortune that, when at a later stage Austin came to be well known in America, some of the more progressive writers in that country found the sources of Austin's reactionary tendencies more deeply embedded in his theorizing than we should for ourselves. The restriction of legal functions which we should see deriving from aspects of Austin's particular view of law tended to be attributcd to Austin's logical analytical methods of proceeding. Any attempt to pin law or a particular system of law down by any definitions or classifications came to be suspected as imposing restrictions on the development of the law in the interests of social justice. The achievement of justice in the law and logical arrangement of the law came to be thought opposed to one another. Insistence on the latter thus came to be seen as itself opposed to reform. Austin's approach was seen as the epitome of this sort of undesirable conservatism, stigmatized as conceptualism or formalism.

On this fundamental matter, however, we see for ourselves the strongest reasons for defending Austin. His scientific, analytical methods, when some amendments are made to them which in fact preserve their fundamental drive, we see as essentially sound and in no way restrictive of developments of the law for social ends. In the manner in which Austin combined a determinedly empirical approach to law with a view that it could be analysed by means of traditional logic, we see Austin's enduring contribution to jurisprudence. In the remaining section of this chapter we look more closely at Austin's logic and general philosophy as a preliminary to later examination of false notions which developed about them and to defending them against more recent logical and philosophical theories.

The enduring theoretical value of Austin's work

Unless the only kind of argument which is worth advancing about Austin's theory of law is an argumentatum ad hominem, we have not disposed of the matter of its truth or usefulness[65] once we have determined whose side he was on politically, what his motivations were, or what his political effects were. What is worth continuing remark about Austin's theory is the particular character of his empiricism when applied to propositions made in law and the social sciences. He believed that they were just true or false, in the simple ordinary sense of truth, understood as what is to be observed taking place. Even when talking of ethics he spoke, curiously to some ears, of ethical truth.[66]

On this kind of question, current legal philosophers who show special interest in the Benthamites, are disposed to attach weight to suggestions thrown out by Bentham himself, wherein Austin differed from him. Among these suggestions are those we have noticed which appear to give fundamental importance to special imperative propositions in the social sciences (the logic of the will) and the suggestion that there are notions in law which can only be explained by propositions indicating their relations to reality (paraphrasis) rather than by representing them as reflecting empirical facts.[67] So, on this kind of issue, there is a 'back to Bentham' movement among modern legal philosophers, insofar as they seek assistance from the Benthamite group at all, though we should not contend that Bentham is accepted uncritically in the current activity or provides more than jumping-off points.

The present writer, on the other hand, regards these propositions of Bentham as unsound and Austin's approach to this kind of matter as superior. What is called for in these respects is a 'back to Austin' movement. Explicitly, Austin's view of the relation of theorizing in law, or elsewhere to ordinary empirical truths is a very simple one. In one statement of it in his lectures, he begins by saying that a true theory is only a compendium of particular truths. It is only the terms of the theory which are general and abstract, so that it abbreviates or condenses particular truths. If, however, the theory is not true of particulars it has no truth at all. Truth is always particular, although language is commonly general.[68]

Thus far, Austin might appear to be confining himself to a discussion of some particular class of theories whose purport is to represent truths, and to be leaving open the possibility that there might be theories which have other objectives and whose 'validity' might be subject to different criteria. But then Austin goes on to exclude this possibility by claiming that if a theory does anything else than represent a compendium of particular truths, it not only has no truth at all, but makes no sense at all. He says:

> Unless the terms of a theory can be resolved into particular truths, the theory is mere jargon: a coil of those senseless abstractions which often ensnare the *instructed*; and in which the wits of the ignorant are certainly caught and entangled, when they stir from the track of authority, and venture to think for themselves.[69]

In the early part of the above passage Austin is reflecting the views of James Mill. John Stuart Mill says that, at some time about his thirteenth year, he happened to suggest that theory could be at variance with practice, whereupon his father became indignant, and left his son fully persuaded that in positing such a variance, he had shown unparalleled ignorance.[70] As Austin proceeds, however, he places an impossible weight on language to account for the fact that, though truth is particular we speak in generalities, especially since he wishes to maintain that the generalities in which we speak are true. As the fact that he called his disquisition on logic the *Excursus on Analogy*[71] shows, he sought to suggest that it is possible for language to fulfil this function because things have resemblances. But resemblances can hardly be anything but shared characteristics, which involves that we observe general features in the particulars we observe. This latter is in effect the basis on which Austin proceeds, using the notions of traditional logic – with reservations about the syllogism[72] – as indicating the most general ways in which shared characteristics of things are to be found in nature in conjunction with other shared characteristics of things – for example, that shared characteristics of things in a species were necessarily related to other characteristics called *propria*. This to us is both right and fundamentally important.

Austin was disposed to leave the deeper aspects of some of these things to Mill. He told his class that Mill would sort out the metaphysical issues because Mill was a metaphysician.[73] What Austin meant by metaphysics, however, one does not know. We should for ourselves reject metaphysics where it speculates on matters which are not open to ordinary observation as inconsistent with Austin's empirical approach that our generalities are simply true of what we observe, or false, or nonsense. While the study of Mill's *Logic* in many matters provides means of developing what we take to be Austin's main message and we accept what Mill says, in others Mill is metaphysical in what we regard as an unsatisfactory sense.

An example is to be found in Mill's account of what explanations are to be given of the fact that we appear to be able, in some cases, to demonstrate necessary connections between characteristics by which we decide to designate a species and other characteristics which we call *propria*. Mill says that this may be due to laws of our nature or something in the constitution of the universe.[74] But Mill does not pretend to be able to observe either the laws of our nature or the constitution of the universe except through their products – in the fact that we appear to be able to observe necessary connections. Surely consistent empiricism requires that we trust what we appear to observe in the first place, that we observe things *as* necessarily connected. To proceed to suppose that there are ulterior explanations seems in much the same category as the supposition of the existence of the will in psychology.

Mill also, undesirably as it seems to us, complicates Austin's simple picture of propositions in the social sciences as reflections of observed reality, by insisting that 'ought' propositions are of a special character.[75] Mill says, in effect, that a proposition in which the predicate is joined to the subject by an 'ought' copula is generically different from one in which the predicate is joined to the subject by an 'is' copula. He concedes, however, that there is an 'is' assertion included. This is that the conduct recommended excites in the speaker's mind the feeling of approbation. There is no problem about representing this in an 'is' proposition. But Mill says that this is not all, because this should not be a conclusive reason to the person himself, nor would it provide a reason for others to approve.[76]

This may indeed lead us to the conclusion, which we accept, that an 'ought' proposition may be represented in more 'is' propositions than one. One further proposition, beyond the speaker's assertion of his own approbation, is the assertion that the approval follows from something approved by both his hearers and himself. This is sufficient to explain why the speaker thinks he is providing a reason for approbation to his hearers. If he is asked why he makes the 'ought' statement, the appropriate course is for him to go as far as necessary to produce conviction in his hearers towards making the common ground explicit. The simplest form of responsive argument, a perfectly ordinary argument comprising 'is' propositions, is: 'All things required for the achievement of X are things that you and I approve', 'Y is a thing required for the achievement of X', 'therefore Y is a thing that you and I approve – even if you have not immediately recognized this.'

The minor proposition in this syllogism is the kind of scientific proposition, which Mill rightly insists is an 'is' proposition, which serves the art in the field in question. But, because it functions as a minor premise in syllogisms of the sort we have given, it may be said to provide a hypothetical imperative. This does not mean that it ceases to become an indicative and becomes instead something different which requires a different kind of 'ought' logic to deal with it. Calling it a hypothetical imperative simply expresses its real relations of implication with other indicatives. That is: Persons who commit themselves to what is required for X (like you and me) are involved in committing themselves to Y.

If Mill himself will not accept this, it appears to be because he will not accept that all imperatives are hypothetical, which, in our own view, is required of one who is to remain consistently an empiricist. Mill, when he looks for conclusive reasons for doing things, is apparently supporting the existence of categorical imperatives which, in some mysterious way, offer reasons to people *whatever* the particular objectives they might wish to support happen to be. As soon as Mill attempts to support his view of the necessity for 'ought' propositions in art, he does what a consistent empiricist would expect to happen. He resorts to metaphysics in a bad sense.

Mill specifies utility as his own fundamental objective for the Art of Life in Society which would be unexceptionable in itself if he were able to give empirical content to that notion. But he does not leave the matter there, going on to claim that the objective of utility admits of vindication. This exercise of vindication is part at least of the subject matter of teleology, the doctrine of ends. To indicate what is involved here, Mill states, without elaborating, that he borrows the language of the German metaphysicians, and calls it the Principles of Practical Reason.[77] This last is a phrase especially associated with the name of the philosopher Kant, with whose name the idea of there being categorical imperatives at all is also associated.

The extent to which Kantian notions are metaphysical, and in what senses is a complex question, because of the distinction which Kant draws between principles which are only formally transcendental of the empirical world, that is to say involve only principles of organization by the mind of empirical entities (phenomena) and principles which are substantively metaphysical in that they set up metaphysical entities beyond the world of empirical observation (noumena). But both notions are metaphysical in the sense which we would think require to be rejected by a consistent empiricist. We have already given reasons for rejecting the former when referring to Mill's suggestion that laws of our mind produce the appearance of necessary connections generally in reality, itself a borrowing of Kantian ideas. The Kantian notion of a categorical imperative, as a formal transcendental principle organizing our own actions so that some come to be regarded as necessary, is in a similar position.

Austin himself had a collection of Kant's major works in original German versions in his library, both dealing with philosophy in general and morals in particular.[78] But we have noticed that Andreas Schwarz's conclusion is that Austin was largely impervious to German philosophy,[79] which appears to be correct. The actual result of this imperviousness is one of the great virtues of Austin's work. The British empiricist philosophical approach from which Austin and Mill began had created an immense philosophical problem by supposing that we can only directly observe individual things as individual, and Kant's work is an immensely sophisticated solution to the problems of how notions of necessary connections are built up in spite of this. Austin escaped this extensive blind alley through his imperviousness. Instead, his no doubt inept and absurdly simple solution that generality was only a matter of linguistic abbreviation or condensation of individual things enabled him to proceed for practical purposes on the correct view that the general features of order in things that we appear to observe are in fact immanent in what we observe and are reflected in the kinds of propositions found in traditional logic. In the ethical field his justification for supporting the objective of the greatest happiness of the greatest number was the simple one that it was an index to the laws of God, and he spent little time on the demonstration of that.[80]

Just as Austin's imperviousness to Kantian philosophy meant that he confined himself in practice to presenting questions of whether something commanded his approval as a question of truth about its relations to the production of happiness, it also meant that in practice he presented the question of whether something was law as a factual question of whether it was commanded by the sovereign. Neither of these questions was a good question to ask. But they were the appropriate *kinds* of questions to ask from an empirical approach, whereas a Kantian approach typically leads to the wrong kind of question being asked, whether about what one might find worthy of one's approval or about what is law. Both Austin's questions can be answered by indicative propositions.

Under a theory like Hans Kelsen's, the propositions constituting a legal system do not have the factual existence for which a physical scientist looks using, as Kelsen sees it, the formal organizing category of causality. They have legal validity in terms of a basic norm which is scientifically arrived at by reference to a different formal organizing principle which produces 'imputation' of predicates to subjects in the propositions of the system. Kelsen did not present this notion as something he derived directly from Kant or even at which he arrived with Kant in mind. But it is in the same family of thought as gave rise to notions like Kant's categorical imperative in morals. Kelsen's legal theory is open to similar philosophical criticisms as apply to Kant's moral theory.

Despite the sharp difference between Kelsen's theory and Austin's theory in the above aspects, Austin's theory is commonly treated as if it sought to separate the formal and substantive aspects of law, and deal particularly with the formal ones. Thus his theory is seen to be concerned with the question of what is a suitable conceptual framework for law. The argument then tends to proceed that these questions are not ordinary empirical questions. They are organizational questions. The question whether propositions about the organization to be used are true or false − in the sense of correctly picturing what we observe or not − does not make sense. But we do not believe either that Austin would have seen his activity in this way or that he would have been right to do so, at least without strong reservations.

Certainly Austin was preoccupied with questions of classification. But the notions he presents as the basis of his work − species and genera − in this respect are what Mill calls 'real' kinds.[81] Though, for Austin, language has somehow to abbreviate them from the primitive impressions we receive from nature, nevertheless Austin supposes that the result of the abbreviation is accurate in relation to what we observe. We believe Austin's result was right, though we think he was wrong in making the assumption at least sometimes that things divide themselves naturally into a single species − or *infima species* − and even a single genus, and that the appropriate definition of anything follows from this. Mill knew that there was a problem of selection of classes to which things belonged for definitional and other purposes according to the interests of the investigator, and while Austin was forced into this in practice, it meant that he was unsystematic in examining the purposes involved, even those which Mill classed for this purpose as scientific. Austin never got to the point of clarifying, for example, in what ways his map of the legal system was important to the interests of an investigator of the legal system and how far it was important for a legislator, whether for the purpose of understanding what the legislator was doing, or recognizing particular classifications in the framing of the system for some official purpose.

There were connected questions which Austin's tendency to simple-mindedness about the degree of simplicity in the organization of what we observe, limited his ability to confront. If all that language does is abbreviate what we observe, and this is its only function, then this involves us in rejecting the view which Mill accepted that the art in any field involves some special function of talking 'in' rules. When we talk law at all, the sharp distinction made between law and fact in some legal language may appear to suggest that we have ceased to talk fact. Austin's work, however, generally suggests that he considered, as his philosophy would require, that when we talk law we are still talking fact and the present writer agrees with Austin in this. Yet there are complexities involved in explaining just what facts we are picturing when we reason legally, and Austin made matters too simple for himself. His account of what we mean when we say that a fact situation falls within the principle of a case seems to be that the situation falls under the same species which was before the court in the former case and the action taken by the court then is taken to be approved by the sovereign for the whole species.[82] None of this explanation is acceptable for reasons we hope to have made clear. Yet the fact remains that Austin posed for himself the problem of presenting law as facts of the kind which could be represented in propositions of traditional logic, even if his solutions were unsatisfactory.

We believe that Austin is the only prominent English jurist who has presented the fundamental philosophical problem of legal theory to himself in that way and the present writer's interest in Austin most particularly derives from the fact that he believes it is the right way. Those, however, who took a particular interest in Austin's approach from the time when his work was published until the mid twentieth century generally failed to interest themselves in Austin from this point of view because they had no broad philosophical or logical interests. They set out to improve Austin's account of legal phenomena, but since they did not see Austin's doctrines in relation to his broad philosophy, they had no interest in their improvements being consistent with that philosophy. Inconsistencies immediately began to develop and Austinianism lost a kind of fundamental motivation which it had for Austin himself.

When interest in the relation between philosophy and jurisprudence revived in the mid twentieth century at Oxford, it was a different kind of philosophy which occupied the stage. The drive was now to say that legal discussion could not be seen as embodying propositions of the simple truth presented in traditional logical propositions. Highly sophisticated presentations of the relation of law to ordinary empirical facts became the vogue. But philosophical fashions ebb and flow. The traditional logic by reference to which Austin sought to present law represents the wisdom of the ages. We venture to believe that as changes in the philosophical climate occur, John Austin's fundamental problems will be remembered and attacked with renewed zeal. There are periodic demands for the presentation of law as fact elsewhere. It will happen in England.

5

The scholarly reception of Austin: development of myth

Analysis versus history

Before Austin's work was even generally known, the description of the kind of jurisprudence which he wrote by the term 'analytical' jurisprudence was already current, particularly when the expression was used in contrast with the expression 'historical' jurisprudence. This contrast is drawn, for example, by James Reddie, writing in 1840, eight years after the first edition of Austin's *Province* was published, but without reference to Austin. Reddie saw scientific theories of law as those which regard it as belonging 'to that by far the largest and most important part of the domain of human knowledge, which the Germans denominate empirical, or *a posteriori*, which embraces all physical existence and event (*sic*) which is so far dependent on, or affected by, time and place, and which can only be acquired by observation and experience'.[1] Reddie placed the Benthamite science of law in this category, as does the present writer. Reddie went on to say that, at the time he wrote, the scientific students of law throughout Europe were divided into two great sects. One was the analytical school, of which Mr Bentham might be called the founder, and the other the historical school, of which Professors Hugo and Savigny were the great leaders.[2] Reddie pointed out that Bentham's views, though supported by a numerous body of admiring pupils and staunch supporters, particularly in London, had made perhaps a stronger impression in the southern countries of Europe than even in his own country through the work of Étienne Dumont.[3]

For England, the contrast between Austin's own work in this respect and the work of the leading English historical jurist whose life overlapped with his own – Sir Henry Maine – was focused sharply in 1861. It was in October of that year that Sir James Fitzjames Stephen reviewed simultaneously Sir Henry Maine's *Ancient Law* and the second edition of Austin's *Province*, which was the first fruit of Sarah Austin's labours after her husband's death.[4]

James Fitzjames Stephen was the son of Sir James Stephen, who was a friend of the Austin family and, as Under-Secretary of State, was instrumental in sending Austin to Malta in 1836.[5] From 1849, Sir James was briefly Regius Professor of Modern History at Cambridge. He died in 1859. James Fitzjames's brother was Leslie Stephen, the celebrated historian of the utilitarians. Fitzjames, as his brother refers to him, was a barrister who took silk in 1868, a professor of law at the Inns of Court, the holder of more than one high judicial office, the author of works on criminal law and evidence, a successful codifier in India and an unsuccessful codifier in England. His brother describes him as in first principles an unhesitating disciple of Bentham and Austin,[6] and in Fitzjames's contentions with John Stuart Mill on political matters, Leslie Stephen notes that both antagonists began from the common ground of John Austin's analysis of law.[7]

Other writings about Stephen indicate that the description of him as a utilitarian is subject to substantial qualifications. But we believe Stephen correctly sums up the *objectives* of Austin's work. Stephen claims that Austin placed jurisprudence upon a basis as systematic and truly scientific as political economy, and as providing a second illustration of a moral science in the true sense of the words.

For Stephen, the test of the truth of any scientific rule is its correspondence with every case which can be put of circumstances which it ought to explain, and the subjects of moral sciences are rules of this kind which refer to human conduct. Stephen shared Austin's enthusiasm for political economy. The difficulties of scientific prediction in the moral field are, in Stephen's view, due to the transience and obscurity of the facts to which principles have to be applied and the difficulties of developing vocabulary. But Austin's propositions on jurisprudence have the same precision and importance as Adam Smith's and Ricardo's propositions on rent, profits and value. Stephen concedes that insofar as Austin's work is definitional, it cannot be said to be true or false, but nothing could be more convenient than his definitions for reducing the entanglement between the actual and ideal state of things.

Stephen introduces his account of Maine's *Ancient Law* by describing Maine's work as in some respects a contrast to Austin's and in others closely connected with it. He takes Maine's object to be the giving of the history of the gradual evolution of several of the principal conceptions by which law is pervaded, and the description of the different influences by which they have been developed. Maine, Stephen notes, had talked about his activity as involving the historical method, and Stephen comments that it is common to talk about the analytic and historical methods as if they are independent roads to the same result, one of which experience proves to be right and the other wrong. But they are not independent roads; they are complementary and equally indispensable. History without analysis is a mere curiosity and analysis without history is blind, as Austin recognized. While, however, on the one hand, Stephen sees Austin as thoroughly aware of the combination of analysis and historical investigation required for the fundamental task of arrival at the truth, and, indeed, as having anticipated Maine's researches into some historical matters, Stephen sees Maine, on the other hand, as less ready to recognize the importance of analysis, even though his inquiries are only rendered possible by the definitions of Austin and Bentham. Moreover, Stephen sees Maine as making, inferentially, exaggerated and confusing claims for the results of historical research. This is because Maine seems to think that once he has succeeded in giving the history of a system or theory, he has done with it. Stephen represents Maine as saying in substance of Natural Law: There is no such thing as Natural Law because Rousseau got to it by adapting for his purposes certain language current among lawyers of his day, who took their ideas from earlier lawyers, who to serve a temporary purpose twisted Roman law ideas, and these ideas in turn were compounded out of earlier ideas which meant something different from what is now understood by natural law. All this may be so, says Stephen, without proving the conclusion. A conviction of the truth may be founded on bad reasons.

Whatever may be said of the detail of Stephen's criticisms of Maine, the present writer finds Stephen's argument about the complementarity of analytical and historical studies cogent. If the development of historical inquiries into law posed any threat to Austinian aspiration to give a scientific account of empirical legal phenomena in the setting of those which are the subjects of the social and natural sciences, it would be because of deficiences in the way historical inquiries into law developed, not because of any virtues in the methods adopted. Mere retailing of historical legal events would produce only 'curiosities' – having about as much importance in the way of stating general truths, we may comment, as Frazer's *Golden Bough*. Certainly this criticism could not be made of Maine's work because he set out to find causes of views being held at given times and in this respect his work was scientific and Stephen recognized it as such. But it was still important to make the point that the reasons why a particular doctrine is held do not dispose of the question of its truth. Stephen might have added, and certainly believed, that the fact that the causes which led to the adoption of a particular stance of the law have disappeared historically, does not dispose of the question of the continuing utility of that stance.

But Stephen's most important point arises out of his puzzlement about what could be meant by the historical method. All that the term 'history' itself suggests is that phenomena are to be studied with an emphasis on the time dimension. This can only be a matter of emphasis, because in assigning causes Maine is bound to leap from one sequence of phenomena to another sequence of phenomena, just as a Benthamite would, in the processes of induction and verification. There must be some method – not suggested by the term history – of the organization of sequences, or at least some perception of the general organization of sequences, and Stephen suggests that in Maine himself this tended to be Benthamite, even though he thought Maine often made a virtue out of simply sticking to the 'facts' in his account. But we may comment that a historical account of law could, for example, be written from a natural law point of view, in which case it would come into conflict with Austinian theory just as much as any other natural law interpretation of any facts. There were seeds of conflict. The material with which Stephen was concerned did not raise for him the more specialized issue of whether the historical development of the law would be frozen by codification, which is an issue independent of the general question of the relationship of analytical and historical methods of investigation, but which was to get mixed up with the general question in England, as it had earlier in Germany.

The Austinian tradition: England and Australasia

The first book written in the Austinian tradition other than by Austin himself was Sir William Markby's *Elements of Law*,[8] and was something of a family affair. Markby was one of Sarah Austin's advisers when she was struggling with ill health and Austin's manuscripts. One of her chief sources of satisfaction near the close of her life was Markby's marriage to her niece Lucy and his appointment as a Judge of the High Court of Judicature at Calcutta. He retained this appointment for 12 years and *Elements of Law*, the first edition of which was completed in 1871, was based on lectures delivered to students in Calcutta in 1870. It ran to six editions by 1905. From 1878 to 1900 he was reader in Indian law at Oxford.[9]

F.H. Lawson was to write in 1968 that Markby was by then almost forgotten and that his book was classified as analytical jurisprudence and neglected as such. Insofar as Lawson himself was prepared to defend Markby's importance, it was on the grounds that his work afforded much general information about law that students would not have otherwise obtained in the then Oxford curriculum, and that it contained much more comparative law than is usually found in more modern books on jurisprudence.[10] In other words, it was defensible by reference to the other things which it contained outside what might be considered central to analytical jurisprudence.

These comments point to the fact that, even at the time when Austinianism was making its initial impact, Austinian scholarship itself was turning inward upon law and losing the vital and continuing inspiration for it which came from the determination to understand legal phenomena on the basis of a general philosophy of the world in general and the fields of the social sciences within it. It was losing, too, its sharp eye for the criticisms of its competitors' errors in scientific analysis. Markby sought to defend Austin against criticisms by relying on the authority of Maine. And the assessment of Austin he attributes to Maine is confusing in the highest degree. Markby says that Maine's view is that Austin's analysis is scientific and not political, based on assumptions rather than historical facts, and an abstraction. But, Markby adds, Maine recognizes 'that it is the only existing attempt to construct a system of jurisprudence by a strictly scientific process, and to found it, not on *a priori* assumption, but on the observation, comparison, and analysis of the various legal conceptions'.[11] This representation of Maine shows Maine holding blatant contradictions in his view of Austin together. That may be a correct representation of Maine, though the substance of his view has to be boiled down from two long, and at times rambling, lectures.[12] But in that case why should Markby accept this as an appropriate defence of Austin? Surely Maine's account should have been attacked for giving a correct interpretation of Austin in the quoted passage and then going on to obscure what Austin had said.

The teaching of analytical jurisprudence in Oxford at this stage was not the exclusive province of Markby. Sir Thomas Erskine Holland was appointed to the Chichele chair of international law and diplomacy in 1874. The first edition of his *Elements of Jurisprudence* appeared in 1880 and ran to 13 editions by 1924, with various reprints after his death in 1926. It is avowedly founded on the work of Bentham and Austin, though he criticizes both of them for being unsystematic. It is symptomatic of what happened to Austin in the hands of his successors that Holland treats as digressions, spoiling Austin's systematic treatment of his subject, Austin's treatment of the psychology of the will, codification and utilitarianism. Holland took the narrowing influence of Austin's definitions a great deal more seriously than Austin did himself, and Holland's canvas is simply not Austin's canvas. Holland further explained that he derived little help from Continental legal literature.[13] Lawson describes Holland as rigorous, dogmatic, intolerant, and hard to budge from any position he had taken up. He praises Holland's work as providing a useful introduction to law, but couples him with Markby in saying that Holland is almost forgotten and his book classed as analytical jurisprudence and neglected as such.[14] While, however, Lawson's remarks may be accepted so far as they indicate a lack of interest in analytical jurisprudence of the style of Markby and Holland, we shall see that by 1968 there was an intense interest in a new approach to analytical jurisprudence stimulated by Hart.

Holland defined his science even more narrowly than it was possible to adhere to himself. Jurisprudence was a formal science dealing with the various relations with which law dealt rather than legal rules themselves. Greater ambitions for jurisprudence were visionary. Comparative law was the material science to which jurisprudence ministered by clarifying ideas like prescription in relation to ownership and actions.[15] Holland is departing from his definition as soon as he begins to explain. It is surely confusing to be told that prescription is a relation with which the law has to deal. Since Holland proposed to use the term 'analytical' as equivalent to 'formal', the effect of his notions on the ideas of his readers concerning what analytical jurisprudence was in Bentham's and Austin's hands was in the highest degree unfortunate. For the rest, his book is in fact a work of comparative law, under largely Austinian headings with some variations and individual criticisms, and particular emphasis on matters of classification.

The picture of gloom presented by work in the Austinian tradition in the late nineteenth-century Oxford is, however, relieved by one shining exception. This is A.V. Dicey's *Law and Public Opinion in England During the Nineteenth Century*.[16] Dicey had been appointed to the Vinerian Chair of

English Law in 1882 and the work in question was based on lectures delivered in Harvard in 1898. Dicey's object in this book was to demonstrate the close dependence of currents of legislation in England in the nineteenth century upon currents of public opinion. The opinions comprising these currents were thought of as dominant opinions, though they might be stimulated by individual thinkers, and were something better than mere self-interest. They were thus something like Austin's positive morality. So that Dicey's work was in effect an exercise in the relation of positive morality and law, which was something Austin himself would have delighted to have written. Certainly some Benthamites would have complained of Dicey's defensive attitudes to features of the law in his own time. In this respect Dicey was typical of legal thinkers of the period, including Stephen. Benthamites would also have objected to Dicey's treatment of Benthamite views as an influence on an era of public opinion which was by Dicey's time passing away.[17] Dicey thought that it was paradoxical that Austin's legal theory was producing an effect at such a late stage. But he was nevertheless sympathetic to Austin[18] and Austin would have thought Dicey's own project in this respect generally Austinian in character.

Since Dicey's book was not by now thought of as dealing with what was centrally Austinian, it no doubt did little to improve what was happening to Austin's reputation in the hands of Markby and Holland even before controversies developed about Dicey's own work. Sir John Salmond on the other hand, wrote a book which deals with the central topics of Austin's theory, and he, like Dicey, was a man of high reputation in particular legal fields as well as in jurisprudence. As the Holmes–Pollock letters show, he commended himself particularly to Sir Frederick Pollock, who had replaced Maine as Corpus Professor of Jurisprudence in 1883.

Salmond was a New Zealander educated at Otago and University College London, the forum of John Austin's lectures. He wrote his major work on *Jurisprudence** in 1902, while a professor in the University of Adelaide. Later, he was to write a work on Torts which was continued after his death with distinguished Oxford editors and a work on Contracts which had a more chequered history. Salmond had more familiarity with the details of the law than Austin did, and was much more familiar with the workings of the English courts than Austin. He makes far less attempt than Austin to

---

* See John W. Salmond, *Jurisprudence or the Theory of Law* (3rd edn, London, 1910). For the purposes of this summary we have used an early edition of Salmond's work, principally to show the kind of impact Salmond's work was calculated to have in his lifetime. He himself said in the preface to the last edition in his lifetime (7th edn, London, 1924) that there were few material changes in the original text and that the seventh did not represent any material departure from the essential doctrine of the earlier editions. He did, however, become uneasy about the lack of fuller attention to continental legal literature, became satisfied that it is not permissible for a book of jurisprudence wholly to ignore the ethical implications of the subject, and that to treat all questions which were not governed by rule as questions of fact could cause misapprehension (See 7th edn, preface vii – ix).

correlate the workings of different systems together. He draws inferences from what he knows. At the same time, his work suffers in comparison with Austin's by his lack of scientific curiosity beyond what he considers to be required for practical purposes. It is not too much to say that whatever broad scientific inspiration remained in the Austinian tradition suffered the same fate in 1902 as was claimed to have overtaken English cricket 20 years earlier. It died, the body was cremated, and the ashes were taken to Australia.

Salmond's stated aims in his preface are the laying of a scientific foundation for legal education and the indication of features of legal theory touching problems of ethical and political science. He divides the science of law into civil (State) jurisprudence, international jurisprudence and natural (natural law) jurisprudence. He includes the last simply because people write about it, though for him it is 'unprofitable'. Civil jurisprudence is divided into systematic (exposition of the law at present, though what is more systematic about it than proper study of other fields he does not explain), historical jurisprudence (legal development) and critical jurisprudence (concerned with the ideal future). Systematic jurisprudence, on which he concentrates, deals with fundamental legal conceptions and the more general part of the law which provides the foundation for study of particular topics.[19]

In Salmond's hands, the 'fundamental conception' which substitutes in effect for the Austinian notion of the sovereign, is the State. Law is for Salmond the body of principles recognized and applied by the State in the administration of justice. It is the State whose force maintains the right. But whereas Austin's sovereign is philosophically an empirical notion, Salmond's State is not. Salmond does not set out to define the State by reference to identifying something actually going on, but tells us instead what he can only mean is its *proper* end, the marshalling of force to control individual brutishness, in the interests of justice, even though he speaks as if this is what actually happens. Bentham and Austin would properly have complained about confusion of the 'is' with the 'ought' in this. The more remote end of marshalling force is for Salmond justice, but at this point the end itself becomes obscure, adding complications to the departure from empiricism involved in defining institutions by reference to their proper ends at all. In explaining how we arrive at justice, Salmond achieves nothing better than homely phrases: sound reason and good sense (like Pollock and Pollock's successor in his Chair of Jurisprudence, Sir Paul Vinogradoff).[20] The present writer has criticized elsewhere the lack of philosophic rigour in ethical discussion which this kind of approach represents and the easy assumption that common sense was to be found in the law itself, which was affecting English jurisprudence at this time.[21] Some 'pragmatic' approaches in the United States of America may be thought analogous. The practical consequence was not only avoidance of sharp and fundamental criticisms of the law but, in Salmond's hands, lack of rigour in its identification. The deficiencies of Blackstone attacked by Bentham and Austin had returned, if in different dress.

These deficiencies were not confined in Salmond's treatment to his definition of the State, but extended to his narrower definitions. One way in which the force was properly exerted by the State was through the courts, and a court was defined by reference to the fact that its proper end was justice. Not all that the courts so defined might do was for Salmond law, but only the rules they acted on. All else concerning the courts was fact at judicial discretion and presumably of no interest to the jurist.[22] What is to be treated as making law in what the courts do — how we determine what makes a precedent — is, for Salmond, whether the question with which the court is concerned is answerable on principle. We determine the *ratio decidendi* of a case by asking what is the narrowest principle of justice (or common sense) required to decide the case. Common sense solves the problem of determining the *ratio decidendi* which Austin strove vainly to solve by logic. For Salmond, common sense is also prominent in arriving at a rule in a case of first impression where there is conceded to be no precedent to follow.[23]

Salmond's habit of identifying institutions by attributing ends extends to his methods of classifying legal rules. Civil justice is identified by reference to the fact that its end is the punishment of wrongs. In civil claims, for example, the end is always restitution,[24] but in criminal proceedings the essential end is deterrence, to which other objectives like prevention of crime, reformation of the criminal, and retribution are said to be accessory. Salmond does not explain in what way he thinks the essential end of an institution is to be identified. At the present point he slips into propositions like: 'We hang murderers not merely that we may put into the hearts of others like them the fear of a like fate, but for the same reason for which we kill snakes, namely, because it is better for us that they should be out of the world than in it.'[25] Salmond presumably does not mean that he has done these things or that he expects his readers to have done so and it is not clear what he does mean. His attribution of particular ends to institutions is *ex cathedra* and dogmatic.

What are proper ends for an institution is a consideration as prominent in Salmond's treatment of constitutional law as it is in his treatment of civil and criminal law. The fact that the ends of the State are to exert force through the courts for the administration of justice, and to wage war for just ends, implies, he tells us, a definite organization. Constitutional law is the body of rules determining this organization, which arise through the reflection in the courts of constitutional practice, which is logically prior to the law. A State exists if it has the necessary legislative, executive and judicial organization for the maintenance of peace and justice, though there are different forms which its organization may take within these limits.[26] In all this there again appear to be easy identifications of the ideal with the actual which reflect the Blackstonian complacency. Attacks on this were the very jumping-off point for the making of distinctions from which the development of a scientific empirical approach to law from Bentham through Austin proceeded.

We must stress that in pressing this kind of criticism of Salmond we are not attacking a 'functional' approach either to law or to legal classification. Modern functional approaches often are empirical, but only when they approach the identification of institutions by reference to objectives actually pursued in them, not when they first determine what are the proper ends and then proceed to identify the actual with the ideal upon a minimum of examination. Salmond's approach might conceivably be adapted to eliminate these criticisms. What we are concerned to stress is Salmond's lack of concern about matters of fundamental theoretical importance to Austin and the consequent disappearance of the springs of scientific and philosophic inspiration in the English jurisprudence of Salmond's time.

There were features of Salmond's treatment which were less affected by his lack of scientific interest, and in which his closer knowledge of English law led him to more realistic views than Austin. His treatment of sources of law exhibits a degree of consciousness which Austin lacked of the extent to which these matters are dependent on the attitudes of those administering a particular system. He makes a detailed study of what are the rules of English law in particular concerning the authority given, for example, to legislation, custom, precedent. He corrects Austin by pointing out that if there is a rule for the acceptance of custom under given conditions there is no difficulty in saying that a particular custom is law before it has been specifically adopted judicially. In dealing with other sources he often accepts Austin's conclusions as valid for English law.[27]

As might be expected, Salmond lacked the scientific curiosity to make a searching examination of the operation of rules about sources of law within the legal system as a whole, of the kind which Hart was later to do. Salmond introduced the subject by saying that every legal system contains rules determining the establishment of new law and the disappearance of the old, which was not a broad enough description to include all that he himself said about sources, for example his statement that an authority confirming an existing precedent is a source of law. He made a highly pregnant statement that among the rules about sources, one or more must be ultimate so that we do not have to trace authority back for ever.[28] For the most significant twentieth-century positivists like Hart and Kelsen, it is this fact which provides a key to the understanding of the organization of the legal system and is important for the understanding of what is involved in the State organization – rather than the implications of what Salmond conceived to be the end of the State. But Salmond leaves this proposition standing, as it were, on a limb by itself.

A further topic where Salmond's work represents an advance on Austin's, at least when empirically reinterpreted, is Salmond's treatment of legal positions, though its permanent value is diminished by the fact that he failed to take full advantage of Hohfeld's highly systematic treatment of legal positions when it became available to him. A legal wrong for Salmond is a violation of justice according to law. A legal duty is to do something the opposite of which would be a wrong. A right is an interest, respect for which is a duty, and disregard of which is a wrong. All duties have correlative rights, says Salmond, rejecting Austin. This involves Salmond in saying that the general public has rights and treating the general public as a person. In developing his ideas on this subject he finds himself talking about incorporeal things, having no concern of the kind Austin did that this might involve a departure from an empirical view of law.

Salmond goes on to deal with what he calls rights in a less strict sense under which he classes liberties and powers. My legal liberties, says Salmond, are the benefits which I derive from the absence of legal duties imposed on myself, while rights are benefits from duties imposed on other persons. Salmond evidently sees no difficulty in envisaging things which I am allowed to do, without having a right in the sense that I may stop others from interfering, and since Austin should not have had any difficulty in envisaging this either, though he did, this is one of Salmond's advances on Austin. On the other hand Hohfeld would scarcely have approved of Salmond's licence to judges and others to call a liberty a right if they feel like being sloppy. In Hohfeld's view, confusion of the notions is a fertile source of confusion in judicial thinking and hence in the law. Salmond defines a power as an ability conferred by law to determine, by someone's own will directed to that end, the rights, duties, liabilities, or other legal relations, of himself or other persons. This is at least a development of things that Austin said in a particular context, in more generalized fashion. But, again, Hohfeld would not have approved of the licence to call a power a right in a slack sense.

Salmond has at this stage used the word 'right' in a broad sense to cover three advantageous legal positions, rights strictly – correlating with a duty imposed on another – powers and liberties. Hohfeld's fourth advantageous position under the law (an immunity) is missing. Salmond then tells us that there is no generic term in the law which expresses the situations of burden which correlate with the benefit situations covered by right in the broad sense. He says the situations of burden are of three kinds: duties, disabilities, or liabilities. But Salmond then goes on to say that some liabilities of a person are burdens correlating with powers in another, while some correlate with liberties in another. This leaves disabilities correlating with nothing that is explained. In the Hohfeldian system they correlate with immunities. That is, an immunity from having one's legal position affected by another involves that the other is under a disability from affecting the former's legal position. Hohfeld further distinguished Salmond's two kinds of liabilities by calling the exposure to acts done by another in pursuance of his privilege (liberty) a no-right (better just called an exposure), and confining the term liability to the burden on a person involved in another's having the advantage of a power.

In comparing the burdensome legal positions with one another, Salmond explains that a duty is the absence of liberty, a disability is the absence of a power, and a liability is the presence either of liberty or power vested in someone else as against the person liable.[29] He thus at this stage defines the first two by reference to what Hohfeld calls their jural opposites: if one has a duty to another in respect of a certain matter one does not have a privilege to do what one pleases in affecting that person and if one has a disability from affecting another's legal position in a matter, one has no power to affect it. On the same basis Salmond should have concluded by telling us that the liability was the absence of two other legal positions, depending on which kind of Salmond's two sorts of liabilities it is. But Salmond had not developed sufficient ideas of legal positions to do this. What Hohfeld says (on the basis that we call one of Salmond's kinds of liability an exposure and reserve the term liability for the other) is that an exposure is the absence of a right and a liability the absence of an immunity. Salmond's scrappiness here is an indication of the greater extent to which Hohfeld's development of the primitive Austinian notions enables us to present legal positions in a systematic pattern.*

It would be pursuing the analogy with cricket too far to represent what happened after Salmond as a struggle for the ashes of Austinian inspiration, for it would grossly misrepresent the degree of interest in what happened to them. But the ashes did cross and re-cross the twelve thousand nautical miles of sea between England and Australia. Sir Carleton Kemp Allen was an Australian educated in Sydney and Oxford, a law fellow at University College, Oxford, and holder of the Chair of Jurisprudence from 1929 to 1931, after which he was for 21 years Warden of Rhodes House. His jurisprudential work, *Law in the Making*, which ran to seven editions by 1964,[30] concentrates, among those subjects developed by Austin, upon sources. It is a useful and detailed book about the English position, as might be expected from a skilful analyst of case law. But he was among those Professors of Jurisprudence in Oxford for whom jurisprudence in its broadest aspects seems to have been a secondary interest and in whose hands the critical development of the more fundamental philosophical aspects of work like Bentham's or Austin's could not be expected to advance.

Allen defines 'sources' as those agencies by which rules of conduct acquire the character of law by becoming objectively definite, uniform, and, above

---

* When Salmond published the seventh edition, the last of his own, he said in a footnote that the analysis and classification of legal rights had been made the subject of exhaustive and acute analysis by W.N. Hohfeld. In another footnote he in effect acknowledged that Hohfeld had made an advance in developing the notion of an immunity, and Salmond therefore acknowledged that his own division of 'rights' into rights in the strict sense, liberties and powers, was not exhaustive. But Salmond made no change to his text, and adhered in these footnotes to using rights in a broad sense, as well as the narrower one, in a way which Hohfeld condemned. (J.W. Salmond, *Jurisprudence* (7th edn, London, 1924), 250, *nn*. (p) and (q)).

all, compulsory. Allen makes it clear that for him these characteristics are acquired historically, by growth of law *upwards* from below, independently of a dominant will. Austin was wrong in imagining law was imposed from above. Sovereign authority with sanctions is a creation of law at some stage. Its character, like that of other sources, cannot be understood independently of its historical evolution. But, though Allen rejects Austin's view, as he understands it, that sovereignty comes from an absolutist sovereign, he is not prepared to reject the different view that there is sovereignty set up in a civilized society as part of its social machinery for the enforcement of law, recognized by common consent, and obeyed as a necessary instrument of government. There is a difference, Allen says, between considering the sanctioning power as the creation of law and considering law as the creation of the sanctioning power. Allen's statement that sovereignty is a creation of law rather than law a creation of the sovereign, might be considered an important advance on Austin if the statement had had the same sort of significance it had even in Salmond's work, and was to come to have in much more systematic fashion in Hart's. But such a statement is not enlightening when law is conceived, as Allen conceived it, vaguely as a kind of hardening of society's arteries. Law arises for him when flexible boundaries of permissible conduct become fixed in the various ways he mentions.[31]

The ashes of Austinian inspiration returned to Australia with the publication of Sir George Paton's *Jurisprudence* in 1946,[32] written, as the author explains, with Sir Carleton Allen's encouragement. Paton had studied at the University of Melbourne and Magdalen College, Oxford, and was Professor of Jurisprudence in the University of Melbourne when he wrote the first and second editions of his *Jurisprudence*. Thereafter he became Vice Chancellor of the University and was succeeded in both posts by D.P. Derham, who wrote the third edition with amendments with which the original author associated himself. The scope of Paton's *Jurisprudence* is much that of Austin and Salmond, but with much more of Salmond's approach than Austin's.

After mentioning briefly the notions and distinctions on which Austin spent most of his time, the authors belabour Austin for believing in universal principles of law, and the suggestion made is that work of his kind will disappear once this is discovered to be untrue. This is a very partial account of Austin indeed, and in the following criticisms of Austin's method there is scarcely one statement of Austinian views which can properly be attributed to Austin himself, and scarcely one statement by way of criticism of the supposed Austinian view of law as a static body of rules which Austin himself did not in fact make of such a view. A sharp distinction is drawn between Austin and Bentham which history does not justify and which Hart had effectively attacked in the *Harvard Law Review* six years before the last edition of this work was published.[33] At this stage Austin ceases to be a real figure altogether. His ashes have been scattered to the winds and he becomes the myth whose significance for twentieth-century jurisprudence will be considered in a later section.*

The Austinian tradition: America

The attention of John Chipman Gray was attracted to the work of John Austin, he himself explains, at a time when it was little read in England and all but unknown in the United States. From what he says, it appears that he might have come across a copy of the first edition of Austin's *Province* before Sarah Austin's edition was published. Gray did not publish his own work, *The Nature and Sources of Law*, until 1909,[34] but tells us that the subject of Austin's work had been little out of his mind in the 50 years since he first read the *Province*. Gray himself was educated at Harvard, a practising lawyer, a member of the faculty of Harvard Law School, from 1875 Story Professor of Law, and, when he wrote his work on jurisprudence, Royall Professor of Law.

As indicated by the above, Gray's work shows as much respect for Austin's as any other important book about the theory of law written in the twentieth century. In background, however, Gray was a good deal more like Salmond than he was like Austin, being primarily a property lawyer, though with more general interests as well. His book resembles Salmond's in that it concentrates on aspects of general theory which Gray sees as important from a practical point of view, his difference with Salmond in this respect being that Gray is very explicit about this while Salmond tends to deny it. Gray uses the word 'academic' in his book in the way that a practical lawyer does,

---

* In the present section we have discussed only major works which confine themselves to treatments of topics which were of central importance to Austin. Austin is additionally accorded a place in many general works on jurisprudence or legal theory which have English associations. Some of these fall for mention at later stages in our treatment of the scholarly reception of Austin. One which does not is W. Friedmann's *Legal Theory* (5th edn London, 1967), which may be taken as illustrating both the virtues and necessary shortcomings of a brief treatment even when carried out with wide knowledge and high skill. Such a treatment is bound to proceed in terms of broad categorisations, or pigeon-holes, on which the comparison with other theories proceeds. Friedmann calls Austin's work the most comprehensive and important attempt to formulate a system of analytical positivism in the context of the modern State (*op. cit.* 258). But he criticizes Austin for not analysing the ways in which judicial law-making was bound to destroy the rigid separation of Is and Ought, of Science and Value, in legal theory (*op. cit.* 265). On the other hand he regards the Vienna school as offering powerful support for Austin's notion of the relation of all legal phenomena to an ultimate law-giving authority (*op. cit.* 264) and says that in the analysis of municipal law the essential features of Austinian theory have established themselves beyond serious challenge (*op. cit.* 264 – 65). He also regards Austin as a source of development of interest in the elaboration of legal concepts and categories, the tools of legal science (at 268). Much of this involves pushing Austin into pigeon-holes which he himself would not have recognized, and lumping him there with theorists whom Austin would have found strange bedfellows. When Friedmann says that the essential features of Austinian theory have established themselves beyond serious challenge in municipal law, one wonders how those essential features are conceived by Friedmann. Austin seems to be subject to current attack in every direction.

as meaning something that does not make any difference to any question of practical importance.

For Gray, jurisprudence is a statement of legal rules in systematic arrangement, and the most useful variety is particular jurisprudence, confined to a systematic statement of the law of a given country. However, Gray thinks it a good idea to include discussion of what the law ought to be on unsettled matters, and therefore approves Austin's discussion of utility in his work. In addition, Gray thinks particular jurisprudence should include a definition of law, distinguishing it sharply from morality and religion, which Gray regards as Austin's feat.[35]

His own definition of law, however, relates it to rules created by the courts rather than those created or adopted by the sovereign as Austin believed.[36] Gray rejects the Austinian notion that the real rulers of society can be found in a sovereign in the official hierarchy, saying that this idea would be ludicrous if it were not so serious. Gray nevertheless believes there are real rulers of society who create the State machinery of which the court machinery is part, even though Gray does not pretend to be able to identify these rulers, and even though he regards the State as an artificial person set up by the law which is created by the courts. So it is not identifiable in empirical process terms. Austin's rejection of artificial persons, except as a convenient way of speaking which must not lead us into misunderstanding the true position, is another matter in which Gray explicitly does not follow Austin. In Gray's view, we must treat the State as an artificial person even if we do dislike that idea.[37]

While Gray concedes that there are dogmatic fictions involved in the notion of legal personality, at the same time he is prepared, on the ground that this is a useful way to think, to go on to attribute characteristics to the State which it could only have if it was a real person. Hence we become lost in the fictions and there is no suggestion that our thinking should keep touch with reality. Gray tells us that it is one of the wonderful capacities of human nature to conceive an abstraction imperceptible to the senses, like the State.[38] Presumably it is also a wonderful capacity of Gray's nature to be able then to say that the State has interests which at times he even calls objects of desire and that it can create rights for itself to protect them. It also has an organized body, and the courts seek their rules from the sources to which they are directed by that organized body. Although Austin would have found all this bewildering, as the present writer does, Gray says that Austin conferred a great benefit by bringing out the fact that law is at the mercy of the State. The State is thus with Gray, as it was with Salmond, a kind of substitute in the functions of Austin's sovereign, but not defined by reference to ends as with Salmond, rather through the miracle of abstraction in legal thinking.

Gray's acceptance of wonderful abstractions imperceptible to the senses is prominent not only in his view of the character of the legal organization, but in his view of legal rules in general as well as in his view of legal positions.

Gray says that law is made up of the rules for decision which the courts lay down; that all such rules are law, and that rules for conduct which the courts do not apply are not law. The judges are the creators rather than the discoverers of the law, because there are only vague limits on the judicial powers to interpret statutes as they please or even to alter the State organization.[39] At this point Gray's proposition that law is at the mercy of the State becomes even more bewildering.

Gray tells us that there is no mysterious entity, the law, apart from rules that the judges make, but Gray talks about those rules, presumably abstractions, as if they were mysterious entities indeed. Hart was later to remark, of a view of law having some similarities to Gray's, that people would think it very odd if we were to define medicine as what doctors do and it might seem equally odd if we were to define law as what courts do. But Gray distinguished the position of law and medicine half a century before Hart compared them. Physicians, Gray says, have not received from the ruler of the world any commission to decide what diseases are, to kill or cure according to their opinion whether a sickness is mortal. But this is exactly what judges do in regard to cases brought before them. If the judges of a country decide that it is law that a man must pay damages, law it is. But all the doctors in town may declare that a man has yellow fever, and yet he may only have German measles.[40]

In this particular example Gray is talking of the fact that the opinion of a court that there is a right, a legal position, makes it so. But he believes the same of general rules. The law of the land is wholly made up of judicial opinions which make what is thought to be so, truly so. What we are then to regard as an authentic expression of judicial opinion becomes a vital point for Gray, facing him with the same problems of circularity which Gray tells us Austin failed to surmount when he attempted to define his sovereign without reference to legal rules. When Gray talks about what fixes a rule in the law as the opinion of the judges, it seems impossible to sort out how far he regards the fact of 'laying down' a rule as itself determined by the rules about precedent in a particular country and how far not. If the question whether a rule is laid down by the judges has to be determined by reference to rules, Gray's definition of law is circular in the way in which, Gray points out, Austin's is circular.[41]

What happened to Austin in Gray's hands was similar to what happened to Austin in the hands of Oxford professors who were lawyers first and legal philosophers second. There was realism in Gray's attack on Austin for his supposition of an official empirically determinable sovereign who really rules. There was realism in his recognition of the extensive law making activity of the courts through what may purport to be only declarations of existing law. But in the more positive parts of Gray's theory realism is virtually explicitly sacrificed to the practical need to create fictions, to make assumptions, to abstract continually in some vague way from the facts. All this is romantically conceived, so that we seem to be expected to stand in awe before the ghosts created by legal technique, which can somehow be fixed like a photographic print through the opinion of those with the appropriate commission from the lurking real rulers of society. By spinning out into a theory some of the elements in practical legal theory, Gray demonstrated one of the paradoxes in practical legal thinking, the extent to which it is 'ivory tower' thinking. Austin noticed the same thing. But he wanted to eliminate it and expose the facts, more especially as he could obviously never get the hang of how you were supposed to manipulate it in practice. But Gray bowed down before it. He could work with it.

At the time when Gray wrote his work on jurisprudence, the *Common Law* of his great contemporary, Oliver Wendell Holmes, Jnr, the holder of high judicial office in Massachusetts and later in the Supreme Court of the United States, had been in print for some 12 years. Gray refers to it from time to time on specific points. This is the sort of reference to Austin which occurs in Holmes's *Common Law*, sometimes with approval, sometimes without commitment, occasionally with condemnation.[42] But Holmes did not at any time make a comprehensive assessment of Austin's work or write a comprehensive jurisprudence himself. Certainly he approached Austin with sympathy. He told Harold Laski in one letter that he did not think that Laski did justice to Austin, and condemned John Zane's indiscriminate attacks on Austin and others. Holmes confided to Laski that he was touched by Sarah Austin's belief in her great man in the way that he was touched by the same belief in the wife of Adams on Equity.[43]

Holmes's views have been associated with Austin's in the first place because of his famous assertion that if you want to understand the law you must look at it as the bad man would look at it. One facet[44] of this is that the specific character of law is associated not with its moral force, but with the coerciveness with which it confronts the man who is unconcerned with moral matters but much concerned with unpleasant legal consequences which may accrue to him from his actions. In the second place, Holmes is in fact aligned with Austin in stressing the importance for lawyers of examining their own fact, the facts of law, in relation to other bodies of fact in adjacent areas.

Another of Holmes's aphorisms, that the life of law has not been logic but experience, is more closely aligned with Austin's views than those who have misrepresented Austin's views may realize, as will be clear from the account we have given of Austin. For all Austin's interest in logic, he certainly did not believe that the law could be deduced from a few first principles, and stressed and approved the creativeness of judicial experience. But in another of his attitudes, Holmes is very much in advance of Austin. This is in his attempt to give meaning to the expression 'law' as what the judges will do.[45] Austin could never get to this point because it is an answer to a problem which could only arise once his theory of sovereignty was rejected.

The outcome of the kind of stimulus which Gray's teachings provided was in relation to much narrower questions than the above. Wesley N. Hohfeld was a graduate of the University of California and then of Harvard Law School, where he formed a close association with Gray. He became a law professor at Stanford in 1905, and then from 1914 for four years at Yale Law School, when he suffered a fatal heart attack. His major work – in fact a series of monographs – *Fundamental Legal Conceptions as Applied in Judicial Reasoning* was published posthumously.[46] Despite the shortness of his career at Yale, he remained a revered figure academically and personally, the latter particularly through the deeply affectionate recollections of Arthur L. Corbin, the author of the standard work on contracts, and the joint editor of the second edition of Hohfeld's work.[47]

Hohfeld's major contribution was to the development of that part of Austin's work which related to what we have called legal positions, but which Hohfeld called sometimes legal relations and sometimes jural relations. Though Hohfeld writes with great respect and deference about Austin and Gray, in these matters he considered they both were at fault in thinking that legal relations could be adequately represented in terms of rights and duties. So he developed the scheme of such relations which has become a standard model, and which we have already referred to in discussing earlier writers.

Hohfeld does not attempt to define what he means by a fundamental legal relation. He says that these relations are *sui generis* and therefore attempts at formal definition are unsatisfactory, if not altogether useless. It is better to exhibit them in a scheme of opposites and correlatives. In the scheme of opposites, a no-right (we have suggested 'exposure') is the opposite of a right, a duty the opposite of a privilege, a disability the opposite of a power, and a liability the opposite of an immunity. In the scheme of correlatives, a duty is the correlative of a right, a no-right the correlative of a privilege, a liability the correlative of a power, and a disability the correlative of an immunity.[48] We have, again in connection with discussing the approach of earlier writers, endeavoured to indicate what Hohfeld seeks to convey by each of these notions and the senses of the terms correlatives and opposites.

Hohfeld's own elaboration in his first monograph concerning his fundamental conceptions consists of appealing to the statements of writers and judges. He does this to show that the judges and writers in question use these conceptions, so that he is not going very far beyond recognized thought and language in advancing them, or to show that if they amalgamate some of them with others, they get into confusion. Some of the conceptions, however, are advanced because, though not used, they are necessary to tie up loose ends left by the lack of systematic character in current legal thinking. We have seen how Salmond's work illustrates this despite his belated acknowledgement of the importance of Hohfeld's analysis.

Hohfeld concludes the monograph referred to with the statement that his eight conceptions seem to be what may be called 'the lowest common denominators of the law'.[49] By reducing fractions in mathematics to their lowest generic terms, comparison becomes possible. It is the same with 'legal quantities'. His second monograph elaborates this, most centrally by elaborating how we may use the conceptions to elucidate the true comparison between rights *in rem* and rights *in personam*. Hohfeld sees the confusions surrounding the use of these broad classifications of the law as being capable of removal only by explanation in terms of his lowest common denominators of the law. For the sake of demonstrating how this is to be done, however, Hohfeld finds it necessary to introduce a pair of adjectives applying to each of his conceptions. Sometimes a right is paucital and sometimes multital and similarly with privileges, powers, immunities and the four correlatives of these. A paucital right, for example (right *in personam*), is either a unique right residing in a person (or group of persons) and availing against a single person (or single group of persons); or else it is one of a few fundamentally similar, yet separate, rights availing respectively against a few definite persons. A multital right (right *in rem*) is always one of a large class of fundamentally similar yet separate rights, actual and potential, residing in a single person (or single group of persons) but availing respectively against persons constituting a very large and indefinite class of people.[50]

As an example of a paucital right, Hohfeld gives the case where B owes A a thousand dollars. Then A has a right *in personam* that B shall do what is necessary to transfer to A the legal ownership of that amount of money. In this case, though Hohfeld does not say so, we are presumably to take it that the right is unique. But if A owns Whiteacre, his right that B shall not enter it, is a multital right or right *in rem*. It is a right fundamentally similar to the rights that A has against other persons generally not to enter Whiteacre.[51] Hohfeld then goes on to consider false and misleading usages which blur the distinction. As against various types of confused people, Hohfeld goes on to assert that a right *in rem*, firstly, is not a right 'against a thing'. Secondly, it is not always one relating to a thing, that is, a tangible object. Thirdly, a single right *in rem* correlates with a duty resting on one person alone, not with many duties (or one duty) resting upon all the members of a very large and indefinite class of persons. In this respect Hohfeld discovers Austin is wrong. Fourthly, a right *in rem* should not be confused with any coexisting privileges or other jural relations that the holder of the multital right or rights may have in respect of the same subject matter. Thus ownership of Blackacre, for example, involves A having vast collections of rights, privileges, powers, and immunities, which must not be confused with one another and here again Austin became confused. Fifthly, a primary right *in rem* should be differentiated from the secondary right *in personam* arising from its violation. Finally, a right *in rem* should not be confused with, or thought dependent on, the character of the proceedings by which it and the secondary right arising from its violation may be vindicated.[52]

In addition to the central material of what he called formal or analytical jurisprudence, indicated in the above two monographs, Hohfeld interested himself in outlining a programme for studies in jurisprudence more generally.[53] In the course of this, he demonstrates that he was a man with broader interests than he is given credit for, as we have sought to show Austin was.

In those central areas of Austinian interest with which Hohfeld concerned himself, his work was classic. His elaboration of legal positions is immeasurably more instructive than Austin's. So is his elaboration of when it is appropriate to use the singular and the plural in talking of the legal position of persons. He made also some improvements in terminology. For example, instead of using the awkward words 'investitive facts' and 'divestitive facts' to relate to facts which make changes in legal positions, he used the economical expression 'operative facts' to refer to all those which have legal effect, the term legal effect being in itself a useful envelope term to refer to such changes. Both the expressions 'operative facts' and 'legal effect' are, moreover, in common legal usage, and one of Hohfeld's objects was to select terms of this sort for his analysis, though giving precise meanings to terms which were employed loosely in professional usage.

In other respects, however, Hohfeld appears more to have hindered progress in areas of Austinian interest, and most particularly in the matter of presentation of law as an empirical study. It is significant that Hohfeld used the expression 'fundamental legal conceptions' as the title of his work on legal positions, whereas Austin uses the expression 'pervasive notions'. Austin does not generally talk about conceptions for opposite reasons, the present writer believes, to those which induced Rat not to talk about his river. If one speaks of what one experiences as conceptions, one suggests that one's own mind is active in constructing them. Austin only seems to talk about 'conceiving' when he is concerned to make the point that we cannot have some experiences without having others at the same time, as we have noticed. One thing is 'inconceivable' without the other.

It was not merely that Hohfeld believed that no general statement can be a matter of observation and involves a mentally creative effort of abstraction. He obviously believed also that an individual legal relation was ideal, and that all legal phenomena are. He attacks any distinction between corporeal rights and incorporeal rights on the ground that all are incorporeal. So the world he chose to make his central study was an ideal one.[54] At the same time he assumed that this world had relations with things that were not ideal in some unexplained way, as shown by his account of the different kinds of jurisprudence.

Probably the springs of his view that the legal world with which he was most concerned is an ideal one lie in his familiarity with Gray. The outflow from this view was a downgrading of his own central work. Others could now say that areas with which he did not concern himself except incidentally got to the actualities of legal happenings in a way his own area did not, with some encouragement to say this from Hohfeld himself. While Austin was concerned to say that his theory represented truth, Hohfeld was concerned to say that his theory 'worked', an approach which Cook also stresses in his introduction to Hohfeld. It is one thing to aim at the truth and go wrong, as Austin often went wrong. But there is a kind of selling out of this area of legal study involved when different criteria from truth seem to be suggested for the satisfactoriness of the theory.*

This aspect of Hohfeld's writing was to achieve greater prominence in the work of Albert Kocourek. What the present writer has treated as of fundamental continuing importance in Austin, Kocourek treats as his aberrations and, most especially, Austin's empirical approach. For Kocourek, Austin was 'really' concerned, however Austin thought of it, with fundamental concepts of the legal system: State, Sovereignty, Law, Jural Relationship, Personateness, Fact and Thing. Kocourek concedes that *Begriffsjurisprudenz* – conceptualism in law – has suffered in various quarters a heavy attack. But he identifies himself with it, and seeks so to identify Austin, even if Austin could not see it. Kocourek says it is not easy to understand how Austin escaped discovering the conceptual nature of the State and sovereignty. The point that Austin missed, Kocourek says, has only recently been elaborated – largely by Hans Kelsen – but the new conceptual extension is merely a step in advance of what Austin, on a lower level of observation and analysis, had already discovered. Kocourek concludes that it is entirely right to say that Austin's analyses are correct and that he deserves to be accorded the rank of primate in the field under discussion.[55]

Thus Kocourek crowns Austin king of what to Austin and the Benthamites generally was an alien land. Kocourek treats writers as having made advances on Austin where we have treated them as turning Austinian

---

* In the above comment and earlier we are assuming that scientific truth and usefulness are distinct, a view which will not be acceptable to those who identify truth by reference to consequences for action, that is, to some pragmatists. In his *Karl Llewellyn and the Realist Movement*, cited above, William Twining points to the influence of a revolt against formalism in the United States, at the time of which we are speaking, on various disciplines including jurisprudence. He refers to Morton G. White's *Social Thought in America: The Revolt Against Formalism* (2nd edn 1957) for the view that pragmatism in philosophy was one manifestation of this and it also affected Holmes in jurisprudence. Such a revolt could also have affected other jurists we have been discussing. But from this point of view the use of Hohfeld, who is highly formalistic in what we should regard as an unempirical 'conceptual' fashion, by realists like Cook and Corbin, is ironic.

The relations between formalism, pragmatism, and empiricism are very complex. It was the famous American philosopher, William James, whose pragmatism, towards the end of his life, though not abandoned, became overlaid with what he called radical empiricism. James, in his radical empiricism, rejected the view that relations are the work of the mind imposed upon original experiences wholly disconnected. Things are observed as being in reality both connected and disconnected. Once this step is taken, in which we would follow James, it is possible to take a view which is empirical and yet formalist. It depends on whether forms are believed to be forms of things – to be immanent in what is observed – or the work of the mind. The present writer calls the latter approach conceptualism, and James called it vicious intellectualism. James's approach, extended by John Anderson in the manner we proceed to indicate in the text, provides an explanation of how Austin could consistently be at once empirical and formalist, as he was. It was not, however, Austin's own explanation, which we concede is unsatisfactory.

studies away from the broader bases of search for truths about law in relation to other social sciences. In this category Kocourek puts Markby, Holland, Salmond, as well as Hohfeld, and other writers like Sheldon Amos and Henry T. Terry. Kocourek sees a parallel on the European continent in the development of the theory of the *reine Rechtslehre*, the pure theory of law, the versions of which to Kocourek are all distinguished by one idea – the conceptual purity of their subject matter. Kocourek detects an American version of the pure theory, distinguished by the fact that it does not deduce from philosophy or metaphysics, but induces from the practical impossibility of dealing with the fundamental elements of legal phenomena in any other way than from the standpoint of pure form. Kocourek thinks that the trend in jurisprudence, in tardy imitation of mathematics, is in the direction of developing an ultimate basis of juristic thought, not on empirical data alone, but on conceptual forms.[56]

Kocourek himself was an LLB graduate of Michigan who practised in Chicago, obtained an academic post in Northwestern University Law School in 1907, and was professor of law there from 1914. He collaborated with Dean John Wigmore in publications in jurisprudence, and his *Jural Relations*[57] appeared in 1927. But its reception was disappointing to Kocourek, as he confessed to an Australian visitor. He attempted a more refined elaboration of jural relations than Hohfeld did, and it failed to take hold, more especially as it required an extensive intellectual investment by the reader, beginning with a special vocabulary. In this enterprise he was encouraged by Wigmore, as Wigmore's introduction to Kocourek's book shows. Wigmore finished with the words: 'May the profession show the courage to master it'. But this prayer was not answered and we refrain from exploring the details.

Kocourek expounds his most fundamental notions dogmatically and even metaphorically. Legal phenomena involve three elements: a system of potential legal rules, situations of fact, and jural relations. The body of legal rules exists in the abstract – potentially – awaiting application in concrete cases. The rule remains abstract until the last stage of judgment and execution is reached. Its existence until that stage may be in formulation in a legislative statement, or as a deduction from other cases, or it may wholly lack literal and logical existence, but in any case its actual application cannot be predicted in advance. Legal rules are therefore both abstract and hypothetical. But nevertheless the law is a force and the outcome of social forces, and it operates upon situations of fact. Jural relations are necessary because it is not enough that there be law in the abstract, set over against social activities. There must be a connecting principle between the force of laws and the material social content upon which they operate and this is the jural relation.[58]

This philosophical interpretation of legal relations is altogether unlike Austin's. It gives away his fundamental objective of presenting legal relations as relations between things that happen, the happening of sovereign commands and other events. But at least Kocourek does not pretend that what he says is what Austin meant. This was what was to happen later.

Despite his 'pure theory' approach, Kocourek's detailed work was not regarded by all empiricists as unimportant, which may be illustrated by the position in the University of Sydney a dozen years after Kocourek's book appeared. At that time the course in jurisprudence was conducted by F.C. Hutley, now a Justice of Appeal of the Supreme Court of New South Wales. Hutley's philosophical predilections were altogether different from those of Kocourek, being those of John Anderson, who came to Sydney as Professor of Philosophy from Glasgow in 1927. J.A. Passmore has pointed out that Anderson set out to show that there is no reality other than the complex, and complexly interacting, objects of everyday experience. Following William James, Anderson insisted that things are experienced, as both connected and distinct, that one experiences things in their relations, not as 'simples' to which connections and distinctions are contributed by the mind.[59] Hence Anderson refused to recognize that connections and distinctions are the construction of formal organizational concepts which are of a different order from the material on which they operate, which is the basis of Kocourek's position. But Anderson also believed that when those who take a view like Kocourek's seek to give an account of their position, frequently empirical equivalents – ordinary empirical truths – may be found in reinterpretation of what they say. It was in reinterpreting Kocourek with objectives similar to Austin's that Hutley sought to develop his course.

The special significance of Anderson for the importance to be attributed to Austin's work lies in the fact that it was he who generalized James's view, that we observe things actually in relations to one another, to the point where Anderson treated the forms exhibited by the propositions of traditional formal logic as simply reflecting in language the most general kinds of relations between things that we observe – relations which *all* the things we observe happening have. Observed reality is propositional. Anderson extended this to treating the syllogistic relations between propositions as relations of implication existing between things which we observe. This is the basis, as we see it, on which Austin, apart from his hesitation about the syllogism, in fact proceeded. Austin's problem was that he accepted in theory that we only observe things as disconnected particulars. But we have sought to show in the last chapter that he cut through this problem by attributing magical properties to language, which enabled us to organize reality in propositions of the traditional logical form – to produce products which were simply *true* of all the particulars we observed. Austin arrived at Anderson's result, for practical purposes, by a feat of logodaedaly.

One consequence of Anderson's general approach as above described is to reject propositons of any other kind than those belonging to formal logic as unempirical, including those of deontic logic in which the copula joining subject and predicate is not 'is' (which indicates that the function of the subject is to locate the predicate spatio-temporally, consistently with the view of reality as happenings) but 'ought'. Insofar as they have empirical meaning, which is equivalent to having any meaning at all, they are propositions which describe attitudes of approval or disapproval, perhaps claimed to be shared with others, to events. From this point of view, the attempt to suggest that one is uttering propositions about something objective outside oneself when making moral judgments is taken to be an attempt to disguise the personal reference of the statement being made. Just as, from the jurist Jerome Frank's point of view, the attempt of a judge to refer his legal decision to an objective rule outside himself functions to enable him to disguise his personal responsibility for what is really a personal decision, so the fiction of an objective morality functions, from Anderson's point of view, to enable a person to disguise his personal responsibility for his own personal values. In all these matters, the present writer generally follows Anderson.*

Austinian myth

With the enthusiasm that scholars interested in Austin showed for revising what Austin said, usually in ways which departed from Austin's own fundamental philosophy, it was inevitable that the picture which scholars have of Austin himself would become obscured. We cannot trace this process in detail. But the results can be illustrated by looking at the characteristics which Robert S. Summers takes to be those currently attributed to legal positivism, of which school of thinking Austin was until recently the principal English representative, and then looking at the lack of relationship between these characteristics and Austin's actual views.

In 1966, Summers[60] said that the phrase 'legal positivism' is used to describe so many different things that it surely deserves to be junked. With citations, Summers describes 10 different views to which the phrase is used to refer. He considers that there is very little evidence that Austin or his successors, whom he classes as the 'older' analytical jurists, were positivists in some six of the senses in which the expression is used. Summers considers that the present writer's 'Some Myth About Positivism',[61] has disposed of one misconception, namely, that Austin believed that judicial decisions were logical deductions from pre-existing premises.

---

* Hutley's experiment in applying Anderson's notions in jurisprudence came to an end with the appointment of Julius Stone as Professor of Jurisprudence and International Law in the University of Sydney from the beginning of 1942. Stone's course was based on the definition of jurisprudence as the examination of law in the light of disciplines other than the law itself. In this scheme Austin's jurisprudence falls for consideration under the heading of examinations of the law in the light of logic. The treatment is embodied in J. Stone, *The Province and Function of Law* (Sydney, 1946) Ch. 2 and Julius Stone, *Legal Systems and Lawyers' Reasonings* (Sydney, 1964) Ch. 2. The present writer has criticized this approach in W.L. Morison, 'Some Myth About Positivism' (1958) 68 *Yale L.J.*, 212. Stone supposes a kind of separation in Austin's mind between logic and empirical fact in a very high degree, so that Austin is presented as one designing a logical dream of law which does not claim to represent either what is or what ought to be in any ethical sense of 'ought'.

Summers's first example of a view commonly attributed to the older analysts is the view that law as it is can be clearly differentiated from law as it ought to be. Austin obviously answered this question in the affirmative. But we have sought to show that the question has relations to a number of different questions. In its simplest aspect, Austin's view was that, if we ask of any provision alleged to be law existing anywhere or at any time 'Is it law?', we answer the question by examining whether it is the command of the sovereign. If we ask 'Ought it to be law?' we answer that question by examining whether it is the provision best serving the happiness of most members of the community in all the circumstances. The answers to the two questions may be the same, but they may not. If they are not, there is a contrast between the actual law and the provision which would serve utility in the circumstances. We believe that the first reason Austin thought it important to distinguish the two was that if we get the two questions confused we will obscure the truth about both. For Austin, it was always basically important not to obscure the truth. But, secondly, in this instance it was especially important not to obscure the truth because it might lead to easy assumptions that the law as it is coincides with the law as it should be, which was Blackstone's great error, whereas attention to distinguishing the two questions focuses what is required for reform.

We may, if we choose, distinguish Bentham's and Austin's concerns by saying that Austin was primarily interested in the first reason, whereas Bentham was primarily interested in the second reason because his primary interest was in what was required for reform. But we do not believe that they would have put the questions in any different way from one another. Getting at the truth about what one was confronted with performed a service towards getting what one wanted and neither of them would have disputed this. Austin confined himself in the first instance, in this context, to developing an account of law in general which would permit us to get at the truth about what the law was at any particular time – to achieve enlightenment. He no doubt exaggerated the utility of enlightenment in the community generally when he was writing his lectures, but he regarded the spread of enlightenment as the central force for good in the sense of human happiness. So he thought he was making a contribution to good.

It must not be supposed, however, that arriving at what the law on a point is at any given time was the only sort of enlightenment which Austin was primarily concerned to serve by presenting the account of law he did. If he did not keep the other objectives as steadily in mind as he might have done, this was in a large measure Bentham's fault. When Bentham said that jurisprudence could be divided into expository jurisprudence and censorial jurisprudence, the natural interpretation of this was that jurisprudence in sum, adding the two together, is concerned with what laws say and what they ought to say. To put it in current terms, exhibiting the influence of the conceptualists with their myriad ways of distinguishing form and substance, we may say that it suggests that jurisprudence in sum is concerned with the content of laws as they are and the content of laws as they ought to be. This is a hopelessly inadequate view of the total of jurisprudential concerns and was put forward by Bentham in a mood of preoccupation with the particular question of what would be a complete expression of legislative will.

When he was not preoccupied with that kind of question, Bentham's language suggested that there might be a science of the way law operated upon particularly the human material with which it had to deal. Austin did at times seek to inquire into the causes of legal phenomena in this spirit, and no doubt again felt that in this inquiry he was serving purposes of a legislator anxious to arrive at laws which would promote happiness. Austin warned, however, against a jurist performing the function of assigning causes, confusing the actual causes to be discovered with those he thought ought to exist. Austin proposed to confine himself to the former kind of question at least in the first instance, no doubt for analogous reasons to those which induced him to concentrate, in the aspect of his work discussed above, on how his account of law enabled one to discover the actual content of laws at a given time. In sum, for reasons going to enlightenment and the service of enlightenment to happiness Austin calls for a sharp distinction between 'is' questions and 'ought' questions, both about the content of law and the causes of law.

It remains to reiterate that Austin did not conceive these various 'is' and 'ought' questions as generally belonging on different logical or philosophical planes. The examination of what a sovereign commands and what is required for happiness, for example, are both just questions of relations between states of affairs capable of representation in the sort of 'is' propositions to which traditional logic is confined. The only interest he showed in finding justifications for the principle of utility itself was to say briefly it was an index to the Laws of God, and what sort of special logical or philosophical problems that sort of statement might raise was a question he left to others.

A second view which Summers finds treated as characteristic of positivism is that only the concepts of existing positive law are fit for analytical study. This is certainly not an Austinian view, despite the stimulus which Austin's work provided for expository text book writing in particular fields of law as we explained at the end of the last chapter. Austin thought the most general notions of what was involved in law were applicable to any community which was not in a state of nature, whether past, present, or future. This goes back to Hobbes. On the other hand, Austin indicated in his remarks on the uses of jurisprudence that he did not expect all his more special classifications used in mapping legal systems to be applicable to any actual system anywhere. Austin, further, obviously rejected the view that the classifications under which a jurist sees the rules of a system to fall will necessarily be 'concepts of the system' in the sense that those administering the system will utilize them for their own purposes. He admired German juristic analyses of the Roman law materials by reference to the German jurists' own classifications, and admired their habit of giving courses in law which would not involve exposition of any particular system. We have suggested that it is a weakness in Austin that he does not consider generally the ways in which the legislator's use of classifications for envisaging the system affect the operation of the system and the effectiveness of what the legislator does. In this aspect there is certainly a contrast to be drawn between Austin and Bentham, unfavourably to Austin.

Summers's third example of a view commonly regarded as positivist is the view that force or power is the essence of law. Certainly Austin treated the control of a sovereign person or body who was habitually obeyed as basic to law. We have suggested that the function of the sovereign in keeping society in a state of peace through the control that he exercised was something that especially appealed to Austin about law, Austin being the insecure sort of person he was. Austin recognized, however, that the degree of control of a particular sovereign who might come within his general definition would vary considerably and in his work on centralization he favoured a high degree of control by the sovereign, even though there might be a good deal of devolution of functions. This was a basic requirement for him of the pursuit through law of higher values than peace keeping itself. This does not mean, however, that he glorified force. The situation he did think ideal was where habitual obedience to the sovereign sprang from an enlightened populace's recognition of the fact that an enlightened sovereign was successfully pursuing the ends of the greatest happiness of the greatest number of the community. This is seen both in his lectures on jurisprudence and his political writings.

Summers's fourth example of a view commonly thought positivist is the view that law is a closed system which does not draw on other disciplines for any of its premises. This is not an Austinian view. It is more suggestive of views like Kelsen's — the kind of view into which Kocourek sought to translate Austin's theory, but without pretending that in doing this he was representing Austin as Austin would have represented himself. Typical of this kind of thinking is an approach to law analogous to the Kantian treatment of general philosophy and morals, in which a scholarly approach is seen as working with formal organizing principles on primitive materials presented to it through observation. It then becomes very important to maintain 'purity' — not to get mixed up between the organizing principles with which we might operate on particular material to arrive at the propositions of one discipline, and the different kinds of organizing principles with which we might operate on the same material to arrive at the propositions of another discipline. We have suggested that Austin was just impervious to this kind of thinking although he was exposed to it in Germany and possessed Kantian literature, and that this is also the expert judgment of Andreas Schwarz. Austin accepted that the same things fall under different classifications, but he did not go on to suppose that this could lead to us producing radically different kinds of propositions which were of radically different kinds of 'validity', in terms of radically different hypotheses, formed with radically different organizing principles. By attributing magical qualities to language, he came to the conclusion that even our most general propositions are just true in some general simple sense. Hence there can be true relations between the truths of different disciplines and the problems of having to think within closed systems do not arise. Austin frequently discussed the relations of other disciplines to law on this basis, both generally at the outset of his course and in particular contexts, and considered how other disciplines should affect the way we look at law. He does not seem to have talked about 'disciplines', a word which suggests that the different sciences are arrived at under different kinds of disciplines of thinking, but just about sciences.

The fifth view which Summers takes to be commonly regarded as positivist is the view that laws and decisions cannot, in any ultimate sense, be rationally defended. This springs from Hart's suggestion that insistence upon the distinction between law as it is and law as it ought to be has been, under the general head of 'positivism', confused with a moral theory according to which statements of what is the case ('statements of fact') belong to a category or type radically different from statements of what ought to be ('value statements'). Hart does not, however, find the latter view one that can possibly be applied to Bentham or Austin.[62]

This is a very complex question because the adherents of different philosophies will have very different notions of what constitutes a rational defence and different notions of how and how far statements of fact and value are to be distinguished, if at all. Some pragmatists, for example, interpret truth in terms of what serves other values than truth, in which case all statements become value statements, what is fact (truth) disappears as an independent question, and the only kind of rational defence possible is ultimately on some basis of usefulness for some other value. Austin, we trust it will by now be clear, was certainly not a pragmatist in this sense. For those who think in Kantian fashion – that rationality is thinking in terms of various disciplines of thought governed by different formal modes of thought – the relations of rationality, fact and value bear a different aspect. The 'rational' defence of any proposition will be concerned with its relations to more fundamental premises within the system determined by the 'category' of thought being used. Kelsen thought of what most people would think of as 'fact' questions, at least of any degree of generality, as being rationally organized under the 'category' of causality. But when we talk about what the law is, and thus when we rationally defend something as being law, as having legal 'validity', we are organizing according to a different formal category of thought. Rational defence becomes something different. The question is the validity of a rule or other norm of a system in terms of premises of the system arrived at using the appropriate discipline of thought. Kelsen apparently, unlike Kant, did not think moral theory could be a discipline in this sense, though law could. Hence he would not have thought, in this sense, that moral views could be rationally defended. But the evidence, we have suggested, is that

Austin never responded to this kind of thinking at all and therefore his views about the rationality of moral thinking are not to be taken as in any way relating to it.

Austin, we have sought to show, regarded the question whether something was law and whether something was morally justifiable as questions to be answered by a general simple test of truth or falsity. One sort of proposition was rationally defensible in the same way as the other, though they were different questions, one about the relation of something to what the sovereign commanded, the other about its relation to the production of human happiness.

The matter would certainly have become more complicated for Austin if he had felt compelled to explore the questions that we have indicated he left to John Stuart Mill. In the first place, we have seen that Mill said that, just so soon as we talk *in* rules or precepts (propositions of *art*) we make imperative statements as distinct from indicative statements. The question then must arise whether imperatives are somehow logically different from indicatives, and an affirmative answer might be expressed in the form that the former are value statements and the latter factual statements. Mill himself jumped through this question very quickly by saying that the Aristotelian logic is satisfactory for reasoning with rules and precepts without asking himself whether there are problems created by the fact that the copula in propositions of Aristotelian logic is 'is'. If he gave any thought to it at all, Austin must have thought that there was some simple answer to the question how imperatives could be rendered as 'is' statements. For, although in the moral field he advocated developing rules and maxims for conduct as a means of reducing individual calculations of the utility of our individual actions, it was precisely in this context that Austin insisted that any general proposition must be just generally true or false of the individual facts to which it related.

We have given our own answer to the problems of how imperative statements are to be understood as a kind of indicative statement in the previous chapter – as statements asserting what are the relations between other states of affairs and the state of affairs constituted by the wishes of the person making the statement, coupled perhaps with other indicative statements. There is, however, a further set of questions which may be thought to arise, the answer to which may be thought to involve value statements, namely the justifications one might make for the broadest propositions by which one expresses one's personal values. Austin justified utility by saying that it was an index to the will of God. For our own part, we do not think it possible to justify our own preferences except by referring to others of our preferences, which may or may not appeal to the person addressed. There are in this sense limits to the extent to which moral views can be rationally defended.

The sixth view which Summers suggests is attributed to positivists is that a logically self-consistent Utopia exists to which positive law ought to be made to conform. Austin's major objectives cannot be expressed in this way.

His initial objective was to find a set of definitions and classifications by reference to which *any* system of positive law could be understood. Not all systems would have all the features falling under all of the classifications included. No doubt there would be some relation between Austin's idea of a system which had all of them and an 'ideal type' of system in the sociologist Max Weber's sense. But the objectives are different. Weber's object was to enable comparisons of different kinds of systems by reference to their approximation to different ideal types. Austin's object was to develop basic notions for the general science of law as he understood it. The fact that a system coincided with an ideal type in Max Weber's sense would not mean that it was specially desirable. The fact that a system had made some provisions under all of Austin's classifications probably would in Austin's eyes say something for the efficiency of its machinery, though this would not preclude its detailed provisions being inconsistent with one another or serving in Austin's eyes undesirable substantive values. It is a safe inference that Austin thought any legislator should carefully attend to his definitions and classifications when framing legislation. But just how many he thought should be in some way officially adopted in any system is a matter on which we have remarked in other connections we find him uninformative or obscure.

Summers's seventh example of a view attributed to positivists is that, in interpreting statutes, considerations of what law ought to be have no place. Bentham and Austin certainly share the view that a judge has no authority to depart from the clear words of a statute, and believe that in case of doubt regard should be had to the legislator's reasons rather than the judge's in the first instance. But Austin is in favour of judicial legislation generally, especially by reference to considerations of utility, and seems to suggest that this might occur by adopting the analogy of statutes as well as judicial decisions. Unfortunately, his work in this respect is incomplete, as he deferred full consideration of the question until after he had explored the nature of analogy, and apparently did not succeed in returning to it.

The eighth view which Summers finds commonly attributed to positivists is that judicial decisions are logical deductions from pre-existing premises. That Austin thought that this is universally the case is hopelessly inconsistent with what both Bentham and Austin say about judicial decisions. The present writer has assembled some of the evidence about this in the article mentioned by Summers. The view appears to derive from the importance which Austin attached to the logic of judicial decisions coupled with a tendency in writers making this assessment to identify logic with syllogistic inference. But Austin had reservations about whether the syllogism – Bentham's 'nonsense physics' – had any substantially useful part to play in logic at all, and Mill's *Logic* certainly leaves it with only a limited place. In cases of first impression, Austin's view, plainly asserted, is that the judge's decision should be determined by a variety of factors centring about utility, and is in fact determined by these or other factors which Austin discusses as causes of decisions.

The ninth view which Summers sees as typically attributed to positivists is that they regard certainty as the chief end of law. Of course, Bentham and Austin regard clarity in legal rules and their economical statement as important for law's effective functioning, including its cognoscibility by the citizens, the simplicity of reforming it as required from time to time and the predictability of its operation in individual cases, even though preoccupation with law as general rules limited the effectiveness of Austin's treatment of other aspects of the system affecting its predictability in operation. But their object in demanding this is ultimately, as always, the contribution of law to the advancement of the greatest happiness of the greatest number.

The final view which Summers sees treated as positivist is that there is an absolute duty to obey evil laws.* Austin rejects this. He says that so momentous is the difference between a bad and good government that, if it would lead to a good one, resistance to a bad one would be useful. The anarchy attending the transition is an extensive, but passing evil. The good which would follow the transition is extensive and lasting.

In sum, of the views taken to be distinctive of the school of which Austin is perhaps the most famous representative, perhaps one in ten is applicable to Austin himself without reservations.

---

* The above ten views sometimes taken of theories of the Austin type are set out on p. 889 of Summers, 'Jurists'.

6

A defence of Austin's philosophy against Hart

A modern empirical theory of law

In the preceding chapter we have looked at theories which were in the Austinian tradition either in the sense that they demonstrate Austinian influence in a number of contexts, while being critical of Austin in others, or because they concentrate upon topics in which Austin had excited interest. What emerges is their lack of interest in, or disagreement with, what we regard as most valuable in Austin: the attempt to represent law as concerned with events which are empirical in the sense of being open to ordinary observation and yet constitute a scientific field of study which can be presented systematically by the methods of traditional logic. The result was that theories which are Austinian in one of the above senses never seriously attacked the problem of correcting Austin's highly unsatisfactory specific theory of law by the use of Austin's philosophical and logical approach. On the contrary, what happened was that these fundamental features of Austin's approach came to be ignored or, still worse, obscured, so that a good deal of myth about Austin's work developed.

The situation was transformed in the United Kingdom with the appointment of H.L.A. Hart to the Chair of Jurisprudence in Oxford in the mid twentieth century, almost a hundred years after Austin died. Now for the first time, both Austin's philosophy and his specific theory of law were squarely examined and perceptively assessed, while many aspects of the Austinian myth which had developed were dissected and attacked. The new theory of law which Hart developed not only pays close attention to those legal phenomena, among others, with which Austin had been especially concerned, but it is an empirical theory of law as well. It is not, however, an empirical theory of the particular Austinian brand which we have just described, and which we may distinguish henceforward by the expression 'naïve empiricism'. The Hart theory, which came to replace Austin in the standard jurisprudential education of the British law student, drew rather on twentieth-century developments in the long history of British empirical philosophy generally.

The present writer wishes nevertheless to continue to defend Austin's empiricism in what he sees as its general drive, both against the different philosophy of Hart and against some aspects of Hart's specific legal theory which we consider implicated with Hart's general philosophy. Such a defence, however, would fall short of being constructive if it did not attempt to show that it is possible to find or develop a theory of law lacking the deficiencies of Austin's own, yet capable of accommodating his philosophical notions without violence to its main tenets. We do not find it necessary to develop one. It is to be found in the legal theory of Harold D. Lasswell and Myres S. McDougal, to the general tenets of which the present writer subscribes. In the present section, we seek to show how the main positive features of this legal theory can be interpreted in terms of Austin's philosophy. In the concluding section we seek to show how some of its critical features, similarly interpreted, can be used to reinforce criticisms of features of the Hart theory which can be made by direct appeal to Austin's philosophy.

Lasswell was a graduate at the Bachelor's and Doctor's levels in the University of Chicago and subsequently a faculty member, and a prime mover in what was called the 'behavioural revolution' in political science. In the 1930s he accepted visiting appointments at the Yale Law School, and became a professor there shortly after the second world war, continuing to work with McDougal until their long association was severed by Lasswell's death in 1978. McDougal is a Southerner from Mississippi who began his academic career instructing in Greek, studied law, and particularly legal history, in Oxford, and, as a professor at Yale, moved from property to international law and jurisprudence. Even before his association with Lasswell, he was associated with a number of jurisprudential thinkers at Yale of the kind classed as realist. The present writer has sought to summarize elsewhere the relation of Lasswell's and McDougal's jurisprudence to twentieth-century legal thinking generally,[1] and confines himself here to their treatment of questions of particular relevance to Bentham's and Austin's work.

While there are some close relations between Benthamite thinking and the Lasswell – McDougal theory, what influence there was appears to have been largely indirect. Benthamite thinking underwent various modifications in the course of exerting influence on the development of the social sciences. Lasswell and McDougal made a close examination of the social sciences in relation to law, and drew their own conclusions for legal theory. In the result, the Benthamite notions which can be discerned in their theorizing have undergone transformation. For example, at a very early stage of the *Principles*, Bentham says that nature has placed human beings under two masters, pleasure and pain. The corresponding proposition in the Lasswell – McDougal theory is that human beings act, at the conscious or unconscious level, to maximize their values. The attempt to quantify values in terms of pleasure and pain had not been found satisfactory in the social sciences generally, and the reference to the unconscious is a specific reference to Freudian psychology which was unavailable to Bentham.

Lasswell and McDougal do not commit themselves to philosophical stances on all the matters on which the present writer does, and has done in relation to Austin's thinking. This is, at least in part, a deliberate matter of Lasswell's and McDougal's policy. They wish to cooperate with thinkers of various philosophies and do not go so far in defining their own positions as would exclude others unnecessarily from cooperation.

For example, they confine their examination of their own values to observations of them on the empirical level, being concerned to specify what empirical results they are aiming at − the results in the world open to ordinary observation. But they do not reject the possibility of justifying these results by reference to 'transempirical' considerations. What they call for is that those who may engage in such justifications specify the results in this world which their own kinds of justifications require, so that there can be common ground about cooperation for achieving those empirical results.

Again, Lasswell and McDougal do not speculate about other-worldly, theological or metaphysical, explanations of what we observe on the empirical level. They do expect it to be possible to present a coherent account of what we observe on the empirical level without resort to other-worldly explanations, but the present writer does not understand that they would want to reject the possibility of such explanations, as the present writer himself would.

Hence, in indicating how Lasswell's and McDougal's theory may be seen in relation to Austin's philosophical problems, we must not be understood as attributing our own philosophical assessment of either to Lasswell and McDougal. Rather we are concerned to show how their theory satisfies the requirements of a philosophical approach like that of Austin and the present writer, as applied to the legal field, without our wholly identifying them with it.

Lasswell and McDougal take their stand, as Austin did, as social scientists specially concérned with enlightenment about law as one of those sciences.[2] This affects their approach to what they describe as establishing their focus of attention − what Austin thought of as the problem of definition. A deficiency in Austin's logic appears to have disguised from him the extent to which the way we define things depends on the direction of our interest. Mill did understand that the great complexity of characters possessed by things we observe means that there is a problem of selecting for definitional purposes those characters, among the many we might choose, which will best serve our scientific purpose if that is the dominant interest we have. Lasswell and McDougal emphasize that what law means in the mouth of the legal official or adviser, when he is determining what the law is on a point, is a quite unsuitable notion for determining one's focus of attention for scholarly purposes.

There are two reasons why professional meanings for words are likely to prove unsatisfactory to the scholar. The first is that the meaning is likely to shift in the mouth of the professional man, especially when confusion may serve his advocatory purposes of persuasion or justification. Bentham and Austin detected a confusion of this kind between the legal and moral and set out to eliminate it by identifying law for their purposes with positive rather than moral law. But their definition of positive law was a disaster, firstly because it was only a minor modification of the professional man's notion of law, and, secondly because it was achieved by appealing to a supposed state of affairs which nobody since Bentham's and Austin's time has felt able to believe in. What Bentham and Austin did was to turn the professional man's notion of legislation by the supreme authority in the system into their own notion of law generally, which involved the supposition that the legislator tacitly approves all the other acts which the professional man regards as being of legal effect. Subsequent positivists fell back on associating law with rules enforced or laid down by the courts, another principal focus of the professional man's concern. In so doing they found themselves abandoning the scientific empirical approach, with varying degrees of consciousness, reluctance, or satisfaction about this. Making empirical sense at all, on the basis of any plausible representation of what goes on, requires a more radical departure from professional notions of law than that embodied in any of the theories so far considered.

The second unsatisfactory feature of professional notions of law for social scientific purposes is that they are so narrow that they do not enable us to consider matters together which must be considered together to make sense for scientific purposes. Vital aspects of situations needing to be considered turn out to be excluded from our focus of attention. A legal administrator puts blinkers on the 'eye of the law' for reasons of rapid dispatch of business in his situation as well as for less cogent reasons. Austin constantly found himself accused of digression. Sometimes this was for bad reasons, but sometimes through his own fault because his definitions were too close to professional notions adopted for purposes alien to his own. He excluded by his definition from law some matters which he especially wanted to teach, such as international law.

In the light of these considerations, Lasswell and McDougal make their focus of attention law in the sense of processes of authoritative and controlling decision among political (power) processes in the community. By 'decisions' they mean the making of commitments in the expectation that this will lead to severe deprivations (frustration of someone's or some definite or indefinite group's objectives) or to high indulgences (rewards). Decisions are 'authoritative' when they are in a significant degree in accordance with community expectations about who is to make them, the criteria to be applied, and the procedures to be followed. They are controlling when the outcome sought by the makers of the commitments is realized in a significant degree. 'Communities', for the purposes of the above, are defined by reference to intensity of interaction within areas ranging from the local to the global.[3]

This notion of law is empirical in that it points to happenings, as Austin's did, though to a much broader range of events mental and physical. It is also empirical in the sense that there is no attempt to find a centre of comprehensive control in a community in order to define law. To attempt to find a comprehensive or omnipotent centre of control is anti-empirical, for we just do not observe this kind of phenomenon by ordinary means. We have to assume or conceptualize or abstract it and empiricists prefer to avoid these activities.

Therefore what Lasswell and McDougal set out to examine is the interactions of decision making processes within different communities, as well as the relations between those processes and other community processes out of which claims come to community decision makers and which the decisions made in turn affect. In this respect, Lasswell's and McDougal's empiricism involves a radical departure from Austin's approach. Austin recognized, as we have seen especially in the first part of chapter 4, that control of the sovereign over the people was very much a matter of degree, but it is unempirical to suppose that there will be a centre of gravity in a modern community at all. What Lasswell's and McDougal's approach involves is that we can find degrees of success and failure in relations between effects aimed at and produced in different kinds of decision making processes within a community.

In the same way as Lasswell and McDougal decline to find a centre of control of the community in any special kind of decision making process, so they reject the notion that there is any systematic body of controlling rules of the kind which substitutes for the notion of a comprehensive controlling decision process in some positivist – and other – theories. Austin's theory could unfortunately be adapted in this direction and was, for example, in the suggestion that the true drive of his theory was in the direction of a theory like Kelsen's.

Lasswell and McDougal do not deny that decision makers' notions of what is 'law' for them, in the sense of what they commit themselves to respect, is a mental factor of importance in influencing decision. But just how important it is is a matter for investigation in each case and greatly varying answers may be found. The sources which they in fact respect may differ a great deal from those which they purport to respect, and so do the degrees of respect which are given, particularly having regard to the complexity of the ways in which sources of law are discussed.

It is, in any case, always the respect actually shown for what emanates from particular sources which has to be examined, and not some mysterious 'binding force' which rules supposed to call for obedience from decision makers or citizens may be supposed to have independently of the extent to which they are in fact respected. A judge, for example, may often speak as if there were some such binding force in such a way that he appears to escape responsibility for what is, from the empirical point of view, a personal decision. But 'Law', as commonly used by lawyers and private citizens, only makes empirical sense as a reference to someone's commitments, the speaker's or someone else's, or both. These commitments are part of what Lasswell and McDougal feel called upon to take under consideration but, as we indicated at the outset, by no means the whole of what must be taken under consideration for a comprehensive view of decision processes and their relations to community processes.

There is a strong body of current opinion which nevertheless defines law by reference to rules, conceiving these as community standards and purporting to relate them empirically to community practices. But this seems inevitably to become conceptualist. They present the supposed common standards as more comprehensive and coherent than they in fact are. The account of what is involved in statements supposed to invoke the common standards comes to contain such complex references to what 'we' mean by them that the only answer one can make is 'speak for yourself'.

A riposte that one may encounter to the 'speak for yourself' response is to the effect that one cannot get away from a rule approach if one is to talk about law at all, that any simple attempt to give an empirical account of rules themselves in terms of stimuli from some source and response to those stimuli will not suffice, and that Austin's example illustrates this. It is undoubtedly the case, as we have seen, that Austin got into difficulties by identifying law by reference to what emanated from the sovereign, and then fell into identifying what was to be attributed to the sovereign by using expressions like 'character' or 'capacity' or 'mode'. These turned out to be explicable only by resort to rules, even in Austin's own mind. But the conclusion we should draw from this is, not that it is impossible to give an account of law in terms of sociological facts of another sort than rules, but that in the particular circumstances Austin involved himself in circularity of definition.

It is not as if the attempt to identify legal phenomena by reference to rules does not have its own circularity problems. To many people Kelsen does not appear to have satisfactorily answered criticisms that an attempt to identify the State, for example, by reference to rules that are generated by what he regards as State organs, is circular. Salmond was aware of problems with identification of the courts if he claimed that law was rules enforced by the courts, when he wished to emphasize that the courts were set up by rules. We have criticized his attempts to deal with this problem by reference to 'ends' of the courts.

We believe the true position to be that even though rules have something to do with who exercises the immediate supervision over the exercise of force on behalf of the community against individuals, the complexity of observed reality enables us to identify courts just by saying that they exercise that kind of supervision. We need not refer to the fact that they answer various other descriptions including those involving rules in an empirical sense. We may, however, find that what answers our definition in a community is not quite what it might be expected to be in terms of someone's rules or somebody's ends. All the better for proper empirical investigation.

In summary, a proper empirical focus of attention on decisions we class as legal calls for attention to a wide variety of decisions without any preconception that we shall find a legal centre of gravity in any community, whether in demands emanating from any one institution whatever it is, or in some governing rules which 'go', however identified, or even in competing sets of coherent bodies of rules. In any community there will be a wide variety of factors determining the relations between the decisions made within particular kinds of institutions – how decision makers within each react to demands emanating from others – certainly with notions of authority having some importance but also operating with various degrees of organization and disorganization. Hence our examination of them always requires us to ask the empirical questions: who is responding to whom, why, and how? There will be other ideas than notions of authority involved, some operating unconsciously, and there will be factors which cannot be classed under the head of ideas at all.[4] And what is true of relations of legal institutions to one another will be true of the relations of legal institutions to outside forces. All this is law for the scholar with the attitude of Lasswell and McDougal.

Our authors' delineation of their focus of attention naturally leads on to the examination of what sorts of questions they will attempt to answer in relation to the field they have so marked out. Our special interest in this part of Lasswell's and McDougal's theory from an Austinian point of view is that, although these questions are very much more comprehensive than Austin allowed himself to ask within the confines of his expository jurisprudence, they are all questions which can be answered in indicative propositions which are true or false in the general simple sense. This, coupled with Lasswell's and McDougal's empirical focus of attention, is why we regard their theory as providing a satisfactory fulfilment of the specific kind of scientific aspiration for law which Austin represents in British jurisprudence.

Lasswell and McDougal classify these questions under five headings, though emphasizing that this is only for the purpose of relative emphasis. They are not proposing to set up mutually exclusive philosophical categories with separate logics. They call the five investigations which they specify 'intellectual tasks'. These are the clarification of their own goal values, the description of trends in decision, the analysis of causal conditions explanatory of those trends, the projection of future trends of decision in the absence of intervention by the investigator, worked out in the light of past trends and their operative causes, and, finally, the evaluation of policy alternatives for the future in the light of the goal values which the investigator has clarified for himself at the outset.

In classifying both their own values for the purposes of clarifying them at the outset, and in classifying the values of others as well for the purposes of the investigations required by the later tasks, Lasswell and McDougal exhibit the kind of indirect Benthamite influence to which we have earlier referred. They have begun, like Austin, with a kind of definition. They proceed as Bentham began in the *Principles* by clarifying their own goal values, which is something Austin never worked out in systematic detail.

We saw that he defined utility, but never proceeded as Bentham did at the beginning of the *Principles*, once he had explained utility, to the classification of pleasures and pains, which is for Lasswell and McDougal the problem of classification of goal values – their own and those of others.

Austin was right in predicting that economics would occupy a key position in the social sciences, but wrong in supposing that Ricardo's and James Mill's works would prove to contain a definitive account of the field. The Benthamite notion that masses of individual wants could be somehow mathematically added up in terms of the degree of satisfaction and dissatisfaction produced, so that one could arrive at the greatest happiness of the greatest number, failed to survive the test of use by economists as it did the test of philosophic criticism. The present writer has attempted to summarize some standard philosophic criticisms elsewhere.[5] Wants, and still more the effective demands with which some economists have been particularly concerned, can only be measured in some kind of market, even if, in the case of individual wants, it might be in the market of the individual mind and heart – in his 'scales of values'.

So Lasswell and McDougal do not speak of pleasures and pains, but they do believe that an account of society can be given by reference to people pursuing values (objectives) of different kinds through institutions in which values of those kinds are pursued and 'disposed of' – in which various successes and failures are achieved – with a degree of specialization in institutions to values of particular kinds. Bentham's classifications of pleasures, and largely correspondingly of pains, were those of sense, wealth, skill, amity, good name, power, piety, benevolence, malevolence, memory, imagination, expectation, those dependent on association, and relief. Some of these classifications stood the test of workability in the social sciences better than his general theory did, and were gleaned from the social sciences, with their own systematization, by Lasswell and McDougal. Hence they emerge with seven of their eight value categories related to those of Bentham. They categorize values into power (pursued and disposed of in political, including legal, institutions), enlightenment (disposed of in educational institutions), wealth (in economic institutions), well-being (in medical and physical educational institutions), skill (in craft institutions), affection (in domestic institutions), respect (in institutions of honour), and rectitude (in religious and civic institutions).

In the goal clarification task, Lasswell and McDougal are seeking to clarify their own values for law and society. To this extent their theory of morals is thus far what Hart calls 'subjective' or 'non-cognitive',[6] and is what the present writer thinks any theory of one's own values must be. Values do not float in the air to be discovered rather than adopted, though Hart's words are, in the present writer's view, advisedly put in inverted commas. A statement about what one approves oneself is just as objective as any statement about what anyone approves and just as cognitive, provided it is understood one is observing one's own relations to projected situations conceived as something one designs to happen. Propositions about this are either true or false in the ordinary way – one may, for example, be deluding oneself about what one stands for.

The term by which our authors refer to their goals in the broadest fashion, the achievement of human dignity, they put forward as an envelope term for eight objectives. These are the widest possible shaping (production) of values and the widest possible sharing (consumption) of values in each of their eight value categories. Even then they seek to make further more precise specifications of what they wish to pursue. They are alert to what is being done by definition and what is to be done by an investigation of what they find their goals to be after exposing themselves to a variety of observations and studies.[7]

Lasswell's and McDougal's second intellectual task, the description of trends of decision, comes closest to comprising an examination of the kinds of authoritative materials which Austin regularly included in his lectures. But the different definition of the focus of attention means, in the first place, that the materials to be examined are much wider. In the examination of any individual decision the concentration is not simply upon the legal positions of the participants in the decision process and those with relations to it, which tended to be Austin's focus as a matter of his practice, but rather the value positions of these persons. That is to say, we are concerned with such matters as their success in enhancing their values through the decision in question or their failures, and the values at their command which they are able to exploit ('base values') in seeking to achieve a favourable outcome (in pursuing 'scope values'). Thus the decisions are examined by reference to the participants in any decision process, their situations, their base values, their strategies, the outcome in the decision and its effects. Legal positions along the lines of Austin's notions of them will certainly be relevant. Claims about legal positions may be a strategy resorted to by some participants and influence the decisions. But the investigator's resort to authoritative materials will be in that kind of context and will fall short of yielding a satisfactorily comprehensive body of information for all that needs to be investigated.[8]

In addition, there is more clarity about the objectives of the 'exposition' – the description of past trends – than there is in Austin's case. We have suggested that Austin did not quite sort this matter out because he seems to have attempted to reconcile the notion of a science like James Mill's political economy with Bentham's notion of an expository jurisprudence. In Lasswell's and McDougal's case, the immediate object of examining trends of decision is to provide material for the discovery of causal factors behind decisions: for the scientific task. An incidental matter they emphasize in this connection, one on which there is some obscurity in Austin, is that they do not expect the classifications they use for their scholarly examination to coincide with the classifications used by the participants in the particular decision making process they are examining. They expect the decision makers' classifications frequently to be bemusing, though they would certainly consider that decision makers would achieve more clarity and effectiveness for purposes they approve if they proceeded in the way Lasswell and McDougal themselves do.

When they move to the central scientific task, and that is what they call it, of detecting causal factors influencing decisions, our authors are especially concerned to find regularities in factors influencing the decisions they have been examining. But they expect to find those regularities to be a reflection of rules appealed to by decision makers only to a very limited extent, although it is always matter for investigation without rigid preconception. The regularities may be in other kinds of influences. In the present writer's view, there will always be *reasons* for decision, which are applications of laws of nature, but they may be reasons the understanding of which only enables us to understand why the rules are in a shambles. Lasswell and McDougal examine cultural, class, interest group, and individual personality factors working upon participants in decision processes.[9] Our authors are, of course, not looking at this point for justifications of the decisions in their own eyes, but explanations, which may show either that decisions are likely to move towards or away from situations in accordance with Lasswell's or McDougal's own values. It is with the aid of the products of the scientific task that our authors move to the predictive task and attempt to make projections of the likelihood of the distribution of values in the future – favourable or unfavourable to what they would like to see – assuming at this point that they do not themselves seek to exert influence over future events.[10]

The major object of the predictive task in Lasswell's and McDougal's scheme is to provide the basis for the performance of their culminating intellectual task, the evaluation of policy alternatives. Here answers are sought to the question: What kind of intervention in future developments might be expected to move those developments in the direction of our authors' own preferred goals.[11] Austin cut himself off from these questions by distinguishing his own expository jurisprudence from the science of legislation, even though he did not intend the divorce to be permanent in his own case. It was a matter of his priorities.

The ideal kind of situation is conceived differently by Lasswell and McDougal from Austin's notions. Like Bentham, Austin favoured a comprehensive code, even though he expected it to be a lot longer in coming than Bentham did, and expected subsequent amendments required by social changes to be in small compass. On the other hand, Lasswell and McDougal are much too impressed by the volatility of social developments to expect policy making at fundamental levels of law-making to be other than continuous.

Lasswell once described the kinds of propositions which represent the products of the performance of Lasswell's and McDougal's intellectual tasks as consisting in 'reporting'. This points to the fact that all the answers to their questions are descriptions of events, including mental events of their

own, of other persons, and relations of mental events to other events empirically understood. Lasswell and McDougal describe the scholar's function as
the intelligence function, in the sense in which that term is used in the armed
services. We believe that this approach would have struck much more of a
chord with John Austin than in merely taking him back to his army days. He
would have seen in it a notion reflecting his fundamental outlook on a world
of which law was part – which exhibited itself in straightforward indicative
truths.

Austin and Hart

There was never a stage at which Austin was discarded from English legal
education. But after H.L.A. Hart's appointment to the Chair of Jurisprudence at Oxford following A.L. Goodhart's resignation in 1952, a new
interest was demonstrated in the assessment of Austin's theory from a broad
philosophical approach, a reassessment in which Hart was the leading
figure. Hart's activity in this respect is shown by his edition of Austin's
Province of Jurisprudence Determined in 1954 and in other ways. It does not
affect this fact that Hart's own book *The Concept of Law* came largely to
replace Austin as the foundation of an education in analytical jurisprudence.
It is the quality of the new interest in Austin rather than its quantity with
which we are here concerned. Hart was subsequently involved in most
extensive activity in bringing Bentham material to light and in reassessing
Bentham.

In his work, *H.L.A. Hart*,[12] in the *Jurists* series of which the present work
is one, Neil MacCormick attributes Hart's initial concern with Austin to the
desire to make a fresh start from the station in which the locomotive of
British jurisprudence seemed to have broken down.[13] MacCormick sees this
choice of starting point as a reaction to the fact that two great movements in
nineteenth-century thought had gone stale. The first was the Bentham
–Austin tradition. The second was the school of historical jurisprudence.
Hart, in MacCormick's view, regenerated British jurisprudence, particularly through resort to recent developments in British philosophy.[14] From
these, Hart was led to the conclusion that the nature and importance of
studies in analytical jurisprudence spring especially from the fact that
clarification of the legal order is linguistic and conceptual in focus and
concern. A fundamental type of question that has to be asked is: 'What do we
mean when we say X?' One fundamental thing which emerges from this
approach, MacCormick says, is that not everything we say is true or false. At
least some statements – by way of example only of large classes of statements which do not answer the 'true or false?' question – are performative
statements, are acts, and may be various kinds of collaborative exercises.
The words do not just 'stand for' things. To understand the use of terms
which do not, it is necessary to reflect upon the contexts in which they are

characteristically used. It is one of Hart's objects to re-examine what is required for legal analysis from this general approach.[15]

Even on the basis of this summary which MacCormick expands as he goes along, it will immediately appear that Austin is treated in the newer legal philosophy as having gone wrong much earlier and more basically than our own account has suggested he did, and that, from the approach of Hart's philosophy, the present writer is fundamentally wrong in respects in which he has presented Austin as being right. What was in practice Austin's simple notion of language as a picture of truth, whether we are talking about legal language or any other kind of language, is astray in areas upon which it is most important to concentrate for legal philosophy. Austin's empiricism was naïve.* In this respect, Bentham is seen as being superior to Austin in ways to one or two of which we have referred incidentally in our own treatment, such as the analysis of a 'right',[16] but in other ways as well which go beyond our own scope here.

The naïve empiricist, in which category the present writer includes both Austin and himself, is compelled to take issue with the new linguistic philosopher, on all of his fundamental planks as they are listed by MacCormick. We have been at pains to stress, in the last section of the preceding chapter, the extent to which we regard as what is most valuable about Austin his insistence that law and morals be approached on the basis that the propositions of which any account of them consists are simply true, simply false, or make no sense at all. We laid a similar stress when we were dealing with the questions which are raised in the course of Lasswell's and McDougal's intellectual tasks, which we saw as raising an adequate range of important legal questions in a way which Austin did not manage. We represented the questions raised by each task in a form in which the answers would obviously be simply true or simply false. We do not believe that we did any violence to the theory by so doing even if, as we acknowledged, Lasswell and McDougal do not have quite the degree of preoccupation with this problem which we do for our present purposes.

It was the same in this respect with matters going to defining the stand of the scholar and to fixing the focus of attention. The state of a man's mind, Lord Bowen once said, is as much a fact as the state of his digestion. This includes references to one's own observations about one's own attitudes to

---

* In 'Positivism and the Separation of Law and Morals' (1958) 71 *Harvard L.R.*, 593, 606, H.L.A. Hart describes a view, which he attributes to the 'Realists' of the 1930s, as 'perhaps too naïve'. The naïve view is described as accepting 'the conceptual framework of the natural sciences as adequate for the characterization of law and for the analysis of rule-guided action of which a living system of law at least partly consists'. Apart from the description of the analysis as being guided by a 'conceptual framework', rather than by beliefs about the common structure of the subject-matters of both classes of sciences the view which is described as 'naïve' is, we believe, that of both Austin and the present writer. From now on, we therefore adopt the expression 'naïve' empiricism to describe that view, by way of contrast with the more sophisticated empiricism which is associated with applying linguistic philosophy.

observable external realities and about one's own intentions to take particular parts of external reality which are capable of observation under consideration. From this point of view, the task of definition is not conceptual. By
this we mean that definition is not represented as built up by the mind with
the aid of organizing principles or in any other way – law, for example, is
not in this sense a 'concept'. It is a slice of observable reality, and all the
definer does is to decide for which slice he intends to use the term, and the
definition does tell us about his intentions in this respect.

The naïve empiricist does not say that words or other things which have
meaning may not function in other ways than by presenting the addressee
with pictures of observable reality. What he does say is that representing the
other functions as conveying meaning is highly confusing, even though in
popular language we may speak in this way, and that it does lead to
confusion. Nor does the naïve empiricist claim that there is any 'one to one'
picture relationship between words that are commonly used and the
observable reality which is pictured if the words have meaning. The task of
representing the sense of a statement once grasped, if indeed it has any, into
a 'one to one' word picture is the traditional task of traditional logic of
putting statements into logical form.

When a philosopher like Hart is explaining what he thinks is the meaning
of special kinds of terms, and proceeds to explain by describing the context
in which special kinds of words are used, he is likely, from the naïve
empiricist's point of view, to refer to considerations which, from that same
point of view, would be important for the purpose of putting the statements
that are made into logical form. But, from the naïve empiricist's point of
view, such a philosopher leaves the task incomplete, claims that it is
complete, and further claims that, in the sense that the naïve empiricist
would look for completion, it can never be complete because the naïve
empiricist is chasing a chimaera in supposing that he can put all significant
language into one or more propositions exhibiting the traditional logical
structure.

The linguistic approach appears to be associated with the view that there
are a number of special logics of different kinds of statements, though Hart
has put 'logic' into inverted commas when he has said that some legal statements have a special logic. For the naïve empiricist there is only one
logic – covering the general propositional and implicational characteristics
which everything we observe has – universally. If the term logic is applied
to more specialized structures, this implies for him that there are different
kinds of realities, which is unacceptable because it is then impossible to
represent the relations of those realities by propositions which would fall
within any of the realities being supposed. If I am told, for example, that
'shut the door!' is somehow a meaningful imperative which is different from
the ordinary indicative, I can only say, following the implications of Austin,
that it does not mean anything to me put like that. It is incomplete. I can put
it into logical form if somebody tells me who is saying 'shut the door' to

whom, and, if I did not know, it would be helpful for a linguistic philosopher to tell me what the sort of context is in which statements like that are used. Then I might look in the right direction for additional information. But it would be no substitute for completing my logical task to the point where it becomes an indicative statement that I can relate to other indicative statements.

It is the same with statements containing 'ought'. I am helped by being told the context, but I must complete the reduction to an indicative statement to make sense of it to myself. A deontic logic does not figure in the present writer's interpretation of traditional logic. There are an infinite number of specialized structures in observable reality. But why are a limited number of classifications of such structures to be singled out as logical?

The answer to this question seems to come back to the conceptualism that is claimed to be a virtuous aspect of an approach like Hart's but which the present writer cannot see in that way. When a philosopher like Hart is describing a legal system, the description does not appear to trace observable reality but, as it were, to hang from observable reality by its head. The top principle is treated as having at least a close relation to sociological fact, but thereafter there is a kind of conceptual building out, and we shall be bound to challenge this when we discuss this approach to the legal system in more detail. It is not as if we objected to conceptions in the sense of checklists of things we encounter in observable reality for purposes of guiding our observations. Austin's map of the legal system is like that. And these might be called 'conceptions' or 'theoretical models' or, in a sense, 'ideal concepts'. Our anxiety in that case is only that the theoretical model may be used too rigidly and we have indicated that we believe that there is often dogmatism when we are told what 'we' mean by some expression. Someone's theoretical model of what we may mean is too easily translated into a list of things we must mean. But this is a mildly objectionable type of conceptualism compared with the sort which builds out conceptually from reality, though the two may well be found in conjunction in the same theory.

In the result, for those who go along with the fresh philosophical approach to legal analysis, as Hart and many following or building upon him do, including MacCormick, further chapters in the correction of Austin since about 1960 are to be found in MacCormick's book, where Hart's relations to Bentham and Austin are pointed out at appropriate points.[17] For the reader who accepts the new philosophy, now is the time to lay down the present book, and continue the Austin story elsewhere. For at this point that reader leaves the present writer at the station where the locomotive of British jurisprudence is said to have broken down, watching the trains of the Hart followers and the Hart correctors and improvers roar through on their way to places undreamt of in the present writer's philosophy.

But they do at least roar through the Austin station. Ronald Dworkin[18] and Joseph Raz,[19] for example, introduce Austin as a jumping-off point for some topics. And here at least may be seen the continuing importance of

Austinian study. Edward Sackville-West and Desmond Shawe-Taylor once wrote of Mozart's Clarinet Quintet that many people have been led to explore the world of chamber music through its gate. For all the unmusical qualities which many find in Austin's style and mode of presentation, it is through the gate of John Austin's work that thousands of people have been led to explore the world of jurisprudence in common law countries – and continue to do so. For those like the present writer who share Austin's naïvely empirical approach to law – and, because they regard this as much the most important thing about Austin, continue to regard themselves as Austinians – the great importance of Austin's work is that it provides a kind of model of what an empirical theory of law is like. The fact that it was worked out in an absurdly simple fashion, with the aid of an enormous misrepresentation about tacit sovereign acceptance of various kinds of decisions, is from this point of view a virtue, just because it enormously simplifies the model as compared with reality. In addition, Austin called attention to at least some of the legal phenomena which have to be taken into account in working out any kind of empirical theory, naïve or otherwise.

From the point of view of a legal philosopher like Hart, Austin's theory is important not only because it calls attention to some legal phenomena which are of importance, but also because it is a convenient method of pointing up contrasts between the newer and the older philosophical approach. The newer legal philosopher points to a great many more features of legal phenomena than Austin was able to explore, mainly in the area of lawyers' talk and its analogies with other kinds of talk, and for this reason has a good deal of interest even to those who do not share Hart's philosophical presuppositions. The naïve empiricist must seek to give his own account of these phenomena, though under constant warning from a legal philosopher of Hart's kind that the naïve account inevitably must fail to grasp essentials if it stays within its own framework. In the remaining part of this chapter we say something, briefly and therefore necessarily impressionistically, about one of these phenomena, as well as some phenomena which Austin did explore but, from the point of view of the new philosophy, necessarily unsuccessfully. The present writer has attempted a fuller account of these matters elsewhere.[20]

An example of the legal phenomena which Austin failed to explore is the performative statement – or performative in a sense going beyond that in which any making of a statement is performative – which MacCormick sees as contrasting with the statement which attempts to give a mere picture of something in observable reality.[21] Perhaps we may call the latter kind the informative statement. To the naïve empiricist, all statements which have meaning, at least in what we should think of as the ordinary meaning of meaning, are informative statements. The naïve empiricist therefore must give an account of what are called performative statements, as of other things, along these lines. There is no lack of illustrative examples in law.

Lasswell and McDougal consider that in giving an account of legal decision processes, we must for a full account look both at the operations involved in the decision making and also the perspectives of those engaged in the decision making. Lasswell and McDougal define perspectives to mean the demands and the expectations of those participants, the term 'expectations' being used in a somewhat extended sense to mean the ways in which they see the past as well as the future. What the participants say in the course of argumentation and decision, for example, in court, includes statements in which they tell about the fact that *they* have certain perspectives, and these statements will therefore at least include a proposition which contains an 'I' or 'me' or 'my'.

The naïve empiricist sees nothing remarkable about these statements, in which somebody informs us about what is going on in his own mind, unless it be that they are commonly expressed in 'ought' language which is generative of the utmost confusion, especially about just whose perspectives are being described. The deliberate or unconscious generation of this confusion is possibly one of the oldest and most persistent tricks of advocacy known to the human race.

Among statements which include this reference to the speaker, there are some which do not merely inform us that something is going on in the speaker's own mind, but that the something relates to the act of making the statement itself – commonly that he hopes for something from that act. This may be that the speaker hopes that by making the statement he will succeed in changing legal relations – that the making of the statement will have a certain legal effect. Kelsen calls this the 'subjective legal meaning' of such statements. Kelsen distinguishes this from the 'objective legal meaning', which may not be the same. We should express this difference, though Kelsen would not, by saying that, while the person making the statement is ('subjectively') claiming that the commitments of the relevant decision makers in relation to his act are what he states, the claim may be ('objectively') unjustified.

When legal draftsmen are informing us that the making of a statement is aimed to be what Austin called an investitive or divestitive fact – but Hohfeld compressed to 'operative fact' – it is customary in some contexts to signal this by putting some of the words in a stereotyped form called 'operative words'. Among examples of this are the words 'Be it enacted' in an Act of Parliament, or 'the order of the court will be' at the end of a law case, or the words 'now this deed witnesseth' introducing the 'operative part' of a deed (following the preambles) or operative words of conveyance such as that the conveyor 'doth hereby grant bargain sell release and confirm'. The lawyer's frequent use of 'hereby', at which the layman laughs, is a reminder of the importance of the performative act to the lawyer.

But the present writer is unable to see in the phenomena just described anything which needs a new philosophy to explain. If I do any one of the above things, or at least those of them which there would be any point in doing in my non-authoritative position, I realize that my *making* of the statement has other objects than communication of information. But I think that the act of communication of information is part of the appropriate strategy for achieving that object in all the circumstances. And if I am told that in the account I have given there is a fundamental failure to grasp what I am about, I am bewildered. And if what I am being told is that Austin was not interested in all the aspects of the situation I have described – in all the volitions involved as well as in what is communicated – I am equally bewildered by this.

Another class of legal phenomena to which the newer legal philosopher gives attention include those with which Austin was centrally concerned, but which are regarded as incapable of satisfactory treatment in terms of his kind of philosophy. In this situation, we have noticed, the exposition of terms like right is included. A naïvely empirical approach to the description of legal positrons might be as follows. Suppose that A has a right as against B that B shall do X. This means that where B does not do X, the courts have committed themselves to imposing a sanction on B at the instance of A. Or suppose that A has a privilege against B that A may do X. This means that courts have committed themselves to refrain from imposing a sanction on A at the instance of B, where A does X. Or suppose that A has, against B, a power to change B's relations in manner X. This means that the courts have committed themselves to give effect to that change when appropriately approached. Correspondingly, if A has an immunity from having his relations so changed, the courts have committed themselves not to give effect to the change.

In the above statement, 'courts' is to be taken to mean those who are entrusted with the immediate supervision of the exercise of coercion on behalf of the community against individuals. When we talk of 'the courts' in the round, of course we cannot mean all courts before whom the matter might come. We are talking of dominant commitments in the way that any social investigator is looking for dominant commitments in any social field. It is very likely that on large numbers of matters no dominant commitments will be found. In this case, the conclusion is obvious. No legal position exists in relation to that matter.* We must further explain ourselves by saying that it is to be understood that the commitment has not been withdrawn, and that also is matter for investigation of the same kind.

Just what kind of investigations we will regard as establishing that the commitment we are looking for has been made, depends on the attitude we take to logic in relation to the law, and varies not only as between naïve empiricists and the newer legal philosopher, but as between different kinds of naïve empiricism. There is, for example, a view that the only point of time at which we can discover the existence of a commitment to a particular indi-

---

* We should not describe absence of commitment of the courts in relation to a situation as a privilege-exposure situation. Having no commitment whether to interfere or not (law unsettled) is not the same as having a commitment not to interfere.

vidual legal position of a person, is at the moment before it is individually implemented by a court. This view appears to be bound up with the notion that there are no adequately definable classes of things. Then, even though we might be able to discover a dominant expression of commitment of the courts to implement rights in all the circumstances falling within class A, this is not a real but a spurious commitment. For the notion of class A is bound to be so vague that what a judge brings within class A and what he puts outside it will be wholly within his discretion in *any* individual case that arises.

The above view is clearly not the Bentham–Austin view, in which enormous importance is attached to accurate classification, despite the tentativeness about what the present writer would think the related matter of the validity and usefulness of syllogistic argument. The difficulty about the view under discussion is that it proves too much. It is a sceptical view. If there can be no real meaning in assertions that, for example, a judge has committed himself to something in general terms – and this is put on broad logical grounds – neither can there be any real meaning in any general statement the sceptic himself makes about anything. Yet some sceptics about law are full of general statements about economics, or justice or morality, or sociological principles which they see as exclusively the determinants of decision.

We must not, however, be understood to say here that the fact that a commitment has been made is determinative of the individual decision, or that the other factors referred to above are causally unimportant either. Commitments, even if the individual judge subscribes to what has been found to be the dominant approach, can be revised, and might be revised in the course of the case. This may happen consciously or unconsciously. One way, for example in which confusion may develop is through surreptitious shifts in the meaning of law in the judge's mouth. As a matter of observation we find that a judge expresses the fact that he sees the judicial fraternity including himself as committed to X, by saying that X is 'law' (We should prefer 'of legal effect'). But sufficient confusion surrounds the fact that this is what is normally meant for shifts to occur, for example, to a meaning of law in terms of 'positive morality'. Of course, the judge may also quite deliberately prefer 'what social standards now require' to what his colleagues and himself have previously seen as their commitments. And if this takes hold, this piece of positive morality becomes legal, what the judges have committed themselves to implement in the course of their duties.

If we do not accept the sceptical view, we may then be prepared to accept that the existence of judicial commitments may be established as matter of inference. One of the fundamental issues betweeen a naïve empiricist and a legal philosopher like Hart seems to be the character of 'matter of inference' in the area of laywers' talk. It is at least implicit in the logical writings of Austin that, in the moral sciences as elsewhere, by reasoning from true premises by appropriate logical methods we arrive at true conclusions. The meaning of the proposition which constitutes the conclusion is its reference to a state of affairs, and this state of affairs exists quite independently of the reasoning by which we happened to arrive at it. We might have arrived at it in a number of different ways.

For a legal philosopher like Hart, however, it appears to be different. The existence of legal propositions, for example, constituting the premises and conclusions of legal reasoning, is never a matter of 'picture of reality' truth, and in most instances the 'validity' of the proposition – its being law – is not independent of the process of reasoning by which the 'lawness' of the proposition is reached as a conclusion. Moreover, the logic involved is regarded as of a special kind.[22] It appears to be largely these features of the approach which make the analysis of rights by a newer legal philosopher such an enormously complex matter, though no doubt there are additional matters involved in the complexity arising out of independent subtleties in what is involved in rights, which our own impressionistic account does not capture. The analysis of rights becomes virtually a science which seeks to be as exact as it is exacting.

In Hart's theory as developed in *The Concept of Law*, the supreme element in the 'recognition rule', which is, on his approach, at the basis of a legal system, is, in the United Kingdom, along the lines: 'What the Queen in Parliament enacts from time to time is law'.[23] On our own approach, what this might be expected to mean is 'What the Queen in Parliament enacts is something the judiciary have committed themselves to implement in the course of their duties'. Thus understood, it is a perfectly ordinary statement which is true or false in the ordinary way, and its truth or falsity may be investigated in the ordinary way. In fact, if it is investigated in this way, it turns out to be false. But, according to the Hart philosophy, this is not what it means, anyhow. The word 'law' does not have a meaning of the kind the naïve empiricist looks for. 'Is law' is sometimes represented by such a legal philosopher as 'counts as law' which indicates the function of these very broad propositions in which it appears. Their function is to specify criteria for the way we are to talk in the course of carrying out the game-like activity involved in legal-rule-guided behaviour – in the way we might specify the fundamental rules of a game before we start if we are explaining them to a newcomer to the game. The *existence* of the rule is something distinct from the truth of anything it purports to say. It is indicated by pointing to what in the case of a game would be the practice of those playing the game when they use the rule and, in the case of law, consists in pointing to the social practices in the course of which a recognition rule is used. This itself can be done in a naïvely empirical way.[24]

Hart claims that the judge, among others, looks to rules to guide and justify him.[25] This certainly seems to express something, or more probably a lot of things, which are true. Hart makes this point in opposition to people like Holmes who represent rules as predictions of what the judge will do. It would certainly be odd if a judge were to act generally with the object of satisfying someone's predictions about him. Hart certainly appears to be right in saying that that particular naïvely empirical account of rules fails to account for the phenomenon to which he refers.

But how is it with our own? In the theory of Lasswell and McDougal there is a proposition which represents a transformation of the hedonistic psychology of Bentham to the effect that people act to maximize pleasure and avoid pain – a part of the Bentham theory which, we have seen, rather troubled Austin because of criticisms to the effect that it seems to turn people into calculating machines. In Lasswell's and McDougal's hands, the transformed proposition is that people, at the conscious or unconscious level, act to maximize their values. And they may be values which the individual sees himself as sharing with his group, in relation to the performance of functions he shares with them – in the case we are considering, the group being the judiciary. On our interpretation, what the judge, typically though by no means always, means when he uses the word 'law' in his discussion of what the law is in the course of his opinion, is a review of these shared commitments. That he should find such a review helpful in the way of guidance does not seem implausible to us.

There is one legal phenomenon in particular which may, however, appear to cast doubt on the above account of what is happening in the 'standard case' of a judge talking law in his opinion. Sometimes a judge may say that 'left to himself', he would come to a quite different view from that to which he feels 'bound by law' to come. This may suggest that he is here thinking of law as something quite alien to his own commitments, and yet it has some mysterious coercive effect on him. If this is right, it would falsify not only our own particular account of the matter we are discussing, but Lasswell's and McDougal's maximization postulate generally. However, the answer seems to lie in the fact that everyone is in some degree a complex of conflicting demands, and the question in relation to the decision he reaches is which lot will win. If he feels 'bound' by the commitments of the group, it is, on the maximization postulate, because he is drawn to them by something in himself, particularly his wish to stay with the group, and in the circumstances we are discussing, it is that in himself which wins.

Just as the naïve empiricist finds himself at odds with Hart's legal philosophy concerning the account to be given of the character of the wider generalities of a system of legal propositions, so he finds himself giving a different account of the more specific ones. In Hart's legal philosophy, the arrival at more specific propositions of a system consists in playing the game involved in legal-rule-guided behaviour with the criteria which have been adopted through the basic 'rules'. The criteria are, through some logic, 'used' to arrive at more specific 'rules'. The existence of the inferior rules is their 'validity' in terms of the criteria. Their validity, which is their 'lawness' cannot be understood – cannot be given meaning – without reference back to the criteria.[26]

For the naïve empiricist, the *meaning* of 'lawness' is quite independent of the reasoning and is the same, however specific the prescription we are discussing. If we say that a particular judgment is of legal effect, we mean typically that the judiciary is committed to upholding it. If we arrive at this proposition in a particular instance by reasoning from more general propositions, the process of reasoning is of the perfectly ordinary syllogistic kind containing three factual propositions, or a string of connected syllogisms. For example, the reasoning might be: 'All things which this Act of Parliament directs to be implemented are law (things we are committed to implement). This is a thing which this Act of Parliament directs to be implemented. Therefore this is law.' This is a perfectly ordinary first-figure syllogism in the mood Barbara. The word 'law' in the major premise has exactly the same meaning in the major premise as in the conclusion – otherwise the *reasoning* is not valid. And the same is true if we broaden our premise so as to find ourselves with the syllogism: 'All things which a current Act of Parliament directs us to implement are law. This is a thing which a current Act of Parliament directs us to implement. Therefore this is law.'

This points to a contrast between the Hart and the naïve empirical approaches. Under the former we *must* give a different account of what is involved in saying that something is law when it appears in what we see as the major premise where, as in our second syllogism, the major premise is a fundamental rule of the system. Under the naïve approach we *cannot* give a different account. If we do, it makes the kind of reasoning which we see as involved invalid. It will be noted that under our older approach, validity is a characteristic of the reasoning we use in arriving at our conclusion. But the predicate of our conclusion is not the term 'valid'. It is 'law', with a quite different meaning. We might say that the conclusion as a whole is 'validly inferred' from something we believe is law. We might even say, in a particular case, that the reason we believe it is law is that we have validly inferred it from something we believe to be law. But that is not what we *mean* when we are asserting it.

For the naïve empiricist, the question arises how far we should be searching for broader generalities anyhow. Among the empiricists, McDougal in particular is profoundly suspicious of 'higher-level abstractions'. When we are talking about judicial commitments there is always a danger of representing particular judicial commitments in more general terms that those in which they actually exist, contributing to the ignoring of distinctions which justice demands. Nevertheless, there is a corresponding danger that if we do not represent them as systematically as the facts do justify, we will get them wrong. In his introduction to his edition of his father's *Analysis of the Phenomena of the Human Mind*,[27] John Stuart Mill stressed the importance in fields of moral science of what is sometimes called 'reducing the hypotheses' – putting the subject matter in the most general terms possible, rather than leaving a multiplicity of narrower principles which in fact are examples of broader ones. John Austin stressed the advantage to the practitioner of discovering the dependence of narrower applications of the law on broader principles. This was, of course, interpreted by some to mean that he thought the whole body of decision making was determined by, and determinate, in relation to a few broad principles, though his detailed work cries to heaven that he meant nothing of the kind. Certainly Austin could not have meant either that principles were to be found covering the whole of the law or that those which were to be found by empirical investigation were not subject to constant revision in the course of decision making.

Hart approaches the most general propositions associated with a legal system by treating it as a system of rules within rules. MacCormick interprets this to mean that Hart thinks of the fundamental secondary rules of a legal system as rules about its primary rules, though, no doubt rightly, he considers that Hart's statements fall short of complete clarity in this respect.[28] Hart's secondary rules of a legal system are its rule of recognition, its rules of change, and its rules of adjudication. The reader may pursue the details of how Hart himself sees the rules in Hart's own work and in MacCormick's book about it.[29]

From the naïvely empirical point of view, we have already indicated that what Hart makes the supreme element in the recognition rule of the United Kingdom is to be treated as an ordinary factual proposition, not as what might ordinarily be understood as a legal rule, and Hart himself does not insist upon its character as a rule, though for different reasons from our own. But is it a proposition about a rule? The naïvely empirical answer to this question is 'no', and the negative answer is based upon the logical character of informative propositions generally from the naïvely empirical approach. When we say that, for example, all A are B, on our own approach, while A *is* B, because that is what the proposition says, it remains true that if the proposition is to be significant – informative of what goes on – 'A' as it appears in the subject, is not recognized as 'A' by its attribute 'B' but by others. Otherwise it is a tautology (B is B) and not significant. This is sometimes put by saying that significant propositions are 'synthetic' – synthesize different attributes, even though the synthesis itself is regarded as existing in reality.

Since we for ourselves think of a rule as a demand (of some degree of generality in what is demanded) which is of legal effect (to which the judiciary have committed themselves), it is important, when we are asserting that something is a legal rule, to avoid thinking of the subject of our proposition by reference to the fact that it is a legal rule. On the Lasswell – McDougal empirical approach, we think of it as a claim, and any confusion of claims with matters going to the judicial response is to be avoided.

On this approach, Hart's supreme element in a recognition rule ('What the Queen in Parliament enacts from time to time is law') is to be understood as a proposition the subject of which is prescriptions, and in its relevant aspects to our present purpose, claims made on decision makers by Parliament. Hart's other elements in the recognition rule are, from this point of view, of the same kind, though best seen as distinct propositions than as other elements in a single proposition, which single proposition would have to be very complex on Hart's own approach, and will turn out to be more complex on our own.

Of course, we may assert propositions about rules. When we do, the subject of the proposition is 'Prescriptions which are law', or some class or specimen of rules in this sense. All we are saying is that any significant proposition in which the predicate is law is not like that, whether it is a proposition asserting what is law of the most general kind we can make on the facts (not an example of a broader proposition with the predicate law) or whether it is highly specific. There is likely, however, to be a difference between the naïve empiricist's notion of a rule used as the subject of a proposition and the notions of it of those of other persuasions. It will be recalled that according to John Chipman Gray, when the judges commit themselves to a demand, something which seems quite miraculous happens. By their say so, they create an intangible something in a way that leaves practitioners of other arts for dead. Nothing like it has happened since Genesis.

The naïve empiricist sees Gray's encouragement to judicial delusions of grandeur as arising in the following way. First, the 'content' of the rule – what is called for in it – is 'abstracted' from its 'context' – the aspect of it in which it appears as a commitment of the judiciary. It then is treated as if it were something separate from just *being* a commitment of people, as if it could have a life of its own separate from that. And Gray did the same with rights as with rules. Austin recognized that it was often convenient to talk as if rights could exist as so disembodied, provided we recognized that this was a fiction. But Lon L. Fuller has pointed out that in theoretical exercises concerning law it is important not to forget what we are doing. We fear that his predecessor at Harvard did in this respect forget what he was doing.

At least if Hart's supreme element in the United Kingdom recognition rule ('Whatever the Queen in Parliament enacts from time to time is law') is reinterpreted in the way we have suggested we should for ourselves reinterpret it, it does not involve the kind of abstraction which appears in Gray's theory. But it seems consistent with ordinary language to call any proposition which amounts to talking 'as if', for the kind of reasons Austin tolerated it, as itself a kind of abstraction. We say what is not true for the sake of economically concentrating attention on one class of features in a situation, while ignoring others, which, if taken into account, would require us to narrow and complicate our propositions. So we oversimplify for the time being – remembering what we are doing. Hart's proposition appears to be an abstraction in this sense.

Some of the reasons why it is abstract are reasons to which Hart has done more than anyone to call attention. We have seen that Hart speaks of three kinds of secondary rules. They all are from the older empirical point of view abstract, and to approach true propositions we have, in a sense, to combine them. We may think of Hart's recognition rules (or elements in 'the' rule) as concentrating attention on what we may call questions of the respective status of a source of law in relation to others, his rules of change as concentrating on the questions of when the judiciary is committed to recognize alterations in prescriptions coming to it from a particular source, and his adjudication rules as concentrating on two different related kinds of question, interpretation and 'umpiring' questions. We may think of Hart's theory, from the older empirical viewpoint, as pointing to the existence of propositions of the form 'Under conditions X, prescriptions from source Y are of legal effect', where X and Y are variables, and X is extremely complex, containing sometimes, though not universally, status conditions, change (we might prefer 'supersession') conditions, and interpretation and umpiring conditions.

On this basis, Hart's proposition that 'Whatever the Queen in Parliament enacts from time to time is law', contains a reference to a source (Y) and a compendious reference to the conditions under which the judiciary commit themselves to recognize changes in the demands from the source in question, in the words 'from time to time'. There is no reference to status conditions, that is, conditions qualifying the circumstances under which the authority of the source is to be recognized, such as that it must be within authority given to the source by some other source, or that the demands from the source will only be recognized if they are not in conflict with demands from other specified sources. But this omission is not the result of abstraction in the sense of which we have been speaking. From the naïve empirical viewpoint, the special feature of a 'supreme' proposition of a legal system consists in the fact that the commitment it expresses is not qualified by the inclusion of status conditions in the way that other general propositions of the system are.

But we do see Hart's representation of the supreme element in the United Kingdom recognition rule as abstract in that it contains no reference to interpretation and umpiring conditions. In the English system, the interpretation of a statute which is made by a court recognized by other courts as having appropriate authority, is to be recognized by those other courts, and the courts' commitment to the statute itself is always subject to that. Further, the adjudication on a particular interpretation (the order of the court between the parties) remains authoritative – for example, for a court in which an attempt may be made to re-litigate the matter – under most conditions, even though the interpretation itself is not authoritative, or is subsequently overruled or departed from. So there are two aspects at least, two kinds of points involved, in what Hart calls adjudication rules, and they put qualifications even on a court's commitments to statutes of the realm. Under the English system, the courts do commit themselves to recognize statutes which are designed to overrule previous court rulings on interpretation, or even individual court orders. But those have to be interpreted and adjudicated upon, too. The emphasis on these matters is one of the strong points in Gray's theory.

In the light of this, the difficulty arises, in the face of regarding Hart's 'supreme element' proposition as true of the position in England, that the bases on which the courts commit themselves to interpret the statute are not capable of being comprehensively and definitely specified. There is always controversy raging in legal academic and professional circles about the principles upon which judges should interpret a legislative prescription. Hart assumes that if we can say on some kind of linguistic basis that the statute is clear, the judges commit themselves to give effect to it. Austin certainly thought that they should, but this was bound up with his special codification ideals. Not everyone shares them, not even all judges. The claim a statute makes on the courts is a stimulus. The response will not necessarily even purport to follow the precise terms of the content of the claim itself.

There are different notions of what are the proper interests to be observed in the way statutes are to be handled. A useful comparison can be made with the Constitution of the United States. It would be an unsophisticated judge who thought that his duty to the American community in handling the Constitution was fulfilled by responding to its words literally. Shifts of interpretation of it from time to time are a matter of judicial history, as are conflicting approaches to interpretation at any particular time. A similar comparison can be made with observance of 'the common law' by judges. Karl Llewellyn approaches the responses to prescriptions coming from earlier judges to later judges by contrasting responses in the Grand Style and responses in the Formal Style.[30] The latter attaches importance to close adherence to language, while the former, which Llewellyn espouses, attaches importance to broader values than linguistic exegesis. There is always a degree of conflict between the two, and neither idea can be precisely pinned down in terms anyhow. And there is something of this involved in judicial approaches to statutes as with the common law. However, with the common law the problems of specifying comprehensively and definitely the conditions under which the judiciary commits itself to prescriptions are even more obviously insoluble, even for the purpose of arriving at areas 'clear' in terms of them.

This is not to say that we do not have clear areas of law, where we would be confident that there were commitments of the judges along particular lines, and that if a judge found the opposite way he would be 'wrong' − would have let the group down. But we think that Fuller convincingly demonstrated in his controversy with Hart over these matters, that when we are confident that the legal position is clear about something we are taking into account more values of the judges than Hart's principles suppose we are. Fuller thinks of these as 'justice' principles and, while we would have some conflict with him over the way he sees these, we must not be led astray into arguing with him. The important point for present purposes is that he does not see these as capable of being pinned down to definite specificity − their essential character for him is otherwise − and neither do we. Thus there is no possibility of correcting Hart's theory by reading specific principles of justice into the conditions which have to be made upon his 'recognition rules' and so rendering them definite. The commitments of the judiciary cannot be specified at the degree of generality of Hart's principles.

The facts that, on translating Hart's principles into the only kind of proposition we understand we find them false, and that on reading what seem to be necessary conditions into them we find them too indefinite to yield conclusions for any particular area, does not mean that we abandon them. For they somehow reflect important ways that lawyers think, and an understanding of the perspectives of the judiciary is one part of our field of inquiry. The clue to how we are to understand them is provided by Llewellyn's article 'The Normative, the Legal and the Law Jobs', to which MacCormick rightly attaches importance. The phenomenon with which we are faced here is lawyers' 'as if' talk, which Austin tolerated or even encouraged when he saw it performing important purposes. In Llewellyn's view, lawyers talk 'as if' the law were settled, which reflects the inevitable drive of a legal system towards unity.[31]

To clarify our understanding, we turn to the methodology of economics, as Austin did, though not in the form in which Austin knew it. Rather we turn to its modern development, by which Lasswell and McDougal were influenced in important points in their modern empirical theory, as we have seen. The modern economist does not necessarily abandon the account of the economy which Austin knew altogether. He may expound it at the initial stage of his exposition, to indicate how certain factors in the economy, isolated from their real context, are interrelated – factors which people like Ricardo and Mill took into account, even though their account must be greatly qualified because they failed to think of, or minimized, others. Thus, for example, Ricardo and Mill minimized the fact that changes take time and assumed generally an equilibrium state of the economy. They failed to realize that equilibrium can be reached without human and other resources being fully employed. They assumed an equivalence between effective demand and wants and needs. They failed to take proper account of the effect of monopoly control of markets. They assumed that the economic unit knew what was going on and acted from self-interested motives in relation to what he knew. After the economist has painted the 'pure theory' picture, he may gradually set out to correct the picture by taking the extra factors into account, thus, as it were, bringing economics down to reality.

This is the kind of pure theorizing the naïve empiricist understands. The pure theory asserts what goes on, just because the Benthamites who advanced this kind of theory were empiricists and believed what they said. What makes it pure theory in the hands of a modern economist is that it is not true and recognized not to be true. The economist who uses it as pure theory, asserts it as if it were true while knowing it is not and not pretending that it is. This deliberate use of empirical untruth as a technique for isolating special factors and interrelationships has been adopted from economics in other areas of social science, for example, by John Rawls in *A Theory of Justice*.[32]

The use of fictions by lawyers for assisting understanding and exposition has been a constant subject of attention by jurists, as will already be clear. Some of them are isolated and no one would dignify them by the name of pure theory. Others are more pervasive and may cause confusion, especially 'contemporaneity' fictions, which are legion. As an example, the judge commonly pretends that all the claims to which he commits himself at a given time are being made on him simultaneously, instead of coming to him from different events at different times. He thinks of a body of law now 'in force'. He could not afford to dispense with the convenience, for instance, of looking at up-dated copies of Acts, though now and again he may need for special purposes to remember the time sequences of amendments. The convenience of this sort of fiction tends, however, to be bought at the cost of confusion about what law is really like, through the ways of talking about law which it develops, especially the way it disembodies the prescription. The fiction with which we are at present principally concerned has at least analogies to contemporaneity fictions. It involves speaking of the law as if a degree of order which it is hoped to approach was already there. The ways this is done are certainly complex enough to be given the name of pure theory and it is of this kind of practitioners' pure theory that we see Hart's account as unprecedentedly perceptive. In the light in which we see Hart's theory, it is superior to those which try to correct it by taking additional factors into account which do not enter into this kind of lawyers' pure theorizing.

This does not mean that the reader is called upon to approve of the practice itself, however ingrained it may be, still less to be deceived by it. We are, rather, all called upon to recognize its existence, for it is an important aspect of the perspectives of lawyers required for an understanding of judicial and other decisions. At the same time, if we use it ourselves, we will do well to recall Fuller's injunction and not forget what we are doing. In this respect, practical lawyers are often more readily able to come down off the pure theory perch, and argue and decide in different terms when they think it suitable, than some legal academics.

We need further to remind ourselves that for major academic purposes – such as those of Lasswell and McDougal in describing past decisions in the course of sequential carrying out of the intellectual tasks – we will not select the same classifications for our study as those selected for emphasis in the account of the pure theorizing of the practitioner which we see Hart as giving. In the latter account, claims are classified fundamentally in relation to the sources from which they come. The practitioner himself selects other classifications for most of his work than classification by source – the kind of classification which Austin refers to in what we called, in our exposition of his work, his map of the legal system. But for a more comprehensive description we need to go beyond the pure theorizing, beyond commitments, beyond judicial perspectives of any kind altogether, and classify by reference to the values disposed of (some value positions of people are improved and some worsened) having regard to all features of all community decisions. Dean Roscoe Pound of Harvard – to whom Lasswell and McDougal acknowledge their indebtedness – has a way of talking which emphasizes this aspect and has been enormously influential. Rather than talking of claims which are legally recognized, he speaks of legally protected interests.[33] However, the term 'interest' tends to be used abstractly in Pound's theory and Lasswell and McDougal have preferred to use 'claim' where Pound would use interest.[34] Moreover, their value classifications are, in the end, closer to Bentham's than they are to Pound's, though the analysis is of the same general kind and Pound's work has relations to Bentham's too. These approaches are mentioned here to indicate that, while the aspect of Hart's central theorizing which we have discussed is vitally important, it is also highly specialized from the standpoint of other modern legal theories.

Having stated our view of the relation of Austin's approach to current developments, we must conclude. The reader is commended, after this summary introduction, to Austin's own work, and to the rich literature on the Benthamites which is continuing to accumulate. From it, the reader can envisage, with extraordinary faithfulness because of the labours of many scholars including particularly Hart, a period of extraordinary vitality. In those great days, leading scholars working in different fields of knowledge and the humanities found themselves much closer together. It was all a hothouse for the development of contextual and inter-disciplinary thinking which we think of as especially modern and almost as if we invented it. And it was with the most earnest attention to the insights available in this environment that John Austin built an early locomotive of British jurisprudence on a broad philosophy of continuing soundness. Newer locomotives run strongly which share its basic philosophical constructional principles while effecting radical transformations in other respects. We have tried to give some inkling of some of these.

Appendix I
Recent commentaries on Austin

It was Austin's practice to append notes to his lectures to permit detailed, or more detailed, discussions of matters which would have unduly disturbed the prosecution of his themes if included in the text. We adopt this expedient for the purpose of referring to articles which have been published since the revival of Austinian study but which are not part of the development of jurisprudence in the light of the newer philosophy. Pre-eminent among these are two articles of Wilfrid E. Rumble (called Alfrid Rumble in the first of them) 'John Austin, judicial legislation and legal positivism' ((1977) 13 *Univ. of Western Australia L.J.*, 77) and 'Divine law, utilitarian ethics, and positivist jurisprudence: a study of the legal philosophy of John Austin' ((1979) 24 *American Journal of Jurisprudence*, 139).

The first article contains a detailed analysis of Austin's approach to judiciary law, calling attention to his account of judicial legislation, the uncertainties in Austin's treatment, and the criticisms which have been made of it. Rumble compares Austin's treatment with modern ones to which he attaches importance.

In his second article, Rumble attacks the view that Austin's ethical theory had little impact on his philosophy of law. He sets out to demonstrate that it had various kinds of impact, influencing in particular his basic ideas of law and sovereignty. He attaches importance to differences which he detects between Austin's and Bentham's ethics, particularly in the aspect of Austin's emphasis on morality as a matter of adherence to rule, rather than generally calling for an assessment of particular acts by reference to the broadest considerations of utility. He does not accept that Austin's empiricism was unqualified and is critical of the empirical interpretation of Austin in the present writer's 'Some myth about positivism' ((1958) 68 *Yale L.J.*, 212).

The attention of the reader is commended to Rumble's work, firstly, because it bases itself in some measure on unpublished materials not available to the present writer, ranging from matter in University College, London, through what is left after the fire in the library of the Inner Temple, to Enid Campbell's unpublished thesis, *John Austin and Jurisprudence in 19th Century England* (1958) in the library at Duke University. Secondly, Rumble's articles contain detailed discussions of important aspects of Austin's theory of a depth not appropriate to a general survey like the present book.

Thirdly, as already indicated, it qualifies the fundamental interpretation of Austin pursued in the present writer's work. The writer has obviously got to expect an assessment of the present work under some such title as 'More myth about positivism'. Rumble concedes, however, that we marshalled a body of evidence for our empirical interpretation in the article to which he refers. We expect to reply to Rumble's assessment of the present work in an article entitled 'Still more myth about positivism'.

Rumble shares with Robert S. Summers ('The *new* analytical jurists' (1966) 41 *NYU Law Review*, 861) the view that Austin was in a degree constructing a conceptual framework for legal study. Summers regards the urge to convert conceptual questions into questions of empirical fact as an old-fashioned kind of error. But, if so, we believe that Austin was guilty of it along with the present writer. At least the predominant view on which Austin seems to proceed is that things really belong to classifications in reality and all that we do is detect them. If Austin fell into error, this was usually because, though not consistently, he spoke as if reality itself labelled one classification to which an object belonged its genus and another one its species. He explicitly accepted the view that there is a difference between the substantial features of an object – its essence – and its accidental features.

In this respect, however, Austin is not more of a conceptualist than the present writer, but in a sense a more extreme empiricist, seeing classifications in reality, for the purpose of determining fields of study, as selecting themselves. All that we have to do is focus sharply on them. For Austin, in jurisprudence there abide three things: Faith, Hope and Clarity. But the greatest of these is Clarity and it is all that is needed in definition. The exercise is purely descriptive in aspects which the present writer would see as involving selection of observed attributes of things on grounds of usefulness for the purposes of the writer. But the reader should attend to Summers and Rumble for a different and more usual view of the character of Austin's work on these aspects.

Herbert Morris's 'Verbal disputes and the legal philosophy of John Austin' ((1959 – 60) *UCLA Law Review*, 27) aims to answer claims of Felix Cohen and Glanville Williams that definitional disputes are merely verbal, or at any rate do not raise questions of truth or falsity, and that this is so in particular in respect of definitions of law. Morris develops an extensive catalogue of kinds of definitions and their functions and demonstrates that there are vast oversimplifications in the generalizations of those he sets out to criticize. The discussion of Austin is an examination of what Austin is seen to be doing in the light of what Morris sees as the functions of different kinds of definitions. He concludes that Austin's is a theory of law concerned with law as it is rather than law as it ought to be. It is a theory concerned with the law laid down and enforced by the sovereign in a community. It is a general theory of the meaning of law and of legal concepts.

However, to suggest that Morris laboured with his great variety of notions of definition to produce this mouse would be to do an injustice to the article. Its importance is in the closer examinations of what Austin says which are made along the way. For the purpose of understanding Austin, the attention of the reader is directed especially to those quotations from Austin where firstly he refers to 'essences' of things, which the present writer would take to be typical of those where Austin was disposed to make the sort of error we have referred to above. At the same time we should argue that Morris fails to give due weight to this feature of Austin's work to distinguish what Austin thought he was doing in defining and what Morris thinks it comes to in terms of Morris's own notions. And the same applies to Rumble's account of the extent to which Austin's ethics influenced his definitions. What Austin meant, and what a writer thinks he ought to have meant, or what influenced Austin without his knowing it, are different things.

Secondly, Morris discusses the statement in Austin which may give a certain fuel to conceptualist interpretations of him (in the Campbell *Austin* xxix): 'The principles of General Jurisprudence will not coincide with any actual system, but are intended to facilitate the acquisition of any, and to show their defects.' What the present writer takes Austin to have meant by this is: 'You will find most of the legal phenomena I discuss in most mature legal systems some of the time, and you will find some of them in all mature legal systems all of the time, but you will not find all of them in any legal system any of the time: that's the slovenly way in which these legal systems are always constructed.' Though Austin speaks here of principles, his main interest in this respect is actually in classifications.

Samuel E. Stumpf's article, 'Austin's theory of the separation of law and morals' ((1960) 14 *Vanderbilt Law Review*, 117) has the thesis that neither Austin nor any other early positivist succeeded in separating considerations of what is in law from what ought to be. Not one of the early positivist jurists ever disengaged the idea of law from the notion of the ends of law successfully. They all begin by announcing that law and morals are two distinct subjects, that law is simply a command. But within the same treatise they deal with the ends or purposes of law. And they deal with the problem of ends in such a way there can be no full understanding of what is meant by law.

We may comment that most people have demands of their own about institutions. But to attribute ends to social institutions themselves is a much more complicated matter. Few were designed complete by anyone as they exist now at a stroke, or even by a group with identical ends or unanimity. They are outcomes of social processes. To specify the ends of an institution in a context of dispute most often functions to identify the supposed demands of the institution with those of the propounder, and then to suggest that they must be also those of the person addressed. As it is with particular institutions in a society, so it is when people talk of the 'ends of society' or 'the ends of the twentieth century'.

Of course, if we want to understand demands emanating from an institution, say, Parliament, to the judicial institutions, we look at objectives of participants in the Parliamentary process. That is what Austin recommended in some circumstances. But as soon as it is claimed that this introduces a 'moral' element into the picture, there is an implication that they are somehow our demands, too. This is at least one of the confusions that the empiricist seeks to resist. The question of whose objectives are being talked about in a statement is vital to him. Objectives do not exist on the empirical level except objectives of people. We must add that this is our own criticism of the widespread kind of approach which Stumpf takes rather than Austin's own. But Austin would have made an allied point. To understand the objectives of the sovereign body in issuing a particular command is one thing. To understand whether the command serves utility is something else again. It may turn out that it does. But what the command is and whether it has utility are matters for independent investigation.

John Underwood Lewis's 'John Austin's concept of "having a legal obligation": a defence and reassessment in the face of some recent analytical jurisprudence' ((1975) 14 *Western Ontario Law Review*, 51) criticizes Summers's approach to Austin in the article referred to above. Lewis's conclusion is, however, that Austin and those who follow or are inspired by him are enabled to ground their theoretical propositions about the structure of legal systems in definitions of 'law', 'obligation' and 'sanction' that are, in relation to one another, purely analytic or formal. But, says Lewis, in reality law is a social institution, and something radically different from an atomic particle or a logico-mathematical system. This means that in reality some notion of justice has to be developed in order even to understand the concept of law in a descriptive way. The present writer sees all this as coupling misinterpretation of Austin's understanding of the kind of activity on which he was engaged with a kind of criticism we believe to be unjustified for reasons we have given in the course of discussing Summers's, Rumble's and Stumpf's views.

Colin Tapper, in 'Austin on sanctions' ([1963] *Cambridge L.J.*, 270) disputes Hart's proposition that it was a virtue of Austin that when he went wrong, he went wrong clearly. Tapper seeks to establish that Hart was wrong by pointing to inconsistencies in Austin's treatment of sanctions. But we doubt whether this quite makes Tapper's point. People are often very clearly inconsistent in different things they write. However, Tapper is rather in favour of Austin's inconsistencies and vacillations where they result from Austin's efforts to take account of different factors which his perceptiveness enabled him to recognize. Tapper finds this stimulating to the uncommitted.

There are some other articles in the period under review which feature Austin's work although the treatment is not confined to Austin, such as Thomas Broden, Jr's 'Straw man of legal positivism' ((1958–59) 34 *Notre*

Dame Lawyer, 530), Mark R. MacGuigan's 'Law, morals, and positivism' ((1961 – 62) 14 *University of Toronto Law Journal*, 1), and the unattributed 'Hart, Austin, and the concept of a legal system: the primacy of sanctions' ((1975) 84 *Yale L.J.*, 584).

Of special interest is the article by Richard A. Falk and Samuel I. Shuman: 'The Bellagio Conference on legal positivism' ((1961 – 62) 14 *Journal of Legal Education*, 213). It discusses the Conference's attempt to make comparisons between Anglo-American and Continental positivist theories.

It is noted in the last-mentioned article that one of the participants in the conference was Arduino Agnelli of the University of Trieste and that 'it might be of special interest to the American reader to know that Professor Agnelli had done the first full-length study of John Austin in any language' (p. 214). But whether this claim is justified is perhaps a matter of definition. W. Jethro Brown's *The Austinian Theory of Law* (1906) is only to be denied the title because of the fact that it includes an amended version of lectures I. V and VI of the Austin text and the 'Essay on the uses of the study of jurisprudence'. For the rest, it consists of commentary on Austin. Unfortunately its value as a materials book is damaged by the author's temerity in re-writing the Austin text in places where the author thought he could communicate what was in Austin's mind better than Austin.

C.E. Clark's *Practical Jurisprudence, a Comment on Austin* (1883) is, on the other hand, a systematic treatise, the object of which is to criticize Austin in the light of the history of legal systems – the Roman legal system especially – and of the methods of analysis appropriate to them. If this book is to be denied the title of the first full length study of Austin, it is because the author sets out to give his own general account of the topics which Austin discussed, working Austin's treatment into the picture at appropriate points. R.A. Eastwood, *A Brief Introduction to Austin's Theory of Positive Law and Sovereignty* (1916) and R.A. Eastwood and G.W. Keeton, *The Austinian Theories of Law and Sovereignty* (1929) can be denied the title of books on Austin only on the possible grounds of brevity or specialization of themes.

Arduino Agnelli's own *John Austin* (1959), in the Italian language, fulfils the claim made for it to be an extensive study of Austin himself and of Anglo-American comments on Austin as well as his European associations. However, it is part of the materials reflecting the European scholarly reception of Austin which have been regretfully excluded from the present work through considerations of space, and of difficulty of access to the materials for the present writer.

Appendix II
Bibliography of works cited

Works marked * are cited in W.L. Morison, 'Some myth about positivism' (1958) 68 *Yale Law Journal*, 212 and not discussed again in the present work.

Works of John Austin

A Plea for the Constitution (London, 1859).

'Centralization' (1847) 85 *The Edinburgh Review*, 221.

'Disposition of property by will — primogeniture' (1824) 2 *The Westminster Review*, 503.

'Joint stock companies' *Parliamentary History and Review* (London, 1826), 709.

Lectures on Jurisprudence (latest edition by Robert Campbell, 2 vols., London, 1885).

Review of Friedrich List's 'Das Nationale System der Politische Oekonomie' in (1842) 75 *The Edinburgh Review*, 515.

The Province of Jurisprudence Determined (latest edition by H.L.A. Hart, London, 1954).

Other references

Agnelli, Arduino, *John Austin — alle origine del positivismo giuridico* (Turin, 1959).

Allen, C.K., *Law in the Making* (7th edn, Oxford, 1964).

Anderson, John, *Studies in Empirical Philosophy* (Sydney, 1962).

Arndts von Arnesberg, Ludwig, *Lehrbuch der Pandekten* (9th edn, Stuttgart, 1877).

Austin, Sarah, *Characteristics of Goethe from the German of Falk, von Müller etc.* (3 vols., London, 1833).

Bellot, H. Hale, *University College, London 1826–1926* (London, 1929).

Bentham, Jeremy, *A Comment on the Commentaries and a Fragment on Government* edited by J.H. Burns and H.L.A. Hart (London, 1977).

_____ *An Introduction to the Principles of Morals and Legislation* edited by J.H. Burns and H.L.A. Hart (London, 1970).

_____ *Church of Englandism* (London, 1831).

_____ *Constitutional Code – for the use of all nations and all governments professing liberal opinions* (London, 1830).

_____ *Defence of Usury* (London, 1818).

_____ *Draught of a New Plan for the Organisation of the Judicial Establishment in France* (London, 1790).

_____ *Letters to Lord Pelham* (London, 1802).

_____ *Of Laws in General* edited by H.L.A. Hart (London, 1970).

_____ *The Limits of Jurisprudence Defined* edited by C.W. Everett (New York, 1945).

_____ *Plan of Parliamentary Reform* (London, 1817).

_____ *Rationale of Judicial Evidence* edited by John Stuart Mill (5 vols., London, 1827).

_____ *Rationale of Punishment* (London, 1830).

_____ *Theory of Legislation* translated from the French of E. Dumont by R. Hildreth (London, 1891).

_____ *The Works of Jeremy Bentham* edited by J. Bowring (11 vols., Edinburgh, 1843).

Blackstone, Sir William, *Commentaries on the Laws of England* (Oxford, 1770).

*Bodenheimer, E. 'Analytical positivism, legal realism and the future of legal method' (1958) 44 *Virginia Law Review*, 365.

Broden, Thomas, Jr, 'Straw man of legal positivism' (1958–59) 34 *Notre Dame Lawyer*, 530.

Brown, Thomas, *Inquiry into the Relation of Cause and Effect* (4th edn, London, 1835).

Brown, W. Jethro, *The Austinian Theory of Law* (London, 1906).

Campbell, Enid, *John Austin and Jurisprudence in 19th Century England* (unpublished) (Duke University Library, 1958).

Carlyle, Thomas, *The French Revolution* (3 vols., London, 1837).

Christie, George C., *Jurisprudence. Text and Readings on the Philosophy of Law* (St Paul, Minn., 1973).

Clark, Charles E., *Practical Jurisprudence – a Comment on Austin* (Cambridge, 1883).

Currey, C.H., *Sir Francis Forbes* (Sydney, 1968).

Dicey, A.V., *Law and Public Opinion in England During the Nineteenth Century* (2nd edn, London, 1914, reissued with preface by E.C.S. Wade, 1962).

Dickens, Charles *Hard Times for These Times* (London, 1854).

Dumont, É., *Théorie des Peines et des Récompenses* (London, 1811).

_____ *Traités de la Législation Civile et Pénale* (Paris, 1802).

_____ *Traité des Preuves Judiciaires* (Paris, 1823).

Dworkin, R.M., 'Is law a system of rules?' in *The Philosophy of Law* edited by R.M. Dworkin (Oxford, 1977), 38.

Eastwood, R.A., *A Brief Introduction to Austin's Theory of Positive Law and Sovereignty* (London, 1916).
Eastwood, R.A. and Keeton, G.W., *The Austinian Theories of Law and Sovereignty* (London, 1929).
Enfield, William, *The History of Philosophy – drawn up from Brucker's Historia Critica Philosophiae* (London, 1837).

Falck, N., *Juristische Encyklopädie* (Kiel,1825).
Falk, R.A. and Shuman, S.I., 'The Bellagio conference on legal positivism' (1961–62) 14 *Journal of Legal Education*, 213.
Fifoot, C.H.S., *History and Sources of the Common Law: Tort and Contract* (London, 1949).
Frazer, Sir James G., *The Golden Bough: a study in comparative religion* (London,-1890).
Friedmann, W., *Legal Theory* (5th edn, London, 1967).
Froude, J.A., *Thomas Carlyle. A History of the First Forty Years of his Life. 1795–1835* (2 vols., London, 1882).
*Fuller, L.L., *The Law in Quest of Itself* (Chicago, 1940).

Gaius, *Institutiones or Institutes of Roman Law* translation and commentary by A.H.J. Greenidge (Oxford, 1904).
Gray, John Chipman, *The Nature and Sources of Law* (New York, 1909).
Grote, George, *History of Greece* (London, 1888).

Hart, H.L.A., *The Concept of Law* (Oxford, 1961).
_____ 'Definition and theory in jurisprudence' (1954) 70 *Law Quarterly Review*, 37.
_____ 'Positivism and the separation of law and morals' (1958) 71 *Harvard Law Review*, 593.
_____ 'Bentham's "Of Laws in General" ' 2 *Rechtstheorie* (1971) 55.
Haubold, D.C.G., *Institutionum Juris Romani Privati Historicodogmaticarum Lineamenta* (Leipzig, 1826).
Hayek, F.A. von, *John Stuart Mill and Harriet Taylor* (London, 1951).
Heineccius, Johann G., *Antiquitatum Romanarum iurisprudentiam illustrantium syntagma secundum ordinem Institutionum Iustiniani digestum*, castigavit, C.G. Haubold (Frankfurt, 1822).
_____ *Leçons élémentaires du droit civil romain, rédigées dans l'ordre des Institutes de l'empereur Justinien* edited by A. Menestrier (Paris, 1808).
Hohfeld, Wesley N., *Fundamental Legal Conceptions as Applied in Judicial Reasoning, and Other Legal Essays* edited by Walter Wheeler Cook (New Haven, Conn., 1923) 2nd edn by the above and Arthur L. Corbin (New Haven, Conn., 1964).
Holland, Sir T.E., *Elements of Jurisprudence* (13th edn, Oxford, 1924).
Holmes, O.W., Jr, *The Common Law* (London, 1887).
_____ 'The path of the law' (1897) 10 *Harvard Law Review*, 457.

Holmes, O.W., Jr and Laski, H.J., *Holmes-Laski Letters* edited by M.D. Howe (2 vols., Cambridge, Mass., 1953).

Hooker, Richard, *The Laws of Ecclesiastical Polity* edited by R.W. Church (Oxford, 1873).

Justinian, *The Institutes of Justinian*, edited and translated by T.C. Sandars (Westport, Conn., 1970).

*Kantorowicz, Herman, *The Definition of Law* edited by A.H. Campbell (Cambridge, 1958).

Kocourek, Albert, *Jural Relations* (Indianapolis, 1928).

_____ 'The century of analytic jurisprudence since John Austin' in *Law. A Century of Progress. 1835–1935* (3 vols., New York, 1937) II, 195.

Lane, P.H., *An Introduction to the Australian Constitution* (2nd edn, Sydney, 1977).

Lawson, F.H., *The Oxford Law School 1850–1965* (Oxford, 1968).

Lewis, A.D.E., 'John Austin (1790–1859). Pupil of Bentham' in *The Bentham Newsletter* edited by J.H. Burns and J.R. Dinwiddy (1979, no. 2).

Lewis, J.U., 'John Austin's concept of "Having a legal Obligation": A defence and reassessment in the face of some recent analytical jurisprudence' (1975) 14 *Western Ontario Law Review*, 51.

* Llewellyn, Karl, *The Bramble Bush* (New York, 1951).

_____ *The Common Law Tradition – Deciding Appeals* (Boston, 1960).

_____ 'The normative, the legal and the law-jobs: the problem of juristic method' (1940) 49 *Yale Law Journal*, 1355.

List, Friedrich, *Das nationale System der politischen Oekonomie* (Stuttgart and Tübingen, 1841).

Locke, John, *Essay Concerning Human Understanding* (London, 1823).

MacCormick, Neil, *H.L.A. Hart* (London, 1981).

McCulloch, J., 'Disposition of property by will – entails' (1824) 40 *Edinburgh Review*, 350.

Macdonnell, Sir John, 'John Austin' *Dictionary of National Biography* (London, 1885) I, 737.

McDougal, Myres S., 'Law as a process of decision: A policy-oriented approach to legal study' (1956) 1 *Natural Law Forum*, 53.

MacGuigan, Mark R., 'Law, morals and positivism' (1961–62) 14 *University of Toronto Law Journal*, 1.

Mackeldey, F. *Manuel de Droit Romain*, contenant la théorie des institutes, précédée d'une introduction à l'étude du droit romain (Brussels, 1846).

*McWhinney, E., 'English legal philosophy and Canadian legal philosophy' (1958) 4 *McGill Law Journal*, 213.

Maine, Sir Henry, *Ancient Law* (London, 1861).
_____ *Early History of Institutions* (London, 1875).
*Manning, C.A.W., 'Austin today: or "The province of jurisprudence" reexamined' in *Modern Theories of Law* (Oxford, 1933), 180.
Markby, Sir William, *Elements of Law* (6th edn, Oxford, 1905).
_____ 'John Austin' *Encyclopaedia Britannica* (London, 1910) II, 939.
Mazlish, Bruce, *James and John Stuart Mill* (London, 1975).
Mill, James, *Analysis of the Phenomena of the Human Mind* edited by John Stuart Mill (2 vols., London, 1878).
_____ *An Essay on Government* edited by C.V. Shields (New York, 1955).
_____ *Elements of Political Economy* (London, 1826).
_____ *History of British India* (9 vols., London, 1820 – 48).
_____ 'Whether political economy is useful' (1836) 2 *London Review*, 553.
Mill, John Stuart, *Autobiography* edited by Jack Stillinger (London, 1971).
_____ *Collected Works of John Stuart Mill* general editor F.E.L. Priestley (19 vols., Toronto, 1963 – 79).
_____ *Principles of Political Economy* (9th edn, 2 vols., London, 1886).
_____ *System of Logic* (8th edn impression, London, 1959).
_____ *The Early Draft of John Stuart Mill's Autobiography* edited by Jack Stillinger (Urbana, Ill., 1971).
_____ 'Austin on jurisprudence' (1863) 118 *Edinburgh Review*, 439.
_____ 'Recent writers on reform' (1859) 59 *Fraser's Magazine*, 489.
Mitford, William, *History of Greece* (London, 1821 – 22).
Morison, W.L., *The System of Law and Courts Governing New South Wales* (Sydney, 1979).
_____ Introduction to *Cases on Torts* edited by W.L. Morison, R.L. Sharwood, C.S. Phegan and C. Sappideen (5th edn, Sydney, 1981).
_____ 'Frames of reference for legal ideals' in *Law and Society* edited by Eugene Kamenka, Robert Brown and Alice Erh-Soon Tay (London, 1978).
_____ 'Myres S. McDougal and twentieth-century jurisprudence' in *Toward World Order and Human Dignity* edited by W. Michael Reisman and Burns H. Weston (New York, 1976).
_____ 'Anderson and legal theory' (1977) 8 *Sydney Law Review*, 294.
_____ 'Frames of reference for legal ideals' (1975) 2 *Dalhousie Law Journal*, 3.
_____ 'Some myth about positivism' (1958) 68 *Yale Law Journal*, 212.
Morris, Herbert, 'Verbal disputes and the legal philosophy of John Austin' (1959 – 60), 7 *UCLA Law Review*, 27.
Mühlenbruch, C.F., *Doctrina Pandectarum* (Halle, 1827).

Niebuhr, B.G., *History of Rome* translated by J.G. Hare and C. Thirlwall (2 vols., Cambridge, 1831 – 32).
*Northrop, F.S.C., 'The mediational approval theory of law in American legal realism' (1958) 44 *Virginia Law Review*, 347.

Packe, M. St J., *The Life of John Stuart Mill* (London, 1954).
Paley, William, *The Principles of Moral and Political Philosophy* (2 vols., London, 1818).
Passmore, J.A., *A Hundred Years of Philosophy* (London, 1968).
_____ *The Perfectibility of Man* (London, 1970).
Paton, G.W., *A Text-book of Jurisprudence* (3rd edn, Oxford, 1964).
Pollock, Sir F., 'Judicial caution and valour' (1929) 45 *Law Quarterly Review*, 151.
Pound, Roscoe, *Jurisprudence* (5 vols., Minnesota, 1959).
Priestley, Joseph, *An Essay on the First Principles of Government* (London, 1771).
Pückler-Muskau, H.L.H. Fürst von, *Tour in England, Ireland and France in the Years 1826 – 1829* (Philadelphia, 1833).

Ranke, L. von, *History of the Popes* translated from the German by Sarah Austin (London, 1866).
_____ *History of the Reformation in Germany* translated from the German by Sarah Austin, edited by R.A. Johnson (London, 1905).
Rawls, John, *A Theory of Justice* (Oxford, 1972).
Raz, Joseph, *The Concept of a Legal System* (Oxford, 1970).
Reddie, James, *Inquiries Elementary and Historical in the Science of Law* (London, 1840).
Ricardo, David, *The Principles of Political Economy and Taxation* being a reprint of 3rd edn, 1821 with an introduction by M.P. Fogarty (London, 1911).
Ross, Janet, *Three Generations of Englishwomen* (2 vols., London, 1888).
Rosshirt, C.F., *Lehrbuch des Criminalrechts* (Heidelberg, 1821).
Ruben, Eira, 'John Austin's political pamphlets 1824 – 1859' in *Perspectives in Jurisprudence* edited by Elspeth Attwooll (Glasgow, 1977).
Rumble, Wilfrid E., 'Divine law, utilitarian ethics and positivist jurisprudence: A study of the legal philosophy of John Austin' (1979) 24 *American Journal of Jurisprudence*, 139.
_____ 'John Austin, judicial legislation and legal positivism' (1977) 13 *University of Western Australia Law Journal*, 77.
Ryle, Gilbert, *The Concept of Mind* (London, 1949).

Salmond, John W., *Jurisprudence or The Theory of Law* (3rd edn, London, 1910; 7th edn, London, 1924).
_____ *The Law of Torts* (6th edn, London, 1924).
Savigny, F.C. von, *Das Recht des Besitzes* (Stuttgart, 1837).
_____ *Geschichte des römischen Rechts im Mittelalter* (5 vols., Heidelberg, 1815 – 29).
_____ *System des heutigen römischen Rechts* (Berlin, 1840).
_____ *The History of the Roman Law During the Middle Ages* translated from the German by E. Cathcart (Connecticut, 1979).

Savigny, F.C. von, Eichhorn, C.F. and Göschen, T.F.L., *Zeitschrift für geschichtliche Rechtswissenschaft* (Berlin, 1815 – 23).

Schwarz, Andreas B., 'John Austin and the German jurisprudence of his time' (1934 – 35) 1 *Politica*, 178.

Seddall, Henry, *Malta: Past and Present* (London, 1870).

Smith, Harrison, *Britain in Malta* (2 vols., Malta, 1953).

Stephen, Sir James Fitzjames, 'English Jurisprudence' (1861) 114 *Edinburgh Review*, 456.

Stephen, Leslie, *The English Utilitarians* (3 vols., New York, 1900).

_____ *Life of Sir James Fitzjames Stephen* (London, 1895).

Stone, Julius, *Legal System and Lawyers' Reasonings* (Sydney, 1964).

_____ *The Province and Function of Law* (Sydney, 1946).

Stumpf, Samuel E., 'Austin's theory of the separation of law and morals' (1960) 14 *Vanderbilt Law Review*, 117.

Summers, Robert S., 'The *new* analytical jurists' (1966) 41 *New York University Law Review*, 861.

Tapper, Colin, 'Austin on sanctions' (1963) *Cambridge Law Journal*, 270.

Thibaut, A.F.J., *System des Pandekten-Rechts* (Jena, 1828).

Thomas, William, *The Philosophic Radicals* (Oxford, 1979).

Twining, William, *Karl Llewellyn and the Realist Movement* (London, 1973).

_____ 'The bad man revisited' (1973) 58 *Cornell Law Review*, 275.

University College London, Faculty of Laws, *Law at the University College London 1827 – 1838. Annotated Catalogue of Exhibits* (London, 1977).

*Vinogradoff, Sir Paul, *Outlines of Historical Jurisprudence* (2 vols., London, 1920).

Wallas, Graham, *The Life of Francis Place, 1771 – 1854* (London, 1951).

Waterfield, Gordon, *Lucie Duff Gordon* (New York, 1937).

White, Morton G., *Social Thought in America: The Revolt against Formalism* (2nd edn, 1957).

Winch, Donald, *James Mill: Selected Economic Writings* (Edinburgh and London, 1966).

Yale Law Journal, 'Hart, Austin, and the concept of a legal system: the primacy of sanctions' (1975) 84 *Yale Law Journal* 584.

Reference notes

Chapter 1: Personal and social influences on Austin and his work

1 Janet Ross, *Three Generations of Englishwomen* (2 vols., London, 1888) I, 13–18, 20–4.
2 op. cit. I, 8.
3 op. cit. I, 9.
4 A.D.E. Lewis, 'John Austin (1790–1859). Pupil of Bentham', *The Bentham Newsletter* edited by J.H. Burns and J.R. Dinwiddy (1979, no. 2).
5 op. cit. 2–3.
6 Leslie Stephen, *The English Utilitarians* (3 vols., New York, 1900) I, 65–9.
7 John Stuart Mill, *Autobiography* edited by Jack Stillinger (London, 1971), 46.
8 Gordon Waterfield, *Lucie Duff Gordon* (New York, 1937) Ch. 1.
9 ibid.
10 Ross, *Englishwomen* I, 35.
11 op. cit. II, 92, 102.
12 op. cit I, 31.
13 Sir John Macdonnell, 'John Austin', *Dictionary of National Biography* (1885) I, 737.
14 John Austin, *Lectures on Jurisprudence* edited by Robert Campbell (2 vols., London, 1885) 4.
15 University College London, *Exhibits*, notes to Exhibit 4.
16 Ross, *Englishwomen* II, 112.
17 Macdonnell, 'Austin', 737.
18 Stephen, *Utilitarians* I, 200.
19 op. cit. I, 214–15.
20 M. St J. Packe, *The Life of John Stuart Mill* (London, 1954) 26.
21 Macdonnell, 'Austin', 737.
22 Packe, *Mill*, 21, 26–7.
23 Stephen, *Utilitarians* I, 185–6.
24 Graham Wallas, *The Life of Francis Place, 1771–1854* (London, 1951) 70–1.
25 Bruce Mazlish, *James and John Stuart Mill* (London, 1975) 4, 59, 150–6. Packe, *Mill*, 9–10.

26 ibid.
27 Mazlish, *Mill*, 3, 152 – 6, 283 – 91.
28 John Stuart Mill, *Collected Works of John Stuart Mill* edited by Francis E. Mineka (Toronto, 1963) XII, 11 – 12.
29 Ross, *Englishwomen* II, 174, 192.
30 Mill, *Autobiography*, 40 – 1.
31 Ross, *Englishwomen* II, 115.
32 Mill, *Autobiography*, 106 – 8.
33 op. cit. 80 – 103.
34 op. cit. 106 – 8.
35 Stephen, *Utilitarians* I, 200 – 6, 213 – 14.
36 op. cit. I, 183 – 4, 186 – 7.
37 John Stuart Mill, *The Early Draft of John Stuart Mill's Autobiography* edited by Jack Stillinger (Urbana, Ill., 1971) 147.
38 Ross, *Englishwomen* I, 42 – 3.
39 Packe, *Mill*, 67 – 9.
40 op. cit. 106.
41 Waterfield, *Lucie Duff Gordon*, 35.
42 Packe, *Mill*, 87.
43 J.A. Froude, *Thomas Carlyle. A History of the First Forty Years of his Life 1795 – 1835* (2 vols., London, 1882) II, 235.
44 op. cit. II, 153 – 4.
45 Mill, *Autobiography*, 46.
46 op. cit. 59.
47 Mazlish, *Mill*, 53.
48 Ross, *Englishwomen* I, 66, 68.
49 op. cit. II, 113.
50 op. cit. I, 47.
51 Mill, *Autobiography*, 71 – 2.
52 Stephen, *Utilitarians* II, 32.
53 Lewis, 'Austin', 23.
54 Andreas B. Schwarz, 'John Austin and the German jurisprudence of his time' (1934 – 5) 1 *Politica*, 178 – 80.
55 Ross, *Englishwomen* I, 63.
56 Packe, *Mill*, 50.
57 Ross, *Englishwomen* I, 47.
58 Schwarz, 'German jurisprudence', 181.
59 Ross, *Englishwomen* I, 55.
60 Schwarz, 'German jurisprudence', 181.
61 Ross, *Englishwomen* I, 53 – 5.
62 op. cit. I, 54.
63 op. cit. I, 49 – 51.
64 See Jeremy Bentham, *The Limits of Jurisprudence Defined* edited by C.W. Everett (New York, 1945), 32.
65 Ross, *Englishwomen* I, 51.

66   Schwarz, 'German jurisprudence', 187.
67   op. cit. 184.
68   Stephen, *Utilitarians* II, 85–8.
69   Mill, *Autobiography*, 94–5.
70   Schwarz, 'German jurisprudence', 185.
71   Campbell *Austin*, 5.
72   op. cit. 6.
73   Ross, *Englishwomen* I, 57. See also Macdonnell, 'Austin', 737; George
     C. Christie, *Jurisprudence. Text and Readings on the Philosophy of Law*
     (St Paul, Minn., 1973), 461; Packe, *Mill*, 127; Sir William Markby,
     'John Austin', *Encyclopaedia Britannica* II (1910), 939.
74   See University College London, *Exhibits* and Lewis, 'Austin'.
75   H. Hale Bellot, *University College, London 1826–1926* (London,
     1929), 97.
76   Ross, *Englishwomen* I, 61–2.
77   op. cit. I, 63–4.
78   op. cit. I, 66–8.
79   Notes to University College London, *Exhibits*, Exhibit 11.
80   Campbell *Austin*, 9, 898.
81   See Mineka in Mill, *Collected Works* XII, 51; Bellot, *University
     College*, 99.
82   Lewis, 'Austin', 21–2.
83   Bellot, *University College*, 99.
84   Ross, *Englishwomen* I, 73–4.
85   Schwarz, 'German jurisprudence', 183.
86   Ross, *Englishwomen* I, 70.
87   See generally as to the Pückler Muskau story, Waterfield, *Lucie Duff
     Gordon*, 51–61, 72–4, 123.
88   Mill, *Autobiography*, 46–7.
89   Packe, *Mill*, 178.
90   Waterfield, *Lucie Duff Gordon*, 44.
91   Ross, *Englishwomen* I, 63–6.
92   op. cit. II, 175.
93   Mazlish, *Mill*, 195–8.
94   F.A. Hayek, *John Stuart Mill and Harriet Taylor* (London, 1951) 89.
95   Henry Reeve, (1874) 139 *Edinburgh Review*, 122. See also comments
     in John Stuart Mill, *Collected Works* edited by Francis E. Mineka and
     Dwight N. Lindley (Toronto, 1972) XIV, xxvi–xxvii.
96   Ross, *Englishwomen* I, 71–2.
97   Campbell *Austin*, 10–11.
98   (1835) 22 *The Westminster Review*, 196.
99   Campbell *Austin*, 11–12.
100 Ross, *Englishwomen* I, 92–5.
101 op. cit. I, 97–123.
102 op. cit. I, 138.

103 ibid.
104 op. cit. I, 132.
105 See his article (1863) 118 *Edinburgh Review*, 139–55. Cf. (1860) 9 *The Law Magazine and Law Review*, 164, 168.
106 Great Britain, Parliament, House of Commons, Parliamentary Papers. *Report by the Commissioners on the Affairs of the Island of Malta.* (1837–38) Session 141, vol. XXIX. Pt. I, 6ff, 27ff, 49ff. (1837–38) Session 141, vol. XXIX. Pt. II. (1839)Session 140, vol. XVII. 13ff, 30ff.
107 See generally as to the above Henry Seddall, *Malta: Past and Present* (London, 1870) and Harrison Smith, *Britain in Malta* (2 vols., Malta, 1953), 26–30.
108 Ross, *Englishwomen* I, 132.
109 Waterfield, *Lucie Duff Gordon*, 2–3.
110 Campbell *Austin*, 13.
111 Ross, *Englishwomen* I, 138.
112 op. cit. I, 151–2.
113 op. cit. I, 162–7.
114 Mill, *Collected Works* XIII, 527–9.
115 Ross, *Englishwomen* I, 189–90.
116 op. cit. II, 5–6.
117 op. cit. I, 191–2.
118 Reproduced in Campbell *Austin*, 16–17.
119 Ross, *Englishwomen* I, 201.
120 op. cit. II, 46–8.
121 (1847) 85 *Edinburgh Review*, 221–58.
122 Mill, *Collected Works* XIII, 706–7.
123 op. cit. XIII, 711–2.
124 op. cit. XIII, 731–2.
125 op. cit. XIII, 733–4.
126 op. cit. XIII, 734.
127 Ross, *Englishwomen* II, 190.
128 op. cit. I, 216.
129 Campbell *Austin*, 8–9.
130 Ross, *Englishwomen* I, 243.
131 op. cit. I, 259.
132 op. cit. I, 280.
133 op. cit. II, 29.
134 op. cit. II, 46–8.
135 op. cit. II, 68–9.
136 April, 1859, at 489. See now John Stuart Mill, *Collected Works of John Stuart Mill* edited by J.M. Robson and Alexander Brady (Toronto, 1977), XIX, 343.
137 Ross, *Englishwomen* II, 72–3.

138   Mill, *Collected Works* XV, 658.
139   Ross, *Englishwomen* II, 91 – 2.
140   Mill, *Collected Works* XV, 674.
141   op. cit. XV, 822 and 822n.
142   (1863) 118 *Edinburgh Review*, 439.
143   Campbell *Austin*, 23 – 4, 25 – 6.
144   op. cit. v.
145   University College London, *Exhibits*, Exhibit 12.
146   Ross, *Englishwomen* II, 151, 163 – 4.

Chapter 2: Literary influences on Austin and his work

1   See generally as to the above Waterfield, *Lucie Duff Gordon*, 12 – 15.
2   See *The Saturday Review*, 14 January 1860, 46.
3   Waterfield, *Lucie Duff Gordon*, loc. cit.
4   H.L.A. Hart, *The Concept of Law* (Oxford, 1961) 19.
5   Waterfield, *Lucie Duff Gordon* 18, 31.
6   J.A. Passmore, *The Perfectibility of Man* (London, 1970) 209.
7   ibid, citing Joseph Priestley, *An Essay on the First Principles of Government* (London, 1771) section 1.
8   Passmore, *Perfectibility*, 165.
9   op. cit. 209 – 10.
10   See Stephen, *Utilitarians* I, 178.
11   Priestley, *Government*, 17.
12   Campbell *Austin*, ix – xiii.
13   Mill, *Autobiography*, 107.
14   See Stephen, *Utilitarians* I, 169.
15   Jeremy Bentham, *Rationale of Judicial Evidence* edited by J.S. Mill (5 vols., London, 1827).
16   Jeremy Bentham, *An Introduction to the Principles of Morals and Legislation* edited by J.H. Burns and H.L.A. Hart (London, 1970).
17   Jeremy Bentham, *Of Laws in General* edited by H.L.A. Hart (London, 1970). See, for an account of this work, H.L.A. Hart, 'Bentham's "Of Laws in General" ' 2 *Rechtstheorie* (1971) 55.
18   Under the title: Jeremy Bentham, *The Limits of Jurisprudence Defined* edited by C.W. Everett (New York, 1945).
19   Bentham, *Principles*, chs. I and II.
20   op. cit. ch. III.
21   op. cit. ch. IV.
22   op. cit. ch. V.
23   op. cit. ch. VI.
24   op. cit. chs. VII – XI.
25   op. cit. chs. XII – XV.
26   op. cit. 187 n.a.
27   op. cit. ch. XVI.

28 op. cit. Preface, ch. XVII, 299 n.b, Appendix at 301 – 11.
29 op. cit. 293 – 5.
30 Bentham, *Laws*, 1.
31 op. cit. 3 – 9
32 op. cit. ch. II.
33 op. cit. 53 – 71.
34 op. cit. ch. IX.
35 op. cit. 145 – 8.
36 op. cit. ch. X.
37 op. cit. ch. XII.
38 op. cit. 156.
39 op. cit. 156 – 69.
40 op. cit. 170 – 6.
41 op. cit. 176 – 9.
42 op. cit. ch. XVI.
43 op. cit. ch. XVIII.
44 op. cit. 232 – 6.
45 op. cit. 246.
46 Bentham, *Principles*, 8 – 9.
47 op. cit. 299 – 300 n. b2.
48 See now James Mill, *Analysis of the Phenomena of the Human Mind* edited by J.S. Mill (2 vols., London, 1878).
49 Gilbert Ryle, *The Concept of Mind* (London, 1949). See on this particular matter Neil MacCormick, *H.L.A. Hart* (London, 1981) 13.
50 See now J.S. Mill, *System of Logic* (8th edn impression of 1959, London).
51 op. cit. 546.
52 Bentham, *Laws*, Hart's introduction at xxxiv.
53 Mill, *Logic*, 616.
54 ibid.
55 op. cit. 616 – 19.
56 op. cit. 619 – 21.
57 Bentham, *Principles*, 8 – 9.
58 op. cit. 293 – 4.
59 See Donald Winch, *James Mill: Selected Economic Writings* (Edinburgh and London, 1966) 188.
60 Mill, *Autobiography*, 41.
61 See Winch, *Economic Writings*, 188 – 9 and David Ricardo, *The Principles of Political Economy and Taxation* (London, 1911) being reprint of 3rd edn, 1821), v – vi.
62 See generally as to the above Mill's own summary at the end of ch. II of the *Elements of Political Economy* reproduced in Winch, *Economic Writings*, 253 – 4.
63 op. cit. ch. III, ss. I – III; Winch 254 – 70.
64 op. cit. ch. III, ss. IV – V; Winch, 270 – 5.

65   op. cit. ch. III, s. VI; Winch, 276 – 7.
66   op. cit. ch. III, ss. VII – XII; Winch, 277 – 99.
67   op. cit. ch. III, ss. XIII – XV; Winch, 299 – 303.
68   op. cit. ch. III, s. XVI; Winch, 303 – 11.
69   op. cit. ch. III, ss. XVII – XVIII; Winch, 311 – 26.
70   op. cit. ch. IV, ss. I – III; Winch, 327 – 37.
71   op. cit. ch. IV, ss. IV – VII; Winch, 337 – 48.
72   op. cit. ch. IV, s. VIII; Winch, 348 – 52.
73   op. cit. ch. IV, ss. IX – XIII; Winch, 352 – 60.
74   op. cit. ch. IV, ss. XIV – XVI; Winch, 360 – 3.
75   op. cit. ch. IV, s. XVII; Winch, 363 – 6.
76   James Mill, 'Whether political economy is useful', (1836) 2 *London Review*, 553 – 72, reproduced in part in Winch, *Economic Writings*, 371 – 82.
77   ibid.
78   Mill, *Autobiography*, 40 – 69.
79   Bentham, *Evidence*, Book I, esp. ch. VII.
80   For a convenient summary of Mill's general approach, see J.A. Passmore, *A Hundred Years of Philosophy* (London, 1968), 17 – 18.
81   See below ch. 3 pp. 97 ff; Campbell *Austin*, 1012, 1013.
82   See generally as to the above Mill, *Logic*, Book I ch. VIII.
83   Given special detailed treatment in op. cit. Book IV chs. VII and VIII.
84   See generally as to the above op. cit. Book I ch. VII.
85   op. cit. Book II chs. V and VI.
86   Neil MacCormick, *H.L.A. Hart* (London, 1981), 18 – 19.
87   op. cit. Book IV ch. II.
88   (1863) 118 *Edinburgh Review*, 439.
89   See below ch. 3 pp. 94 ff.
90   Mill, *Logic*, Book I ch. III s. 10.
91   Campbell *Austin*, ix.
92   Schwarz, 'German jurisprudence', 190 – 1.
93   op. cit. 191 – 6.
94   op. cit. 194 – 7.

Chapter 3: Austin's jurisprudence

1   The best current editions of the material of the *Province* are in John Austin, *The Province of Jurisprudence Determined and the Uses of the Study of Jurisprudence* edited by H.L.A. Hart (London, 1954) and Campbell *Austin*.
2   Lecture I is in Campbell *Austin*, 86 – 103 and Hart *Province*, 9 – 33.
3   Lecture II is in Campbell *Austin*, 103 – 22 and Hart *Province*, 33 – 58.
4   Paley was a Cambridge professor and then an ecclesiastic, fear of whose book anticipating Bentham was one reason for the forced publication

of the *Principles*. An attack of the sort in which Austin indulges here on a highly respected scholar is a mini-exercise in the tradition of Bentham's attacks on Blackstone.

5 Lecture III is in Campbell *Austin*, 122–40 and Hart *Province*, 59–82.
6 Lecture IV is in Campbell *Austin*, 140–66 and Hart *Province*, 82–118.
7 Lecture V is in Campbell *Austin*, 167–214 and Hart *Province*, 118–83.
8 Campbell *Austin*, 214–19; Hart *Province*, 184–91.
9 Lecture VI is in Campbell *Austin*, 219–338 and Hart *Province*, 191–361.
10 Campbell *Austin*, 355–6.
11 op. cit. 398.
12 op. cit. 353.
13 op. cit. 679.
14 op. cit. 354.
15 op. cit. 404–5.
16 op. cit. 409–10.
17 For a general account of the above developments see Stephen, *Utilitarians* I, 267–312.
18 See now the second J.S. Mill edition (London, 1878).
19 See generally as to the above Campbell *Austin*, 410–34.
20 op. cit. 435–43.
21 See generally for Austin's development of the operation of sanctions op. cit. 443–507.
22 op. cit. 1001–20.
23 op. cit. 1013.
24 See generally as to the above op. cit. 509–33.
25 op. cit. 524.
26 op. cit. 627–8.
27 op. cit. 536–43.
28 op. cit. 543–9.
29 op. cit. 567–75.
30 op. cit. 576–620.
31 See for example op. cit. 663–6.
32 op. cit. 625–8.
33 (1789) 3 Term Rep. 151.
34 Campbell *Austin*, 620–81, 989–1020.
35 op. cit. 1001–5.
36 op. cit. 663–4.
37 op. cit. 665–6.
38 op. cit. 638–41.
39 op. cit. 634–6.
40 op. cit. 624–5, 989–91.
41 op. cit. 577–80, 991–5.

42 op. cit. 632 – 4, 989 – 1001.
43 op. cit. 647 – 81, 1021 – 39, 1092 – 1100.
44 op. cit. 31 – 73.
45 op. cit. 917 – 88.
46 op. cit. 683 – 93.
47 op. cit. 626 – 7.
48 op. cit. 744 – 60.
49 op. cit. 773 – 89.
50 op. cit. 793 – 802.
51 op. cit. 810 – 29.
52 op. cit. 829 – 55.
53 op. cit. 856 – 69.
54 op. cit. 870 – 97.
55 op. cit. 51 – 3.
56 op. cit. 53 – 60.
57 op. cit. 60 – 63.
58 op. cit. 65 – 6.
59 op. cit. 67 – 72.
60 op. cit. 72 – 3.
61 op. cit. 840 – 3, 846 – 7.
62 op. cit. 704.
63 op. cit. 768 – 9.
64 op. cit. 347 – 55.
65 op. cit. 794.
66 op. cit. 710 – 12.
67 op. cit. 1071 – 91.
68 Hart *Province*, 365 – 93.
69 Campbell *Austin*, 1071 – 5; Hart *Province*, 365 – 9.
70 Campbell *Austin*, 1075 – 8; Hart *Province*, 369 – 74.
71 Campbell *Austin*, 1079 – 81; Hart *Province*, 375 – 9.
72 Campbell *Austin*, 1082 – 8; Hart *Province*, 379 – 87.

Chapter 4: Austin: conservative or reformer?

1 2 *The Westminster Review*, 503.
2 *Parliamentary History and Review* (London, 1826), 709.
3 Review of Friedrich List's 'Das Nationale System der Politischen Oekonomie', 75 *The Edinburgh Review*, 515.
4 85 *The Edinburgh Review*, 221.
5 (London, 1859).
6 Eira Ruben, 'John Austin's political pamphlets 1824 – 1859' in *Perspectives in Jurisprudence* edited by Elspeth Attwooll (Glasgow, 1977) 20.
7 op. cit. 20 – 1.

8 Summarized op. cit. 31–2, citing *Parliamentary History and Review*, 717–20, 721, 723.
9 See op. cit. 32–3, citing esp. 75 *The Edinburgh Review*, 522–3, 527–8, 544, 550, 556.
10 See op. cit. 23–5, citing esp. 2 *Westminster Review*, 507–9, 511, 529, 546–7, 550–2.
11 op. cit. 23.
12 See Campbell *Austin*, 118–21, 287, 292–8.
13 Ruben, 'Pamphlets' 22, citing 2 *Westminster Review*, 550.
14 Campbell *Austin*, 123–40.
15 Ruben, 'Pamphlets', 24–5.
16 See, e.g., 2 *Westminster Review*, 550.
17 See Ruben, 'Pamphlets' 22, citing Austin's *Plea for the Constitution*, vi.
18 op. cit. 36.
19 op. cit. 36–7.
20 op. cit. 38.
21 ibid.
22 op. cit. 24–5, quoting 2 *Westminster Review*, 507–8.
23 op. cit. 24.
24 ibid, citing 2 *Westminster Review*, 550.
25 op. cit. 26.
26 op. cit. 27, quoting *A Plea for the Constitution*, 21–2.
27 op. cit. 27.
28 op. cit. 25.
29 op. cit. 38.
30 op. cit. 29.
31 Campbell *Austin*, 114–7.
32 Ruben, 'Pamphlets', 21.
33 See chapter 2, p. 34.
34 See chapter 1, p. 11.
35 See chapter 1, pp. 9–10.
36 See chapter 2, pp. 48ff.
37 See chapter 2, pp. 39ff.
38 See chapter 1, pp. 22–3.
39 See chapter 2, pp. 42–3.
40 See chapter 3, pp. 64–8.
41 ibid.
42 ibid.
43 See chapter 3, pp. 66–7, 77.
44 See chapter 3, pp. 80–2.
45 See chapter 3, pp. 98–9.
46 See chapter 3, pp. 78–9, 102–3.
47 See chapter 3, p. 106.
48 See chapter 1, pp. 25–7.
49 See chapter 2, p. 47.

50 See chapter 3, pp. 93–4.
51 See, e.g., C.K. Allen, *Law in the Making* (7th edn, Oxford, 1964), 6–7, where the author comments on its appeal to practical minds and continued vitality despite academic criticisms.
52 See C.H. Currey, *Sir Francis Forbes* (Sydney, 1968), 7,299–300.
53 Dixon, C.J. in address to the High Court of Australia from the Bench, reported (1964) 110 C.L.R. xi.
54 P.H. Lane, *An Introduction to the Australian Constitution* (2nd edn, Sydney, 1977), 230.
55 22 & 23 Geo. V. c. 4.
56 Sir F. Pollock, 'Judicial Caution and Valour' (1929) 45 *L.Q. Rev.*, 293, 297.
57 See Chapter 5 pp. 149–51.
58 *Note*, (1894) 10 *L.Q. Rev.* 99, 100.
59 Chapter 3, pp. 94–7.
60 Bentham, *Laws*, Ch. XVIII.
61 *Vaughan* v. *Menlove* (1837) 3 Bing N.C. 468, 474–5.
62 *Blyth* v. *Birmingham Waterworks Co.* (1856) 11 Ex. 781, 784.
63 Bentham, *Principles*, 69–70.
64 [1932] A.C. 562, 580.
65 As to the latter, see chapter 1, pp. 28–9 and chapter 3, pp. 118–24.
66 See, e.g., Campbell *Austin*, 135.
67 See chapter 2, pp. 45–7 and chapter 3, p. 86.
68 Campbell *Austin*, 115–16.
69 op. cit. 116.
70 Mill, *Autobiography*, 20.
71 See chapter 3, pp. 97, 105–6, 120; Campbell *Austin*, 1001–20.
72 See chapter 2, pp. 56–71.
73 See chapter 3, pp. 97–8 quoting Campbell *Austin*, 1013.
74 See chapter 2, pp. 58 citing Mill, *Logic*, 85.
75 See chapter 2, pp. 46–7 and references to Mill, *Logic*, in nn. 51–6 thereto.
76 Mill, *Logic*, 620.
77 ibid.
78 See Campbell *Austin*, x.
79 Chapter 2, pp. 61–2 and fn.
80 See Campbell *Austin*, 106–7.
81 Mill, *Logic*, 81.
82 Campbell *Austin*, 1009–10.

Chapter 5: The scholarly reception of Austin

1 James Reddie, *Inquiries Elementary and Historical in the Science of Law* (London, 1840), 1–2.

2 op. cit. 50.
3 op. cit. 50 – 1.
4 (1861) 114 *Edinburgh Review*, 456.
5 Leslie Stephen, *The Life of Sir James Fitzjames Stephen* (London, 1895), 49.
6 op. cit. 204.
7 op. cit. 317.
8 See now Sir William Markby, *Elements of Law* (6th edn, Oxford, 1905).
9 See F.H. Lawson, *The Oxford Law School* 1850 – 1965 (Oxford, 1968), 74, citing *Memoirs of Sir William Markby KCIE By his Wife* (1917), 24.
10 ibid.
11 Markby, *Elements*, 5 – 6.
12 Sir Henry Maine, *Early History of Institutions* (London, 1875) 342ff.
13 Sir T.E. Holland, *Elements of Jurisprudence* (13th edn, Oxford, 1924), vii.
14 Lawson, *Oxford*, 74 – 5.
15 Holland, *Jurisprudence*, 6 – 9.
16 (1905) but see now A.V. Dicey, *Law and Public Opinion in England* (2nd edn, London, reissued with a preface by E.C.S. Wade, 1962).
17 op. cit. 413.
18 Lawson, *Oxford*, 65.
19 Salmond, *Jurisprudence* (3rd edn, London 1910) ch. 1.
20 op. cit. ch. 2.
21 W.L. Morison, 'Frames of reference for legal ideals' (1975) 2 *Dalhousie L.J.*, 3 – 6 and in *Law and Society* edited by Eugene Kamenka, Robert Brown and Alice Erh-Soon Tay (London, 1978), 18 – 20.
22 Salmond, *Jurisprudence*, ch. 3.
23 op. cit. ch. 9.
24 But see chapter 4, p. 136 above concerning Salmond's work in Torts.
25 Salmond, *Jurisprudence*, ch. 4.
26 op. cit. ch. 5.
27 op. cit. chs. 6 – 8.
28 op. cit. ch. 6.
29 op. cit. ch. 10.
30 C.K. Allen, *Law in the Making* (7th edn, Oxford, 1964).
31 op. cit. ch. 1.
32 See now G.W. Paton, *A Text-book of Jurisprudence* (3rd edn, Oxford, 1964).
33 op. cit. 5 – 14. Hart's association of Bentham and Austin is made in H.L.A. Hart, 'Positivism and the separation of law and morals' (1958) 71 *Harvard L.R.*, 593.
34 John Chipman Gray, *The Nature and Sources of Law* (New York, 1909).

35   op. cit. ch. 7.

36   op. cit. ch. 6.

37   op. cit. ch. 3.

38   op. cit. ch. 2.

39   op. cit. ch. 5.

40   op. cit. 100–1.

41   op. cit. chs. 9 and 10.

42   O.W. Holmes, Jr, *The Common Law* (London, 1887) 48, 81–2, 107, 383, 384.

43   O.W. Holmes, Jr and H.J. Laski, *Holmes-Laski Letters* edited by M.D. Howe (2 vols., Cambridge, Mass., 1953), 182.

44   For a review of other facets of Holmes's notion, and especially its relations with the importance of prediction in legal theory, see William Twining, 'The bad man revisited' (1973) 58 *Cornell L.R.*, 275.

45   See especially on the above matters O.W. Holmes, Jr, 'The path of the law' (1897) 10 *Harvard L.R.*, 457.

46   Wesley Newcomb Hohfeld, *Fundamental Legal Conceptions as Applied in Judicial Reasoning and Other Legal Essays*, edited by Walter Wheeler Cook (New Haven, 1923).

47   Edited by Cook and Corbin (1964).

48   Hohfeld, *Essays*, 1st edn, 36.

49   op. cit. 63–4.

50   op. cit. 71–2.

51   op. cit. 73–4.

52   op. cit. 75–114.

53   op. cit. 332–84.

54   op. cit. 27–31.

55   Albert Kocourek, 'The century of analytic jurisprudence since John Austin' in *Law. A Century of Progress* 1835–1935 (New York, 1937) II, 195, 198–201.

56   op. cit. 201–21.

57   See now Albert Kocourek, *Jural Relations* (Indianapolis, 1928).

58   op. cit. 1–3.

59   John Anderson, *Studies in Empirical Philosophy* (Sydney, 1962) with introduction by J.A. Passmore, x–xi.

60   Robert S. Summers, 'The *new* analytical jurists' (1966) 41 *New York University L.R.*, 861, 889–90, elaborating matters discussed in H.L.A. Hart, 'Positivism and the separation of law and morals' (1958) 71 *Harvard L.R.*, 593.

61   W.L. Morison, 'Some myth about positivism' (1958), 68 *Yale L.J.*, 212.

62   Hart, 'Positivism', 624.

Chapter 6: A defence of Austin's philosophy against Hart

1   W.L. Morison, 'Myres S. McDougal and twentieth century jurisprudence' in *Toward World Order and Human Dignity* edited by W. Michael Reisman and Burns H. Weston (New York, 1976)3.
2   op. cit. 5 – 13.
3   op. cit. 14.
4   See generally as to this op. cit. 14 – 48.
5   Morison, 'Frames of Reference', 2 *Dalhousie L.J.* 3, 26 – 7; *Law and Society* 18, 37 – 8.
6   Hart, 'Positivism', 624 – 5.
7   See generally as to the task of goal clarification Morison, 'Myres S. McDougal', 48 – 53.
8   op. cit. 53 – 5.
9   See op. cit. 55 – 61.
10 See op. cit. 61 – 4.
11 See op. cit. 64 – 7.
12 Neil MacCormick, *H.L.A. Hart*, (London, 1981).
13 op. cit. 19.
14 op. cit. 18 – 19.
15 op. cit. 12 – 18.
16 op. cit. 88 – 9.
17 op. cit. 6, 18 – 19, 24, 25, 36 – 7, 46 – 7, 57 – 8, 76, 79, 86, 88, 119 – 20. 140 – 1, 159 – 60.
18 See, e.g., R.M. Dworkin, 'Is law a system of rules?' in *The Philosophy of Law* (Oxford, 1977) 38, 38 – 43.
19 Joseph Raz, *The Concept of a Legal System* (Oxford, 1970), 5 – 43.
20 W.L. Morison, *The System of Law and Courts Governing New South Wales* (Sydney, 1979), 317 – 69.
21 MacCormick, *Hart*, 14 – 15.
22 H.L.A. Hart, 'Definition and theory in jurisprudence' (1954) 70 *L.Q.Rev.* 37 at 38, 41, 46 – 7.
23 See Hart, *Concept*, 112.
24 op. cit. 107. For a brief summary of the contrasts between naïve empiricism and Hart's approach see W.L. Morison, 'Anderson and legal theory' (1977) 8 *Sydney L.R.*, 294, 298 – 300.
25 Hart, *Concept*, 10 – 11.
26 op. cit. 106 – 7.
27 Mill, *Analysis*.
28 MacCormick, *Hart*, 104 – 5 citing Hart, *Concept*, 92.
29 See MacCormick, *Hart*, 104 – 21 and the citations to Hart's work there given.
30 Karl Llewellyn, *The Common Law Tradition – Deciding Appeals* (Boston, 1960) passim.
31 Llewellyn, 'The normative the legal and the law jobs: the problem of

juristic method' (1940) 49 *Yale L.J.*, 1355, 1364–5.
32   John Rawls, *A Theory of Justice* (Oxford, 1972).
33   Roscoe Pound. *Jurisprudence* (5 vols., Minnesota, 1959) III.
34   I have made some comparison in 'Myres S. McDougal', 39–42.

Index

233